A DAD'S PURPOSE

One Man's Search for the Reason

Nobody is Listening to Him

By W. Bruce Cameron

Edited by Cathryn Michon

A DAD'S PURPOSE

Published by W. Bruce Cameron
Edited by Cathryn Michon
Cover Photo by Leslie Rockitter

For Bob Bridges

Acknowledgments

Writing acknowledgments is always my most difficult task, because I simply don't know where to *stop*. Yes, I, like most writers, labor alone, spending hours and hours by myself, procrastinating. But I also needed the tools of my craft to be invented, so thank you Microsoft for all the opportunities you have given me over the past many years to rewrite columns that were lost during a computer crash. Thank you email, for enabling me to send my columns to my readers and to receive, in return, opportunities to provide my bank account number and receive 9,892,100.00 USD, which, by the way, is not going to be enough.

So let's assume I'm grateful for all of that.

And then there are the people who were directly involved. Cathryn Michon, who I tricked into marrying me not long ago, started giving me an editorial read of my work virtually the day I met her. She's an accomplished humor writer herself, so my readers immediately noticed I started using what they called "quality." Thank you, Cathryn.

A few years into my emailed column, a reader popped up out of nowhere and offered to do the difficult and tedious job of copy-editing my stuff. Now, copy-editing is, to me, frustrating and not very interesting, but Bob loves the language, and he made it an art. Bob Bridges is the reason why my editor at the Rocky Mountain News praised me for having such clean copy. With eternal gratitude, Bob.

Those columns were all I had to show agent Jody Rein when, upon reading my ninth novel (unpublished to this day) she said "I can't sell this novel, what else you got?"

Most literary agents would scoff at the idea of being able to accomplish anything with an emailed newsletter that goes out to 50,000 readers on a schedule that was random and capricious, but she bundled up a dozen and took them to the Rocky Mountain News, and then I was suddenly a professional humor columnist!

So many people to thank at the Rocky. John Temple, the fearless editor and publisher—without his approval, none of this would have been possible. Then there was Mary Winter, who for many, many years was my direct editor. Mary was an absolute joy to work for. Mike Pearson was features editor and not only supported me, he gave me a raise! And then Maria Cote took over, and Maria was my direct editor and was fun and supportive to work for. I owe each and every one of them a great debt.

I was also internationally syndicated by Creators. For this I first must thank Colonel Oliver North (Ret.), who had me on his radio show on a Father's Day to try to explain, as the *8 Simple Rules for Dating my Teenage Daughter* guy, why teenager girls don't respond when issued direct orders. While I agreed with him that families would run better if organized like the military, I could only tell him, "good luck." Col. North asked me during a commercial why I wasn't syndicated. He offered to write the head of Creators Syndicate for me and I said, "okay, sure," knowing he wouldn't do it. Then he did it. Thanks to Richard and Jack Newcombe for steering me through those waters. Anthony Zurcher was my editor at Creators for many years. Thanks for everything, Anthony.

Now I've got a whole new team! Trident Media: Scott Miller, my agent, who always tries to get me exactly what I want, even if it's probably impossible. And the team who put this book together: Alicia Granstein, Nicole Robson, and Emily Ross. I couldn't have done it without you!

Elliott Crowe was dragged into this process because he simply can't stand to watch me screw up and leaps in to fix my messes. Thank you, Elliott, for taking over and doing everything I was supposed to do.

Oh, and of course I'm grateful for my family, who provided me with so many things to write about over the years. They're still doing it, in fact.

And then there's you. No, I mean it, I'm looking right at you. You are one of my readers and without you I would not have a career and wouldn't have any reasons to procrastinate! It all started with people like you reading my email columns, then my Rocky columns, then my Creators columns, then my humor books, then my novels. I am forever grateful to you for giving me this life.

--W. Bruce Cameron, Chief Procrastinator

Contents

From the Editor

When I was first dating W. Bruce Cameron, I was a sort of a pound puppy of romance.

I had married badly, very young, and then I got divorced and was sent back to the pound, also known as Los Angeles. Los Angeles is a place where the standards for female excellence are so impossibly high that Nobel Prize–winning supermodels spend their days being driven around in limousines, feeling old and fat and dumb. Mere mortals like me, a divorcée in her thirties, drive around in Volvos feeling absolutely invisible. We *aspire* to be old and fat and dumb.

When I introduced Bruce to my family, it was a tough sell on paper. He was divorced, with three kids, and he was older than I. Bruce came to lunch and was polite to the adults but focused most of his attention on the kids. He did a form of what I call "Bruce humor" that works very well with children: He pretends to be the dumbest adult they've ever met, asking four-year olds to drive him places or to explain to him why he can't have a pet giraffe.

"But what if I get one with a *really short neck?*" he challenges.

After the lunch, my four-year-old niece Maya proclaimed, "Bwuce Cameron is da funniest friend you ever had, he da funniest man in da whole world!"

And honestly, I think she may be right.

This collection of Bruce's columns is entitled *A Dad's Purpose* because, just as the dog in the acclaimed *A Dog's Purpose* book series, he keeps, as a dad, being reborn. First he was a father of babies, which he likens to having someone throw grenades into your life— grenades that poop. Then he was the father who wrote *Eight Simple Rules for Dating My Teenage Daughter*, saying that they went from cute, cuddly girls to teenage

1

mutant ninja daughters overnight.   Meanwhile, his parents, high-functioning professionals, retired and turned him into their technical support call center. And most people say Bruce gives off a "dad vibe," seeming to believe he is, in real life, some kind of fatherly superhero—a   superhero   who   clearly   has   no superpowers at all, except perhaps for his delusional willingness to embrace the mantle of his "dad-hood" and applying it to the world.   He acts as if constantly and proudly proclaiming that he is "the dad," causes any of his children to think that means he is "in charge," or to even acknowledge that he is, in fact, talking.

If you are a dad, or have a dad, or have met a dad, you probably know what I am talking about.

Bruce's "Dad Man" persona isn't limited to his own children. We cannot go to a mall anywhere without him looking at the sullen gaggles of teenage girls dressed as if they just got off shift at the local Hooters, without his muttering about the need for all young women to wear goose-down parkas at all times, including on the beach.

Actually, *especially* on the beach.

It's not because he's a prude; it's because he worries for all of them. He has to—it's a dad's purpose.

I met Bruce's real-life children, Georgia Lee, Chelsea, and Chase at the time in their lives where their younger selves were being played by Kaley Cuoco, Amy Davidson, and Martin Spanjers on the ABC sitcom based on Bruce's book *8 Simple Rules for Dating My Teenage Daughter*.

Bruce's kids are three of the funniest people I know, and are also what professional stand-up comics often refer to as "a tough room." They appreciate good comedy, but you better be actually funny, and also they

2

will start making fun of you about five minutes after meeting you.

Bruce's kids have been gracious about being made fun of by their dad on television and in newspapers, but when interviewed on TV talk shows, even as teens, they could make fun of him as effectively as he lampooned them.

Like their dad, they would take the essential truth and tweak it slightly. So, for example, when Bruce's older daughter, Georgia Lee, told a national television audience that her dad always used to embarrass her by mowing the lawn in shorts and black socks with sandals, it was both (a) not true (they didn't have a lawn and he doesn't own sandals) and (b) very funny.

If he didn't want her making up funny stuff about him off the cuff on TV, he shouldn't have started it. Funny parents make for funny kids.

Which isn't to say the stories in this book aren't true; they mostly are, though occasionally they have been, well, perhaps slightly enhanced. But, as an example, his girls really *did* have a car accident, with each other, in their own driveway, and every single column about phone calls with his parents could have been written by a court reporter. They are that accurate—I've heard the actual conversations on speaker phone.

As I said, funny parents make for funny kids.

Now two out of the three of Bruce's kids have children of their own, and as any parent will tell you, that is the best thing ever, and also the best revenge. I look forward to the grandchildren's comedy stylings because even now, just in the way they throw applesauce, I can tell they're going to be hilarious.

For a decade of our lives together, the weekly deadline for Bruce's nationally syndicated newspaper column was like the sword of Damocles hanging over his head. If you don't know what that is, it's a mythological sword hanging by a thread over a mythological guy's head and you never forget there is a sword up there, aimed at your head, it never goes away, and trust me, it would always feel really bad if the sword fell.

So for seventeen years, week in and week out, without fail, Bruce dodged the sword and wrote an award-winning 700 words, to the word. Often his first draft would be exactly that, an even 700 words. "I can just tell when I'm done," he explains—something that doesn't seem to apply when he's eating fried chicken.

Creators Syndicate didn't hold him to that seemingly impossible goal; they told him the length wasn't critical, it was his personal standard, and it's a sign of his artistry and discipline.

It's not just my niece Maya who thinks Bruce is funny. His column won the Robert Benchley Society Award for humor and, he was named Columnist of the Year by the National Society of Newspaper Columnists in 2011.

Although Maya's praise is my favorite, my second favorite accolade for my husband's particular brand of wit happened on *The Oprah Winfrey Show*. Oprah loved Bruce's book *How to Remodel a Man* so much, she devoted an entire hour of her show to it. Oprah's audience that day seemed to feel that devoting an entire hour to fixing men was nowhere near enough time, so the show taping ran really long. With Bruce on the show was Jay Leno, and at one point, Bruce said something that he made up on the spot about how impossible men can be, the audience laughed uproariously, and then burst into applause, some of them standing and literally cheering. Jay, a comedy pro to be sure, began nodding his head as the applause continued, and then just pointed to Bruce and said, "Now *that's* funny."

When a legendary comedian is willing to admit in front of his audience that the other guy on stage with him is the one actually being funny, that's the highest compliment a comic can give.

In other words, Bruce isn't just funny to four-year-olds.

So when the opportunity to publish this collection of columns came up, Bruce asked me, who had been his in-house editor, to pick the best ones. Basically, I had to become King Solomon for my own husband, cruelly rejecting brilliant material because there was only room in a book for one tenth of these gems.

So I'm sorry that this book isn't longer, because there's a lot of great stuff that isn't in here. Not to make you bitter, but you are missing out on a lot of funny. But unlike my delusional husband, you, the readers, actually *do* have a superpower. If you tell other people how great and funny this book is, there will be more books!

Please enjoy the funniest man in da whole world, my husband, W. Bruce Cameron.

—*Cathryn Michon*

Introduction

I'll never forget the day my first child was born, when the nurse came up to me, smiling, and ever-so-gently handed me a small, warm bundle of hospital bills. Being a father, I realized, was going to cost me more money than I had. (Over time, I realized I was wrong. It was going to cost twice that amount.)

Men believe babies represent a problem to be fixed. All we need to do, we reason, is figure some things out, find a *solution* to this demanding new creature who has so disrupted the routine, and then our lives will get back to normal again. It takes many, many days before it dawns on us that life will *never* be normal again.

This means coming to grips with a lot of new realities. Like, I had to face the fact that I would never realize my lifelong dream of being the member of a wildly successful rock 'n roll band, because being blessed with children there was no way I could fly off to London and Paris to perform in concerts. Also, I had never really learned to play an instrument, but the main thing here is the kids holding me back.

So okay. I became a dad, growing into the role through a process the Marines call "boot camp." One moment I'm sitting around trying to summon up the ambition to call for pizza delivery and the next moment I'm not sleeping, I'm running around all night, I've got a four-day-old drill-sergeant-in-training screaming at me, and I don't have enough money for food.

When my kids became teenagers, I looked back on those first shell-shocked days as a parent as among the easiest in my life. It seemed like one day my daughters went to bed wearing bunny slippers and the next day came downstairs dressed for their school's first Show Off Your Breasts Day. Then my son, who

6

always woke up in the morning as if someone had darted him with adrenaline, turned fourteen and decided he rather sleep in until he was fifteen. His metabolism, which had previously converted vast amounts of food into a berserk energy he deployed to break my things, now switched gears and began cranking out indifference and sloth in equal proportions.

So as a Dad, I found my purpose. It was to say things like this:

- You are not leaving the house dressed like that!
- Son, would you please empty the trash before the dog does it?
- Put on more cloth. *Much* more.
- Son, would you please clean up the mess the dog made of the kitchen when he knocked over the trash can?
- You can go on a coed camping trip as long as it is in my backyard.
- Son, are you conserving your energy for something important? Because I'd sure like to see what it is.
- So what happened to the left fender of the car, and is it related to what happened to the right fender of the car?
- Son, the dog threw up in the basement. The moment you have any brain activity, I want you to clean it up.
- Some boy called. No, I didn't take a message. I didn't think it was necessary because I told him you'd moved to Wisconsin.
- Son, the dog was getting sick again so I put him in your room.

I'm also a member of the sandwich generation, meaning, my father always expects me to fix him a sandwich. My mother thinks everything I do is cute; my father thinks I should get a real job.

Now, I think we can agree that the world would be a better place if everyone would listen to their fathers, or, barring that, just to me. I often come up with excellent points of fact and logic that my dog finds utterly inarguable. (Everyone else pretends that I'm an idiot, but that's just an act. Secretly, they are thinking things like, "I'm sure glad my dad told me not to go to Europe," and, "I would have been so sorry if I had gone to that party instead of shoveling snow like he made me.")

That's why I've taken what my children lovingly call my "big fat opinions" and "completely distorted events" and compiled them into this book, so that you can read about my life and say to yourself, "wow, everyone in Bruce's life is completely wrong about everything and he does not need to go on a diet or listen to some other kind of music or replace perfectly good sweatshirts that have maybe at the most three holes in them."

When you're finished reading, please feel free to go on social media and express the above point of view. I hope you enjoy these dispatches from the life of a dad!

- *W. Bruce Cameron July 24th, 2016 – writing from Los Angeles with a dog at his feet*

Instructions for My Funeral

My dear children, you are now all old enough to realize that life is a precious but finite quantity, and that I, your father, will not live forever. This has caused you great concern, and you have all shown compassionate interest in the topic of whether or not you will be inheriting anything from me. You also spend a lot of time debating which of you should get my car, which suggests the disquieting notion that all three of you are convinced I won't outlast the vehicle.

Nobody likes to contemplate his own mortality, especially if he thinks it might somehow be related to how often he changes his oil. But having done so, I'm prepared to give you instructions as to the final disposition of my remains.

My funeral should not be held immediately after my passing, as I would want the news to reach the far corners of the world so that the citizens of this planet can respond appropriately, probably by stitching together a giant quilt to be permanently draped over some otherwise unused land, like Wisconsin. Elton John will write a song about me that will become an instant hit, even though it will sound suspiciously like another one of his tunes. Children will spontaneously build cute memorials out of flowers and stuffed animals—children who don't participate in this outpouring of love should be punished.

The funeral itself should be held in some place large enough to accommodate all the mourners, but let's not have one of those messy bidding wars like what happens for political conventions and the Olympics. Each city can prepare its case as to why it is the ideal location, but the losing cities can simulcast the event in theaters (and, of course, it will be televised live).

There will naturally be a lot of competition for front-row seats. I would like to see these reserved for family members and weeping supermodels. When the president of the United States arrives to escort in the other heads of state, everyone should stand in respect, but let's not forget that this whole thing is all about me.

Being so grief-stricken, none of you will be able to speak, of course—but then, who will? I suspect that you'll have to hire professional actors who can work past their anguish. Keep the thing short: Even though there will be so much to say, more than ten hours and people will begin to get fidgety. Certainly it's inevitable that small children will become fussy and want to go out and play—these children should be punished.

I suspect you will be unable to prevent a candlelight vigil and people tearing off their clothes and biting their own arms and all of that, but I think it will avoid a full-scale riot when the president declares a week of silence. This could be an annual event, even, though I will be disappointed if the holiday turns into an excuse to sell refrigerators and automobiles. (If people do want to sell things, they must do it in silence. If they speak, they should be punished.)

Now, I must warn you that once the shock has worn off, a sizable number of people will come forward and insist that I am not, in fact, dead. Reports will circulate that I've been seen eating hamburgers in Kalamazoo, Michigan, or that I'm actually Ashton Kutcher. Suspicions will grow when it turns out I didn't have an autopsy, though it will calm people somewhat when the pathologist comes forward and explains he just couldn't bring himself to "mar such perfect flesh" with a scalpel. Calls will surface in Congress for an exhumation, but you should fight this, pointing out that since my memorial is over one hundred stories high, digging me up is pretty impossible. Let me rest in peace, even if it means, for so many millions of people, that life just seems pointless without me.

Finally, revisionist historians will eventually come along and try to sell the theory that I was not as important as people think. Although this ridiculous idea will die out as its proponents are executed, you should still argue against it. Why else, you should point out, did they put my face on the American flag?

About Boys

Dear Teenage Daughter:

Though I would prefer you wait a few more years before you begin dating (in this case, "a few" being defined as "twenty"), I recognize that this is impractical unless I am willing to invest in the barbed wire, guard towers, and German shepherds necessary to provide a boy-proof environment. But just because you have grudging permission to associate with the males of your species doesn't mean I approve of your tendency to hang out with persons who possess Y chromosomes and yet are missing so many others. Allow me to identify for you the types of young men who are specifically not invited to come over here:

Boys with metal puncturing their faces in random patterns. I cannot believe you think it attractive for a person to have his face dotted with what look like stainless-steel pimples. I also can't believe that the young men who willingly turn their heads into voodoo dolls don't understand that when they finally grow up and remove the scrap metal, the holes will remain. You could use their cheeks to strain spaghetti. I read once that some people become addicted to the flow of endorphins released when the mystified brain experiences all this unexplained pain and tries to do something about it. Regardless, unless it is shrapnel somehow put there in the service of their country, boys with heads that look like they have been outfitted to provide extra traction in the snow are barred from my door. I don't want to have to worry about you getting too close to one of them and becoming impaled on his face. If it's pain they're addicted to, let them come over with their studs in full bristle to try to take my daughter on a date, and I'll be happy to oblige.

Boys with tattoos. Tattoos have been used throughout history as a means of identifying sailors who have gotten really drunk the night before. At least in their cases, those same sailors, upon awakening and noticing the name "Norma" inked into their arms beneath a flowery heart, had the satisfaction of being able to say to themselves, "Who's Norma?" Some of the boys I've seen around here lately aren't even literate enough to be able to *write* a tattoo, and have chosen instead to go with pink hearts, yellow moons, orange stars, and green clovers, as if they're trying to be magically delicious. These boys are not welcome here; I'm afraid some of the stain might rub off on the furniture.

Boys with dented cars. I'm not saying your boyfriends are reckless, I'm saying they are "wreck-*full*." Dents mean previous accidents, and previous acts are a strong indicator of future performance. Much as I approve of learning by the trial-and-error method, I do not want said errors to occur while you are in the passenger seat. There is nothing to be gained from the experience of having an airbag inflate in front of your face. If a boy wants badly enough to take you on a date, his mother can drive.

Older boys. It is the natural process for boys to grow into men, and then for men to have a midlife crisis and become adolescents. I have trouble enough with the concept of you going out with males; I need a few dozen years to adjust to the idea of you dating "men." You may associate with boys your age or younger— they are less mature and you won't be able to tolerate being with them, which suits me just fine.

Boys who slouch, mumble, and evade my eyes. These boys make me very suspicious. I know they're up to something.

Boys who look me in the eye, address me as "sir," and shake my hand. These boys make me very suspicious. I know they're up to something.

I think we can both agree that this is a very reasonable list of prohibited boys, or at the very least _I_ can agree it is, and should be considered effective until such time as you introduce me to a boy that (a) you like and (b) I approve of. Since this strikes me as (c) impossible, I think you should count on (d) living with these rules until you get married.

Tech Support for Mom

When my mother calls and says, "Do you have just a second?", I know I'd better find a comfortable chair because this is going to take a while.

"Your dad and I want to watch a DVD and I can't remember how to make it work," she says.

"Okay," I say. "Is the DVD player on?"

"Should I turn it on?"

"Yes, that would probably help."

"Okay. Do I use the DVD remote or the TV remote?"

"The DVD remote."

"Or, what's this? This is the cable remote."

"The DVD remote."

"Is this . . . there's another one here, what's this one?"

"Use the DVD remote."

"Okay. The DVD remote. What button do I push?"

"The one that says 'Power.'"

"Okay, I pushed it."

"What happened?"

"The lights went out on the DVD player."

"Oh, okay, that means it was already on. Push the button again."

"I don't remember turning it on."

"Push the button again."

"Would I have had to turn it on to put in the DVD?"

"Yes. Push the button again."

"Okay, I did. The lights came on and then went off."

"Did you push the button twice?"

"I did what you told me."

"Okay, push the button again."

"Again?"

"Push the button again."

"Okay."

"Do you see lights on the DVD player?"

"Yes."

"And what do you see on the TV?"

"A duck."

"A duck?"

"A goose. Some sort of animated thing."

"Is it the movie you wanted to watch?"

"No! That's really funny. Why would I care about a goose? No, the movie has Al Pacino. Is that his name?"

"Okay. Get the TV remote."

"Do you ever watch this? You like animation."

"Mom. How can I know what show you're watching? I can't see what's on your TV."

"Well, I can't either."

"You can't see it?"

"I mean I don't know what show it is."

"Point the TV remote at the TV and push the button that says 'Menu.'"

"Okay. Whoa! Now there's text all over the screen!"

"Those are menu selections. What do they say?"

"Well, I don't know."

"What do you mean?"

"When I saw the words, I pushed the menu button again and they went away."

"Why did you push the menu button twice?"

"You had me push the DVD button twice."

I sigh. "You're right. Okay. Push the menu button once, then read me the words you see."

"It says, 'Signal,' 'External Input . . .'"

"'External Input.' Highlight 'External Input' and push 'Select.'"

"Okay. Whoa!"

"What happened?"

"The dog just about knocked me over."

"Are you okay?"

"Of course."

"Did you push 'Select'?"

"I can't remember."

"What does it say on the screen?"

"Nothing."

"Nothing? Did you push menu again?"

"No. Let me ask your father."

"Wait, why?"

"He took the remote. He said he was getting impatient. Bill! Do you want to watch the movie or not?"

"Was he able to get the DVD working, then?"

"He says he doesn't care if we watch the movie. But I do. It's got that actor in it, Mel Gibson. Do you like him? He was so good in Da Vinci Code."

"He . . . you mean Tom Hanks?"

"Who? Was he in the Godfather movies?"

"No, that was Al Pacino."

"What did I say?"

"You said Mel Gibson."

"Well, that's not what I meant. Who played Indiana Jones?"

"That was Harrison Ford."

"Okay, not him."

"Mom, why don't you either hand the phone to Dad or have him give you the remote back."

There's a loud rustling sound, and then my father comes on the line. "Hello?" he barks gruffly.

"Hi, Dad, I'm trying to help you get the DVD going. Do you have the remote?"

"Me? No, I handed it back to your mother."

"Why did she give you the phone, then?"

"I don't know, she traded it for the remote."

"Maybe you should give her the phone back."

There's a rustling sound, and my mom comes back on.

"Hello?"

"Hi, Mom, so what's on the screen now?"

18

"The movie!"

"What? You got the DVD player working? How?"

"I don't know, I was just pushing buttons."

"Well, if you don't know how you did it, how will you watch DVDs in the future?"

"Oh, that's simple," she says brightly. "I'll just call you!"

The Hypothetical Father

Once when my son was around eight years old, he asked whether we could go see a movie (one we had just seen the previous weekend) and I said no, we couldn't. "If we're not going to see a movie," he demanded in anguish, "then why did you have me?"

He was always pretty good at asking questions—like this one, a particular favorite of mine: "Dad," he asked, "If I were a werewolf, where would I go to the bathroom?"

At dinnertime my son would leave the table, too full of kinetic energy to do more than briefly touch his bottom to his chair before launching himself off in another direction, like a baseball player rounding first. I'd long given up trying to make him sit still, accepting that in order for him to make it through a meal, he'd have to hang from the banister, throw himself on the floor, and stand on his head on the couch. It was during these nightly gymnastics that he would hit me with what politicians call "hypotheticals."

"Dad?"

"Son, please stop jumping on the couch. Come over here and do another drive-by on your mashed potatoes."

"Dad? If we were sitting at the picnic table?"

"Yes?"

"And there was a flood? So we had to climb on the picnic table and float out to sea?"

"Sure, could happen."

"And then one day when we were sitting on the picnic table in the ocean, a big sea turtle swam up and climbed up to be with us?"

"Yes?"

"Could I keep it?"

"Sure."

He would fix me with prosecutorial eyes. "Then why can't I have a gerbil?"

As is often true with boys, he was fascinated with scenarios involving machine guns, rockets, and catapults—all items he apparently believed I owned but was keeping hidden until he was old enough to play with them.

"Dad, if someone fired a rocket at our house? Could we take a catapult and fly up and shoot the rocket with machine guns?"

"I don't see why not."

"If a goldfish were big enough, could it bite off your finger?"

"I guess so."

"Where does the devil play cards?"

"What?"

"If a man came in here with a gun and said we didn't have to clean the garage this weekend, what would you say?"

This was a familiar theme, and I knew where it was going. If I said I'd catapult the man into the next yard, he'd reply the guy was too heavy for a catapult. The assailant would be similarly invulnerable to machine guns, rocket fire, and goldfish attacks. Cutting off all retreat, my son would force me to admit that even with a masked man holding a gun to the family's collective heads, I'd still insist on cleaning the garage that weekend, a chore everyone loathed (including me).

"You love the garage so much you wouldn't even care if I was dead!" my son would accuse bitterly.

"That's not true."

"Dad? If I were dead because you made us clean the garage?"

"Yes?"

"Would you bury me in the back yard?"

"Sure."

"Like Scooter?"

Scooter was a rabbit we adopted against all common sense. She lived a long and productive life—"productive" in this case meaning she must have manufactured several hundred pounds of rabbit poop, all of which was carefully cleaned up by me, the one person in the family who had vehemently voted against Scooter from the beginning. When Scooter died, we had a nice funeral in the back yard, an event that must have made quite an impression on my dog, because he snuck out later and dug Scooter up.

By the time the dog had finished with it, Scooter was a flat piece of fur, lying on a rock in the sun as if Ted Danson was airing out his toupee. Clearly my son was worried this might happen to him.

I told him no, I wouldn't let the dog dig him up. And I continued to answer his hypotheticals as best I could, believing that despite their outlandish nature, they were helping him form an understanding of his world.

Truthfully, I enjoyed it, and wouldn't have stopped, not even if a man came in with a gun . . .

My Time as Montgomery Moose

Though I am positive the wealth and fame promised me by a recent fortune cookie is no farther away than the next Powerball drawing (though I don't buy lotto tickets, so that cookie needs to be really *strong*), I sometimes take on odd jobs to help keep my family income from sliding into a recession. So when a neighbor called to tell me she would pay me to attend her daughter's birthday party, I was enthusiastic: This sounded like my kind of work! Then I grew suspicious.

"Wait a minute. I don't have to dance and take off my clothes, do I?" I demanded.

"Oh no!" my neighbor cried, gasping in such horror that I wondered if I should be insulted. "My daughter's only five years old. We want you to come as Montgomery Moose. We'll supply the costume."

This hardly sounds like the sort of dignified work I should be doing at this point in my career. I could picture the Pulitzer committee poring over my résumé: "Wait a minute, he was a *moose*?" But when my neighbor offered fifty bucks, I suddenly saw real potential in the position, and agreed to be the entertainment at the party.

So now I'm in the kitchen while a gaggle of children mill around in the other room, waiting for the "special surprise." The costume I'm wearing is ridiculous—the head is the size of a beach ball, with a dark veil of material in the grinning mouth my only source of illumination. Peering through this curtain, I can see virtually nothing. The rest of my body is covered in what looks like cut-pile carpeting, and my feet stick out a good thirty inches. I feel like I'm wearing a space suit from a third-world country. Worse, after only ten minutes, the temperature inside the thing has risen to the level of moose soup.

My neighbor comes in. "Okay," she whispers excitedly. She grabs the mitten that is Montgomery's three-fingered hand. "Let's go!"

The party guests are gathered around a table. Their mouths drop open at the sight of a blind, sweating moose barging into the dining room. "Hiya, kids!" I cry, my voice as muffled as someone trapped in the trunk of a car.

Several of the children begin weeping.

"Samantha, look who is here," my neighbor says to a solemn little girl at the head of the table. I start to walk, but my feet drag and I pitch forward. My neighbor reaches out to arrest my fall, but the moose head clunks her right in her skull and we go down together. The birthday girl screams. I'm disoriented, trying to see, aware only that I am sprawled on top of the girl's mother.

The little girl's father chooses that moment to enter the room. His expression indicates he had not expected to arrive home to find his wife rolling around on the floor with a large moose.

The two parents manage to haul me into a standing position. The children are no longer afraid— apparently Montgomery Moose only takes down adults as his prey.

"You're not Bullwinkle," someone accuses. I turn in the direction of the small voice, my head striking the chandelier. "No, I'm Montgomery Moose!" I exult from inside my sauna.

"Can I punch you in the stomach?" demands someone else.

"Samantha, it's your favorite," my neighbor encourages. The birthday girl folds her arms and looks away. I bumble my way toward the head of the table, knocking over a chair. Samantha runs from the room.

The girl's father appears in my vision. "She's just shy," he explains.

A little dog bounds into the room, sees me, and comes to a dead halt. His expression is one of complete astonishment. I bend down to pet him, and he sinks his teeth into my yellow mitten, growling. "Hey!" I shout.

"Miggs! Let go!" the mother commands. But the dog has decided on a meal of cartoon moose and refuses to release his grip. I yank, hard, and there's a tearing sound as I suddenly pull free. I stagger backward, reaching blindly for support. "Look out!" the mother cries. My floppy feet crash into a pile of birthday presents and I go down again, this time without anyone's wife to cushion my fall.

Giggling, several children jump on top of me, bruising my internal organs.

It is not until a few hours later, as I stand in the front door waving goodbye to the departing guests, that Samantha finally comes into view. Unexpectedly, she throws her arms around me and presses her head into my padded stomach. "I love you, Montgomery Moose," she whispers—which suddenly makes it all worthwhile.

That, and the fifty bucks her father gives me.

Spam-o-Gram

I am pleased to announce that I have recently received an offer via e-mail to transfer $25,589,000 directly into my bank account—I'm rich!

I have no idea why I, among the millions and millions of e-mail users, was singled out for such lavish treatment, but I assure you, I will not be selfish—once I have the money, I plan to share it, generously spending it on highly visible luxury automobiles and enormous yachts so everyone can see my wealth and enjoy it.

Lest you doubt the veracity of this deal, allow me to quote verbatim from the e-mail in question:

Dear Sir: I am most unfortunate to thinking you may not suspect me as real for we do not now know or been introduced, but allow me to say I am Song Lou. I work for Heng Suck Banq, Ltd, and have the proposition for you of transferring $25.589 million USD directly to your bank account which will be of mutual benefit to you once we have established cordial cooperation and modality. Please GET BACK TO ME ASAP....Song Lou

Here's how I know this is legitimate: (a) The dollar amount is very specific—I'd be suspicious of a rounded off figure; (b) he works for a Suck Bank—I'm a customer of a Service Sucks Bank, which is probably a subsidiary; and (c) he needs me to GET BACK TO him ASAP—legitimate business people are always in a big hurry. I responded to his e-mail the day I got it:

Dear Mr. Lou: So delightfully I am partaking of your recent e-mail! I would most cooperatively accept your transfer of $25.589 million because that's exactly how much I need! With much insomnia I beg for your response....W. Bruce Cameron

He wrote right back!

Dear W.: My associates are speaking most excitedly on this matter. We are requiring only of some informational proceedings for rapid facilitation of transfer. Please to forward bank account name, number, routing, and phone for reaching....Song Lou

Great! I decided I just needed a little bit more informational proceeding myself and I'd be good to go.

Dear Song: Most unctuous and florid greetings upon your eyebrows. My concerning is for how the transfer is working. Would you please snorkel your immediate describings of the next notes in the opera? Yours longingly....W.

Dear W.: Some puzzlement has befuddled us during your last communications. However, we are confident with you as our partner in business for $25.589 million and can lay the goodness of an additional $10 million USD. However URGENT for response with banking informational details preceedingly requested. Yours truly....Song Lou

Dear Song Sung Lou: Blessings upon you and your puppies. I have spoken with high regard to all my appliances of your keen business skills and shavings. Though much of my lust is bestirred by the $10 million, I am requisite of a total of $50 million and am inquiring of any possibility you and your associates may emerge from their medications with this additional transfer. Also, through the subscriptions of their loins my parents have blessed me with a sister through all perplexity, and she, too, would be willing for a limited time only to accept a $50 million transfer.

Dear W.: Though our history suggests you can be trusted with our worthiness, many among us are suspect of you unseriously misdirecting our associations. Please be aware of our availability to the $50 million only if you can be convincing of your honesty! We have no wasting time! Yes, your sister please also bank information with 24 hours for transferring or we will be withdrawn to other matters. Yours truly....Song

Dear Song: All of my follicles are emerging from the dark winter of their trousers and turning their taste buds to your luscious wrists! Most joyously do I face the soup of your embalming of my sister. My beamings are upon all of the Suck companies, with wishes for continued integrity at every turn of the pipe. Yours most impeded....Bruce

They never wrote back, but I'm sure the transfer is coming soon!

Dear Santa

My son and Santa Claus have been pen pals every Christmas since he first learned to write. Traditionally, letters to Saint Nick are stuffed in the stockings hanging over the wood stove we call our "fireplace," and are answered via the same mysterious process that allows the jolly old elf to descend down a six-inch stovepipe every Christmas Eve.

Though it seems rather early for this to start, my twelve-year-old son, believing that the earlier the forewarning, the better his chance of netting some of the loot he's requested, has already hung his stocking and begun stuffing notes into them by Thanksgiving.

Dear Santa:

For Christmas this year I would like a guinea pig. I have other stuff I want, but I wanted to get the guinea-pig request in early.

Signed, the Best Boy in the World

Dear Best Boy:

You are not getting a guinea pig. Are you forgetting what happened to the goldfish you had, and also to the mice you were given for your birthday? Please ask for something reasonable, like a new rake to help your father in the yard. That request I can fill immediately.

A DAD'S PURPOSE

Dear Santa:

Well, the directions never said you can't take goldfish into the bathtub with you, so how was I supposed to know? And the thing with the mice was not my fault, it was the cat's fault.

I also want a go-cart.

Dear Pet Boy:

Surely you knew that sitting on the fish would not be good for them. And I hardly think the cat can be blamed for its instinctive pursuit of the mice once you left the cage door open. I'm sorry, but you may have no more rodents, and that's final.

Regarding your new request: You have already demonstrated an unnerving tendency to succumb to the gravitational pull of the earth, hurling yourself headfirst off of your bicycle and your skateboard. A go-cart would merely accelerate this process. How about instead of a go-cart you get a wheelbarrow to help haul the leaves you'll be raking.

Dear So-Called Santa:

A guinea pig is not a rodent, it is a member of the pork family.

How about you get me a little trailer for my go-cart and I'll haul leaves in that.

Plus I also want a drum set.

Oh, and I think you should know, my dad is not using the exercise bike you got him last Christmas.

Dear Drummer Boy:

No pigs of any kind, including those related to rats. No catapulting yourself headfirst from a go-cart into the emergency room. No banging on drums, or doing anything to create any noise except the sounds of yard work.

And your father is planning on starting his exercise program just as soon as his schedule settles down.

Dear Saint Nick Picker:

Well, excuse me for thinking that Christmas was for something besides better homes and gardens.

If I can't have a go-cart, I want a snowmobile.

Oh, and I think you'd better take another look at my dad: All he has on his schedule is watching TV and drinking beer. If he settles down any more, he's going to slide off of his chair and onto the floor. My sister says the only way to tell that he's still alive is by his belches.

Dear Incorrect Boy:

Your father works hard and occasionally takes in a game on TV to relax. There is nothing wrong with this.

And a snowmobile? Are you crazy? Not only are they dangerous, do you have any idea how much a snowmobile costs? Please pick something affordable.

Dear Santa Flaws:

Well, why do you care what it costs? I thought you had a bunch of dwarfs working for you who built everything in your workshop.

If I can't have a guinea pig, I want a monkey.

Dear Cost Unconscious:

A monkey? You cannot have a monkey.

Dear Chris Crumple:

I'm the only kid in my school without a pet.

Dear Petless:

I refuse to believe anybody in your school has a monkey. It is illegal.

Dear Santa Laws:

Well then, can I have a guinea pig?

Dear Attack by Attrition:

Well . . . we'll see.

The Eight Simple Rules for D? Teenage Daughter

Whenever boys come over to date my daughter, I do my best to give them the impression that if they were looking for fun, they should have picked some other girl. My motto: Wilt 'em in the living room and they'll stay wilted all night. To assist their understanding, I have come up with some basic rules, which I have carved into two stone tablets on display in my living room.

Rule #1: If you pull into my driveway and honk, you'd better be delivering a package, because you're sure as heck not picking anything up.

Rule #2: You do not touch my daughter in front of me. You may glance at her, so long as you do not peer at anything below her neck. If you cannot keep your eyes or hands off of my daughter's body, I will remove them.

Rule #3: I am aware that it is considered fashionable for boys of your age to wear their trousers so loosely that they appear to be falling off their hips. Please don't take this as an insult, but you and all of your friends are complete idiots. Still, I want to be fair and open minded about this issue, so I propose this compromise: You may come to the door with your underwear showing and your pants ten sizes too big, and I will not object. However, in order to assure that your clothes do not, in fact, come off during the course of your date with my daughter, I will take my electric staple gun and fasten your trousers securely in place around your waist.

Rule #4: I'm sure you've been told that in today's world, sex without utilizing a "barrier method" of some kind can kill you. Let me elaborate: When it comes to sex, *I* am the barrier, and I *will* kill you.

Rule #5: You may believe that in order for us to get to know each other, we should talk about sports, politics, and other issues of the day. Please do not do this. The only information I require from you is an indication of when you expect to have my daughter safely back at my house, and the only word I need from you on this subject is "early."

Rule #6: I have no doubt you are a popular fellow, with many opportunities to date other girls. This is fine with me as long as it is okay with my daughter. Otherwise, once you have gone out with my little girl, you will continue to date no one but her until she is finished with you. If you make her cry, *I* will make *you* cry.

Rule #7: As you stand in my front hallway, waiting for my daughter to appear, and more than an hour goes by, do not sigh and fidget. If you want to be on time for the movie, you should not be dating. My daughter is putting on her makeup, a process that can take longer than painting the Golden Gate Bridge. Instead of just standing there, why don't you do something useful, like changing the oil in my car?

Rule #8: The following places are not appropriate for a date with my daughter: Places where there are beds, sofas, or anything softer than a wooden stool. Places where parents, policemen, or nuns are not within eyesight. Places where there is darkness. Places where there is dancing, holding hands, or happiness. Places where the ambient temperature is warm enough to induce my daughter to wear shorts, a tank top, a midriff T-shirt, or anything other than a goose-down parka zipped up to her chin. Movies with a strong romantic or sexual theme are to be avoided; movies that feature chain saws are okay.

My daughter claims it embarrasses her to come downstairs and find me attempting to get her date to recite these eight simple rules from memory. I'd be embarrassed too—there are only eight of them, for crying out loud!

My mother says I'm being too hard on the boys. "Don't you remember being that age?" she challenges.

Of course I remember. Why do you think I came up with the eight simple rules?

First Class

Recently I arrived at an airport gate and was sadly informed by the agent that my flight was overbooked, meaning there were more passengers for the plane than there was room to put them. Based on my years of squeezing into coach-class seats, I'd say that is always the case, but I guess in this instance the situation was so bad, they were going to have to start "bumping" people off the flight.

"Bump off?" I repeated nervously. "Isn't that the same as 'rub out'?"

The gate agent assured me that the airline would never do anything to harm its customers. "Then you obviously haven't had your breakfast burritos," I countered.

She asked me if I would volunteer to be bumped to a later flight. "If you volunteer, we'll put you on the next flight," she offered tantalizingly.

"Such a good deal!" I admired. "But no."

"Well"—she leaned forward seductively—"how about if we fly you first class?"

"First . . . first class?" I responded, stunned. "Me?"

I had never in my life done anything first class. She exchanged my boarding pass for one embossed in gold flake, and my hands trembled as I accepted it. "We'll move your bags off of this plane," she explained, typing into her computer, "and into the first-class luggage compartment of your new flight."

"My bags fly first class too?" I exclaimed.

"Well, of course, sir," she replied, already treating me differently. "You wouldn't want your luggage mixing with that of the . . . common folk."

"No, obviously not," I agreed smugly, getting with the program.

"Now, for preferences. Back rub, foot rub, or both?"

"Oh, I think both."

She nodded, clicking her computer keys. "Good. And would you prefer to be seated next to a supermodel, or an actress?"

"I believe I'd rather have an actress," I decided.

"Um . . . " she scanned her screen. "I've got both Broadway and screen in here."

"Does the Broadway one have a Tony?"

She shook her head mournfully. "No, just two nominations."

"Guess it will have to do," I sighed.

A few more questions (I elected to have the chocolate facial but skip the manicure) and I was done. I was the first person in line to get on the plane—I wanted to make the most of my first-class experience. I settled into the pillow-soft seats, extended my legs to their full length, and sipped champagne as the coach passengers filed past to their own section. "Hi, I'm in first class," I'd murmur as they went by.

The gentleman across the aisle from me rolled his eyes at the crowd of people. "I don't know why they can't somehow load them from the back; it is really upsetting to see these lower classes," he muttered to me.

"Just so, old boy, just so," I agreed.

We shook hands, professing delight at meeting each other. "I specialize in helping people invest amounts of ten million dollars or more," he told me.

"Ten million!" I hooted. "Why even bother?"

He seemed to appreciate my point of view, and invited me to come visit him in his home in Aspen.

"Don't you find that Aspen is, oh, I don't know, so over?" I challenged him gently. He paled, nearly choking on his caviar. "Just kidding, old boy," I assured him hastily.

We had a jolly good laugh over that one, I don't mind telling you.

Turns out we had a lot in common. We both preferred Lamborghinis over Ferraris, and we both rued the fact that all the best islands in the Caribbean were already sold. Neither of us had ever been successful in efforts to purchase professional sports teams, but we weren't particularly bitter, acknowledging that in some ways it was better to "just own the stadium" instead.

"You still have great seats, plus there's something about seeing your name above the scoreboard that makes you proud," my new friend confessed during the acupuncture.

When the plane landed, I was the last to get off, taking one last lingering look at the first-class cabin that had been my home for two and a half hours.

It's the only way to fly.

Chili Judge

Recently I was honored to be selected, as an Outstanding Famous Celebrity in My Community, to be a judge at a chili cook-off because the original person called in sick at the last moment and I happened to be standing there asking directions to the beer wagon when the call came. I was assured by the other two judges that the chili wouldn't be all that spicy, and besides, they told me I could have free beer during the tasting, so I accepted this as being one of those burdens you endure when you're a celebrity. Here are the scorecards from the event:

Chili #1: Mike's Maniac Mobster Monster Chili

Judge #1: A little too heavy on tomato. Amusing kick.
Judge #2: Nice, smooth tomato flavor. Very mild.
Cameron: Holy smokes, what is this stuff? You could remove dried paint from your driveway with it. Took me two beers to put the flames out. Hope that's the worst one.

Chili #2: Arthur's Afterburner Chili

Judge #1: Smoky, with a hint of pork. Slight jalapeño tang.
Judge #2: Exciting barbecue flavor, needs more peppers to be taken seriously.
Cameron: I'm not sure what I am supposed to taste besides pain. I had to wave off two people who wanted to give me the Heimlich maneuver. Shoved my way to the front of the beer line. The barmaid looks like a professional wrestler after a bad night. She was so irritated over my gagging sounds that the snake tattoo under her eye started to twitch. She pounded me on the

back; now my backbone is in the front part of my chest. She said her friends call her "Sally." Probably behind her back they call her "Forklift."

Chili #3: Bubba's Black Magic

Judge #1: Black bean chili with almost no spice. Disappointing.
Judge #2: A hint of lime in the black beans. Good side dish for mild foods, not much of a chili.
Cameron: My nose feels like I have been sneezing drain cleaner. I felt something scraping across my tongue but was unable to taste it. Sally was standing behind me with fresh refills so I wouldn't have to dash over to see her. When she winked at me, her snake sort of coiled and uncoiled—it's kinda cute.

Chili #4: Linda's Legal Lip Remover

Judge #1: Meaty, strong chili. Cayenne peppers freshly ground, adding considerable kick.
Judge #2: Could use more tomato. Must admit the cayenne peppers make a strong statement.
Cameron: My ears are ringing and I can no longer focus my eyes. I belched and four people in front of me needed paramedics. Really irritates me that one of the other judges asked me to stop screaming. Sally saved my tongue by pouring beer directly on it.

Chili #5: Vera's Very Vegetarian Variety

Judge #1: Thin yet bold vegetarian variety chili. Good balance of spice and peppers.
Judge #2: The best yet. Aggressive use of peppers, onions, and garlic. Superb.

Cameron: My intestines are now a straight pipe filled with gaseous flames. No one seems inclined to stand behind me except Sally. I asked if she wants to go dancing later.

Chili #6: Susan's Screaming Sensation Chili

Judge #1: A mediocre chili with too much reliance on canned peppers.

Judge #2: Tastes as if the chef threw in canned chili peppers at the last moment. I should note that I am worried about Judge #3; he appears to be in a bit of distress.

Cameron: My tongue's gone supernova. I've lost the sight in one eye, and the world sounds like it is made of rushing water. My clothes are covered with chili, which slid unnoticed out of my mouth at some point. Good, at autopsy they'll know what killed me. Go, Sally—save yourself before it's too late. Tell our children I'm sorry I wasn't there to conceive them. I've decided to stop breathing; it's too painful, and I'm not getting any oxygen anyway. If I need air, I'll just let it in through the hole in my stomach.

Chili #7: Helen's Mount Saint Chili

Judge #1: This final entry is a good, balanced chili. Sorry to see that most of it was lost when Judge #3 fell and pulled the chili pot on top of himself.

Judge #2: Nice blended chili, spicy enough to declare its existence.

Cameron: Momma?

My First Nap

My mother says that when I was a newborn baby, I didn't take a nap until I was twenty-eight years old. I think this is probably an exaggeration—after all, this is the same woman who claims that when it came to my birth, she was in labor for the entire Johnson administration.

I do understand wanting little children to sleep—I've always said that having a newborn in the house gives parents a good chance to catch up on their awake. Until kids are old enough to be left on their own, you dare not take your eyes off of them long enough for a nap, and every cough or nightmare in the night awakens you in an instant. Then you've got a small window of opportunity for a few years before they start dating and staying out past curfew, and the sleeplessness starts up again.

This is a story, though, of when my children finally hit that sweet spot and became DNE (Dad Nap Eligible). My kids were ten, seven, and three. It was a snowy Saturday, and the three of them were huddled around the TV like it was a camp stove while I sprawled on a couch nearby, willfully forgetting my promise to fold laundry, my consciousness racing for the exits.

"Kids," I told them sleepily, "I'm going to take a little nap. Wake me if anything happens, okay?"

I closed my eyes, deciding that if it were up to me, I'd give a Nobel Prize to the person who invented the couch. I was just drifting off when I heard the light patter of my son's three-year-old feet, and his tiny hand touched my face. "Daddy, you nap?"

"Yes, son."

"You nap?"

"Yes, son. Go watch the movie."

"You nap?"

"No, I'm just going to lie here motionless and snore."

That seemed to satisfy him. He returned to his movie, and I returned to that luxurious prelude to sleep. Suddenly a wet blast hit me: My dog had discovered me and was trying to inhale me through his nose. "Hey!" I protested. The dog licked my face just in case there was anything to eat on my cheeks. "Stop it!"

There was a short silence, and then I felt the couch cushions sag: The dog—thinking that if I were going to sleep in the middle of the day, all the rules of the house must be suspended—was trying to climb up on the couch. "No! Get off! Lie down!" I commanded.

His look indicated he was very disappointed in me. Groaning, he collapsed on the floor, clearly suffering great pain from having to lie on the carpet instead of the couch.

"Dad," my oldest child yelled, "can I make popcorn?"

"Do you know how?"

"I think so!"

I thought about it. "Good enough." I figured that it was for situations like these that God made smoke alarms.

"Dad?" It was my younger daughter. "Can I make popcorn too?"

"You can take some of your sister's popcorn and put it in your own bowl," I suggested seductively. Unfortunately, the word "bowl" was one my dog recognized, and he leaped to attention, sure we were talking about feeding him.

"I don't want *hers*, I want mine," my younger daughter wailed.

My dog barked. "It's not dinnertime," I hissed at him.

My pet gave me a *Oh yeah? Check* this *out* expression and did the only trick he knew: "Shake." Since I was lying down, his paw did "shake" with my nose.

Ouch! My sleepiness was leaving like children who ring the doorbell and run away. *Come back*, I mentally begged. "Okay, you can have some popcorn if you'll just lie down," I promised my dog.

"Dad!" my older daughter shrieked. "We're out of popcorn!" The dog glared accusingly at me.

"Just watch the movie!" I told her. I pointed at my dog. "You too," I said.

The dog slunk off. Muttering about the lack of popcorn, my kids returned to their movie. *Ahhh, peace at last.*

I was groping for sleep, trying to embrace it, when my son's tiny fingers lifted my right eyelid. I looked at him blearily.

"Daddy, you nap?"

"No, son, not today," I sighed.

My Mother the Sports Writer

I did not have a normal mother growing up, nor do I have one now. The difference is that back when I was a boy, everyone knew my mother wasn't normal because she was a sports announcer, literally broadcasting the message into my friends' homes that "I'm Bruce's mother and I don't have a normal job."

Back then (the Paleozoic era), mothers in my neighborhood didn't work outside the home. That's just how it was supposed to be. Freddie Spitznogel's mom wore a black beret and smoked a cigarette at the end of a long holder and would stage political rallies in her basement to Support the Oppressed Workers of the World. Most of the kids went to these because she gave out free cookies with her leaflets. Every May first she would stand at the end of her driveway and shout unintelligible complaints at anyone driving a luxury car. Freddie used to complain about his mother the Communist agitator, but I'd say, "Hey, at least your mom is normal."

My own mother went to work at a local television station, where everyone seemed astounded at the very concept of a woman sportscaster. Most of the time, they would have on-air conversations like this:

Announcer: And of course we also have with us Bruce's abnormal mother here in the broadcast booth today to help with color commentary. [These might not be his exact words.]

Abnormal Mother: That's right.

Announcer: And you're a woman.

Abnormal Mother: That's right.

Announcer: A female woman, I might add. Here in the sports booth. Doing sports just like a man.

Abnormal Mother: That's right.

Announcer: Yes, but do you understand sports?

I might have the exact words wrong here too, but you get the drift of the conversation. Every time they would cut to my mother, the announcer would point out that the audience was about to hear from their "female sports reporter," as if warning the males in the audience that they might want to stick their fingers in their ears and sing a song for a couple of minutes. Though my mother was there to provide comments like "That's the fourth free throw he's missed today" and "Bruce Cameron, pick up your room!" (again, I might be remembering this a little inaccurately), all the announcers wanted to hear from her was how strange she felt being a woman sportscaster, and probably how impossible it was for her, a (mere) female, to do this job. They acted like they had some strange and fascinating freak of nature in the booth with them—a talking fish, perhaps, or a Cubs fan.

I would go to school and be laughed at by the other boys, who were all born of women who did normal stuff like staging violent demonstrations against the Nixon administration. "Ha ha," they would say, "your mother is a sportscaster, so we hate you."

Well, even if they didn't use exactly those words, I'm pretty sure it's what they were thinking. I was mortified, and used to try to make my mother feel guilty by walking around the house saying things like, "I can't find any clean underwear—I sure hope I don't have to ride in an ambulance today!"

Apparently I was too subtle, because my mother always ignored these desperate ploys and went off to do her job of thoroughly humiliating her son.

And she still has the same job—embarrassing me, I mean. Long retired from the TV station, she now operates in more private venues, announcing at dinner parties that "Bruce slept with a stuffed bunny until he was eighteen years old!" (Which is as false as it is ridiculous: I lost that bunny when I was a sophomore in high school.)

I guess, though, that as hard as it was for me, it must have been terribly difficult for her. She was one of the first women to have such a job, and faced condescension at best and rank sexism at worst every day she sat in front of the microphone. It was years before the novelty wore off and they let her talk about something other than the fact that she was "doing sports just like a man."

Doing sports even better, in my opinion.

Yoga Puts Me in a Bad Position

Experts tell you that to stay in top physical condition, you should keep your strength and cardiovascular workouts in even proportion with your stretching exercises. For years I have done this, keeping all three at the same level, which is to say, zero. But when a newly opened yoga studio sent me a letter telling me I could come in for a free lesson, I was eager to go because it stated the program would be tailored very specifically for my personal needs, which I took to mean there would be a wine-and-cheese party afterward.

"Yoga" is a Sanskrit word for "smarter than the average bear." It is based on the belief that if you lie twisted up on the floor, one arm behind your neck and the other sticking out between your legs, ankles on opposing shoulders, your knees grinding into your backbone, you will find yourself in a state of mental and physical serenity that only a chiropractor can fix.

When I arrived at the yoga studio, I was disappointed to see that I wouldn't be able to take a lesson after all, because a new Mexican café had opened up across the street and was giving out complimentary samples. One has to have priorities in life, and my priority is free food. While I was in the restaurant, however, I ran into two yoga students who enthusiastically sold me on the number one benefit of yoga: Each lesson ends with a nap! It's called "kielbasa," I think they said—the instructor turns off the lights, gives everyone a blanket, and lets you lie there like a kindergartener at rest time.

I told the woman at the yoga center that I wanted the lesson that ended with the nap that sounded like sausage. Within a few minutes I was led into a large gym and guided to a flat mat on the floor.

The instructor was a painfully slender and fit woman whose arms and legs glowed with fake muscle tone. "Before we begin," she announced, "are there any special needs or requests?"

"I'm not sure if it is a need or a request, but I'd like a pillow," I told her.

She laughed—apparently this wouldn't be "full service" yoga kielbasa. "Let's begin," she said, and within minutes was talking us through a series of complex exercises like this: "Take the outer part of your inner right thigh and push it toward the center of your lower left knee, opening your hips." I fell to the floor as if I'd been tossed from a moving bus. "Now reach for the ceiling," she coaxed softly. "Try to feel your rib cage shatter, as your ligaments snap and your muscles shred. That's right. Feel your organs fail and your brain stem swell."

This might not be exactly what she said in her quiet, evil chant, but it is how I interpreted it. Then she had us bend at the waist, feet and hands flat on the floor, at which time it occurred to me that I'd eaten a bean burrito for lunch—and that I was just moments away from having it occur to other people as well.

The sensation was similar to what happens when you swallow an air hose and then become a professional contortionist. Nearly sobbing with effort, I concentrated on not becoming a human Hindenburg while the instructor continued her sadistic drills without any hint of the promised Polish sausage.

"Up down," she commanded. "Ache hurt. Pain die."

Finally she had us twist ourselves into a position for which the word "impossible" was invented, and I experienced what I suppose might be termed "explosive decompression." It sounded like a tuba player being sat on by an elephant. Everyone looked at me in alarm.

"It's okay, I feel a lot better now," I assured them. The people closest to me were so relieved, they had tears in their eyes.

By naptime nearly all the students had left, which I thought was rather odd. After all that work, why wouldn't they stick around for kielbasa? It was the best part!

Dry-Eyed Ted

Many years ago, I attended a "sales convention," a weeklong bacchanalia where the attendees devised their new market strategies, which mostly consisted of deciding to have another sales convention. At that point in my career I had gone from selling automobiles to selling software—something of a step down for me, because when I was a used car salesman, at least my products *worked.*

I was housed in a nice condominium on a golf course, which was good because salesmen need to play golf because it helps them think. There were also a lot of bars, because salesmen need a friendly, nonthreatening place to gather together to brainstorm ideas about golf.

I shared the condo with three other men, one of whom, Ted, turned out to be a teetotaler. One evening I joined Ted at his table in the bar, where he sat nursing a soda and staring glumly at the stack of car keys in front of him. "I'm the designated driver for the whole convention," he muttered.

"And we thank you," I told him.

"It looks to me like staying sober is going to be an impediment to my career," Ted observed, watching a half dozen of our fellow software salesmen warble their way through a karaoke version of "Close to You." Two of them were crying.

It turned out Ted was neither a reformed alcoholic nor a religiously motivated nondrinker —he just eschewed alcohol because it was his observation that "booze makes people stupid."

I had no argument with this.

Tonight, though, Ted announced he was going to cross over to the dark side and have a few margaritas. I tendered my opinion that this wasn't a very good idea, but he was adamant—he wanted to be "one of the gang." So I stuck by his side and watched him morosely attack his sobriety with tequila. When he started laughing uproariously at my jokes, I knew he'd had enough.

"Time to walk home, Ted," I urged him. (The resort where we were staying was relatively small—the only reason to drive was to get to the golf course faster.)

"What do we do with all the car keys?" he wanted to know.

"We'll take them with us," I suggested.

Naturally, Ted thought this was hilarious.

Back at the condo, I pushed Ted in the direction of his bedroom and went to bed myself. At about 2:00 a.m., though, I became conscious of the living room lights streaming in under my door, and walked out to find Ted standing in the middle of the room.

"You okay, Ted?"

He nodded solemnly.

"Do you want to throw up?" I asked.

"No, thank you," he responded.

"Can I ask what you're doing?"

Ted told me that one of his contact lenses had dried and was stuck in place and that he was afraid if he fell asleep, his eye would swell closed. His solution was to stand in the middle of the living room, reasoning that he couldn't very well fall asleep in such a position. That seemed to be about as far ahead as he had planned—he told me he could think of no way to remove the lens from his eyeball.

In one of those odd bursts of inspiration that so rarely come to me anymore, I remembered that the ice maker in the freezer had a thin rubber tube wrapped around the metal arm that measured the level of ice in the reservoir, there to insulate the metal arm and keep it from getting frozen to the cubes. It further occurred to me that if I removed this rubber tube, I would have a flexible, six-inch hose that I could use to literally suck the contact lens right off of Ted's eyeball.

I had Ted lie on the couch, and I straddled him, the tube in my mouth. I bent over, placed the tube in his eye, and began to suck—and it was at this exact moment that our two other roommates blundered into the room, stopping dead when they saw Ted and me on the couch.

I nodded calmly at them. "Yes, gentlemen," I told them, "this is *exactly* what it looks like."

The Boat Ride

I am a member of that nearly extinct generation of Americans that actually thinks it possible to enjoy a vacation without hours and hours of cable television. I believe that a lake can be fun even if you don't rent jet skis and blast around at high speed, and when I come up with a list of exciting things to do on a trip, "go to the mall" is not likely to be on it, even if they do have factory-outlet stores.

Because of my antediluvian attitude, I have forced my children to suffer through several "horrible vacations," including one just last summer in which my younger teenage daughter "almost drowned."

She didn't almost anything. I took her out in a rowboat by promising her an opportunity for one-on-one quality time with her father, during which the two of us could talk intimately about anything she wanted and then I would pay her twenty dollars.

I know it sounds as if I were bribing her to spend time with me, but in my view, she was going to get the money out of me anyway, "borrowing" it so that she could go shopping later. This loan would join all the others in a non-interest-bearing note that will eventually accumulate enough value that I can use its proceeds to retire as long as I die first.

At any rate, we rowed along for a while, enjoying a silence disturbed only by the occasional gurgle when my oar dipped into the water. Then she took me up on my offer to discuss anything she had on her mind, which turned out to be this:

"Can we go back now?"

"We've only been out for five minutes; let's drift for a bit," I suggested.

"I can't believe this boat doesn't have a motor."

"I don't mind rowing. Do you want to try it? It's a lot of fun," I offered seductively.

"No."

"I brought a rod—do you want to try to catch a fish?"

"No."

"What do you want to do?"

"Go back."

"Wouldn't you rather be out here on the lake?"

"No."

It was, I reflected, one of our more pleasant conversations.

"Dad, what's with the water?" She pointed at my feet.

I frowned. A steadily growing pool of water was forming on the bottom of the boat. As a sailor of considerable experience, I immediately recognized we were in the nautical condition known as "sinking."

"The plug fell out," I noted.

"Oh my God!" my daughter shrieked.

"Don't be afraid. We won't drown," I assured her.

"These are new shoes!"

"Just put on a life vest." I held one out to her.

She glanced at it disdainfully. "Could they *pick* a more hideous color?"

"I'll get us back to the dock." I began heaving on the oars, but the boat had gained considerable weight and responded sluggishly. Not wanting my daughter to panic, I decided to distract her with a question. "Well, we seem to be taking on about a gallon a minute. With every gallon, our speed slows down by about one percent. Our current rate of travel is around a foot a second, and we have a hundred yards to go. How long will it take us to get to shore?"

Her eyes bulged. "The boat is sinking and you want me to do *math?*

"It's an interesting problem, don't you think?"

"You're making me nauseated."

"You could take that coffee can and bail."

She gingerly picked up a rusting can. "It has dirt in it."

"Right, that's where they keep the earthworms."

She dropped the can. "Ew!"

"But if you bailed a quart of water every ten seconds . . . "

"If a boat were sinking an inch a minute, how long would it take my dad to realize he's a complete dork?" she wondered out loud.

We didn't sink, but by the time I got us to shore, a considerable amount of lake had joined us in the boat. Our pants were soaked, and my daughter couldn't wait to tell her siblings that in the midst of drowning, I insisted on torturing her with algebra.

Also, her shoes were "ruined," so the twenty dollars I gave her would go toward a replacement pair.

She borrowed the rest.

House of Horrors

When my son was ten years old, he surprised me by announcing that he was operating a house of prostitution.

"Oh, *horror* house," I finally realized with relief. He and his entrepreneurial buddies had been running a lemonade stand for a week, but had eventually concluded that accumulating wealth a nickel at a time was no way to get rich, especially since they were selling mainly to each other. Their new venture seemed more promising: charging people fifty cents to crawl around on the floor of my garage with the lights off.

"We've got all kinds of terrifying spectaculars," my son promised me as he eagerly escorted me to the entrance.

"Right, like the Haunted Bike You Never Put Away," I concurred. I gave him a dollar and agreed that my change could be considered a "tip" if I was truly satisfied. I got down on my hands and knees, the hard concrete cool and unfriendly in the darkness.

My son held a flashlight under his chin. "I a-a-a-am the ghost of the *Titanic*," he warbled at me. The light snapped off, and I heard feverish whispering. The flashlight came back on. "The captain of the *Titanic*," he corrected. "Who are you?"

"I'm your father."

"Dad! Come on."

"I'm Bruce."

This satisfied the captain. He extinguished his light and grabbed my hand, thrusting it into a bowl of cold noodles. "Th-e-e-e-se are the guts of Frankenstein," he quavered.

My hands encountered what felt suspiciously like Frankenstein's meatballs. "Wait, did you get this out of my refrigerator?" I demanded.

"Follow me to the Wolfman," my son replied, scrabbling off into the darkness.

"That was supposed to be dinner," I fumed. I bumped along the floor. "Hey, Captain, where are you?"

"The horror of the Wolfman!" one of his buddies shrieked from over by where I kept the lawnmower, his preadolescent voice squeaking.

"Now the Wolfman will s-u-u-u-ck your blood," my son promised, thrusting my dog at me from the darkness. What ensued was less like bloodsucking and more like finger-licking, as the Wolfman eagerly cleansed me of Frankenstein's spaghetti.

More whispering, followed by the rather incongruous scent of a martini. The flashlight popped on. "Th-e-e-e-se are the eyeballs of Dracula," my son advised, showing me a plate with a handful of green olives. (Apparently Dracula had lots of eyes before the neighborhood kids removed them.) Suddenly something sinister appeared in the flashlight's circle of light, going straight for the eyeballs: the snout of the Wolfman! "No! Bad dog!" my son yelled, dropping the plate. The flashlight clicked off, and I heard what sounded like a wrestling match. I waited patiently.

"He ate all of them," someone finally muttered in disgust.

"Okay, keep coming," the ghost of the captain of the *Titanic* commanded me. The flashlight illuminated a boy named Ben lying on his back and holding a wooden stick to his stomach. "This is the l-a-a-a-st man who revealed our secret location."

"If you keep it a secret, how are you going to get any customers?" I wanted to know.

"Dad."

Ben decided he would look more dead with his tongue hanging out. He turned his head so I could admire this new effect.

"Phew!" someone whispered from behind me. I heard rustling. The captain swung his flashlight up, irritation on his face.

"Your dog just f-a-a-a-rted," a voice intoned. The flashlight snapped off, and I lay there for what seemed like ten minutes, listening to the boys giggling in the dark.

When they had regained their composure, they led me over to a stepladder. "Now for the hot blood of Frankenstein," my son proclaimed. Warm liquid splattered on my neck: tomato juice.

"That's enough!" I shouted. The Wolfman blew olive fumes in my face, and I pushed him away. "Turn on the lights!"

The boys stood blinking in the sudden brightness, looking embarrassed. I drew a calming breath and explained to them that once you turned a shirt into a Bloody Mary, there was no going back, and they agreed to forego the tomato juice for future customers.

As it turned out, there were no future customers, but the boys made five dollars that day anyway.

Cleaning up the garage of Frankenstein.

Christmas with Mom

I am a firm believer in the old adage that doing the same thing over and over again and expecting different results each time is the definition of my mother.

At Christmas, my mother always expected that if she prepared carefully enough, every single aspect of the holiday would turn out to be perfect, despite ample evidence that the closest my dad could come to "perfect" was "incompetent." It started with the tree, which by tradition my father purchased from a place that seemed to specialize in arboreal deformities.

"Only six bucks!" Dad would beam, showing us the twisted, bent trunk, thin branches poking out like broken fingers. We'd do our best to fix it up with handfuls of tinsel and ornaments, but when we were done, the thing always looked to me less like a Christmas tree than some kind of military weather station. The only family member who seemed delighted with the tree was the dog; finally he, too, had a bathroom in the house.

Then there were the presents, which my mother wrapped with painstaking attention to sharp edges and crisp bows and my father put together by slapping on tape like it was a coat of paint. Often when he did this, the tape became twisted during its application, which meant his gifts came coated with a festive layer of carpet lint. Pick up a present from my father and you'd have a tough time setting it back down without losing a layer of skin.

Dad was also responsible for putting up the outside decorations, something the kids wanted done the day after Thanksgiving and he preferred to do never. Nothing could make him more grumpy than when the string of lights became tangled, and at some point he always lost patience and just threw the whole mess on the roof, so that our house was entirely dark except for one blazing clump over the door.

"It's the Christmas supernova," he explained to anyone who asked.

Our yard display consisted of a plastic snowman whose illuminated interior had become stained from a year in a leaky basement, so it appeared that his white skin was covered with prison tattoos. Next to him stood Rudolph the Headless Reindeer, who despite his mysterious decapitation still possessed a working nose bulb. It dangled from his neck stump like a glowing eye socket, which gave me nightmares for years. When my mother saw the ghoulish display, she always went to bed with a migraine.

Christmas morning my mother orchestrated so as to end in a climactic crescendo, each gift more treasured than the last until the final, "big" gift of the morning, which didn't always work out.

Me: This is nice, but why do I need film? I don't have a camera.

Mom: It's always a good idea to have film around, even if you don't own a camera.

Dad: Maybe someday really, really soon, like, later this morning, you'll have a use for that film.

At this point my mother would whirl on my father and hiss, "You're ruining Christmas!"

Other times, one of us would be unwrapping when my mother would suddenly lunge and snatch it out of our hands. "Not yet!" she'd bark. This always made my baby sister cry.

Because it's so difficult to figure out what's in a box when it's all wrapped, my mother always wrote little codes on the wrapping of each present, which she read aloud with a bewildered look on her face, unable to figure out her own cipher.

Mom: "BBG"? What could "BBG" stand for?

Dad: Baseball glove?

Mom: You're ruining Christmas!

Later, my parents, nerves frazzled from listening to their children destroy toys all afternoon, would serve a huge turkey. My dad would slice the big bird and make the same comment every year: "Looks overdone." He would have said this even if my mom had served turkey sushi. My mother would throw down her napkin and storm off, my dad following and apologizing for ruining Christmas.

I've always said my mother believed that the lesson of Christmas is that when things go wrong, they go wrong for a reason—and that reason is my father.

The Awful Truth about Calories

After considerable research, I have reached the conclusion that some foods contain insidious, evil little things called "calories."

A "calorie" is the amount of energy it takes to raise 1 kilogram of water (2.2 pounds) by 1°C. A gallon of vanilla ice cream has 2,320 calories in it, which is why, if you accidentally knock a carton of ice cream into a sink full of water, the water will instantly start boiling.

Food has calories so that you'll look fat at your high school reunion. They sneak into your body with every mouthful, so the best way to reduce them is to chew carefully and then not swallow.

Ironically, calories themselves are tasteless, but the foods that taste the best generally have more calories. (When I say "ironically," I mean "tragically.") For example, I can have tuna noodle casserole for dinner and my body will absorb almost no calories, but that's mainly due to my gag reflex. Ice cream, however, is another matter.

When I eat ice cream, I try not to scoop out the very bottom of the carton, because I'm convinced that's where most of the calories are lurking. Also, now that I know about calories causing heat, I try to eat more slowly so my tongue won't burst into flames. (I also use chocolate sauce as a fire retardant.) This means that a dinner of tuna noodle casserole with a chocolate sundae for dessert will consist mainly of chocolate sundae dessert. The calories that I get from dessert are offset by the calories I don't get from the casserole, so-called negative calories. If I eat 800 calories of chocolate sundae, I must therefore *not* eat 800 calories' worth of tuna noodle, though if I want to lose weight, I should probably not eat maybe 1,000 calories.

Many foods now come with a label explaining how many calories are contained in a single serving. A "serving" varies depending on how badly the food manufacturer wants to trick you. So a single potato chip can be "15 servings," leading you to conclude that you can eat a lot of potato chips, washing them down with 12 servings (1 can) of cola, and not get enough calories to worry about. If you start using the food labels to calculate how many calories you are actually eating, it is time to stop reading the food labels.

If you're concerned that you're gaining too much weight, you should first ask yourself a question: Do you *have* to go to your high school reunion? Why not skip the thing and just visit a Dairy Queen?

If you're determined to go because you still believe, deep down, that you've got a shot at sitting at the popular table, you're going to need to experience what's called a "calorie deficit," which is just a fancy way of saying "pain." There's only so much tuna-noodle casserole you can't eat, so you'll have to start adopting more effective measures, like eating only the ice cream from the top of the carton.

Exercise "burns" calories, which is why exercise causes a "burning sensation" and should be avoided. Lying on the floor watching TV burns about 80 calories an hour, though I assume you lose a lot more weight watching a hockey game than a wedding movie. (Hockey is such an active sport that those guys sometimes start punching each other just to get some *rest*.) If you watch 10 hours of hockey a day, you'll burn up 800 calories, which is a lot, in my opinion. If every 8 calories equals 1 pound, you can lose about 100 pounds before you've even made it through the playoffs.

The problem is, of course, that 8 calories does not equal a full pound. (Did you really think it was going to be that easy?) You have to burn 3,500 calories for 1 pound, which is why the Dairy Queen is starting to look better all the time. 3,500 calories! No one can watch that much hockey. Thank goodness we have baseball; those games can last for hours.

That's why, if you come to my house, you'll find me on the floor, watching sports.

I have a reunion coming up.

The Accident Report

The following accident reports were filed in conjunction with an automobile collision in which my two daughters somehow managed to run into each other in their own driveway. Both of my vehicles sustained damage.

Older Daughter Report: It wasn't my fault. I was backing out of the garage and she picked that minute to pull into the driveway. She hit me. Now I'm late, and I promised Margie I'd meet her at the mall.

Younger Daughter Report: It wasn't my fault. I was in the driveway and if she had been watching where she was going instead of putting on her makeup in the rearview mirror, this would never have happened. I tried to steer around her, but then I would have hit Dad's bike, so which was better, hitting the bike or the minivan?

Older Daughter Report: Well, you took my makeup from the bathroom, which is why I had to use some that I had in the minivan. And anyway, I hate driving the minivan. If you had come back on time like you were supposed to, this never would have happened, because I would have taken the Jimmy instead.

Younger Report: Well, but this Jimmy is falling apart. It has almost 200,000 miles on it and is all rusty. I am really embarrassed to be seen in it. Maybe we should take this as a sign from God that we need a new car.

Older Report: Yeah, why don't we get a new car?

Officer Dad Report: Why on earth would I invest in a new car when you two can't even get out of the driveway without smashing up the ones we have? And the accident report fails to explain the damage to the garage freezer, which now looks like it was dropped from a building, and to my bicycle, which has a rear tire bent like a yoga instructor.

Older: I find this whole thing very insulting.

Younger: Well, look, I told you that I had a choice between hitting the minivan and the bike, didn't I? So after the first time we hit, I had to do something.

Officer Dad Report: Are you telling me you ran into each other *twice*?

Older: Well, because like an idiot, she kept going!

Younger: Well, what was I supposed to do—she started backing out of the garage again!

Older: Well, after I ran into the freezer, I had to back up, didn't I?

Officer Dad: Why did you run into the freezer?

Older: Well, because she ran into the back of the minivan, duh!

Younger: I did *not* run into the back of the minivan, she ran into me!

Officer Dad: And then you ran over my bicycle.

Younger: I was taking evasive action because you were still driving like a maniac and putting on your makeup!

Older: No, I was the one who had to be evasive and run into the freezer, or you would have smashed into me again!

Younger: That's stupid—why would I run into you a second time?

Officer Dad: Especially when the bicycle made such an inviting target.

Older: Well, you *did* run into me a second time—who knows why you do these things?

Younger: I'm not going to say anything more because you are being so stupid.

Older: *You* are the one being stupid.

Younger: You are stupid to infinity.

Older: You are stupid infinity plus two.

Officer Dad: So the sequence of events is, the minivan is backing out of the garage, the Jimmy is coming down the driveway, you run into each other, stop, the minivan runs into the freezer, stops, backs up, hits the Jimmy a second time, stops, and then the Jimmy runs into my bicycle. Does that cover it?

Younger: Except that she was putting on makeup.

Older: And I wasn't moving the whole time.

Officer Dad: Except when you hit the freezer.

Older: Well, duh, except for that.

Officer Dad: Okay, any questions before I ground you both until you are too old to drive?

Older: Yeah, so how am I supposed to get to the mall?

Younger: If we get a new car, can it be a Jeep?

Bruce the Answer Man on Birthdays for Women

Welcome to another edition of Bruce the Answer Man! Today's topic: Human relationships, are they possible? Let's go with the first caller.

Caller: Hello, Answer Man, long-time listener, first-time caller. Oh, and due to the sensitive nature of my topic, I want to remain anonymous.

Answer Man: Tom?

Caller: What?

Answer Man: You're my next-door neighbor, Tom.

Caller: Wow, you *are* the Answer Man.

Answer Man: Plus I have caller ID. So, by "sensitive nature," I suppose you mean that thing about you how cry at wedding shows?

Caller: Uh, no, that was something I wanted to keep secret. I only told you that because you admitted you really don't like basketball and I didn't want you to feel unmanly.

Answer Man: Ha ha, of course I like basketball, now you're making stuff up, you silly bridesmaid, you.

Caller: This is actually about what to get my wife Emily for her birthday.

Answer Man: So what's the question?

Caller: What do I get my wife Emily for her birthday.

Answer Man: When's her birthday?

Caller: Last week.

Answer Man: Hmmmm . . . .

Caller: I told her it was late because I was getting her something really special, even more special than last year's gift.

Answer Man: Which was?

Caller: A sweatshirt with the name of her bank on it.

Answer Man: And you said you'd get her something more special than *that*?

Caller: I know, it's her favorite bank.

Answer Man: I was being sarcastic. Was this the same week last year that you had to sleep on the couch?

Caller: Yeah, but I figured that was just a coincidence.

Answer Man: So this year she's expecting something really, really nice. Like, a new bass rod.

Caller: But she doesn't like to fish.

Answer Man: I know, but if you had a new bass rod, I could borrow it when we go out in your boat.

Caller: I'm really hoping not to sleep on the couch this year.

Answer Man: So sleep on the boat.

Caller: Any other great ideas? And not a fly rod either.

Answer Man: Now you're insulting me. I wasn't going to say fly rod, I already own a fly rod.

Caller: Sorry.

Answer Man: Well, what are some of her likes and dislikes?

Caller: I know she doesn't like *you*.

Answer Man: That's helpful.

Caller: She also doesn't seem to care much for bank-logo sweatshirts, though I don't know why.

Answer Man: Because a sweatshirt is such a high-end clothing purchase, women can be very particular about them.

Caller: Okay, but this one was free, so what you just said doesn't apply.

Answer Man: Buying clothing for a woman can be really difficult. If you buy something too large, they think you're saying they're fat. If you buy it too small, they put it on and feel fat.

Caller: So what do I do?

Answer Man: I'm afraid I'm back to the bass rod.

Caller: What about if I took her on a nice trip?

Answer Man: Like to a fishing tournament?

Caller: You're right, I already did that for our anniversary.

Answer Man: You must be getting tired of that couch.
Caller: You have no idea.

Answer Man: What if you invited your next door neighbor over for some of your world-famous barbecue ribs? What woman wouldn't want a festive party with a favorite friend?

Caller: She's doing a vegetarian diet this summer.

Answer Man: So it will be a *surprise* party. What time should I be there?

Caller: Maybe if we could come up with something that you wouldn't like—if you don't like it, chances are she will.

Answer Man: Hey, I wouldn't want a stupid bank-giveaway sweatshirt.

Caller: You're just jealous I locked in a 0.01% rate on a CD for two years.

Answer Man: What about a diamond tennis bracelet?

Caller: Emily doesn't play tennis.

Answer Man: Women don't wear tennis bracelets to play tennis, they wear them to show they can afford to waste money.

Caller: I guess I could buy jewelry. I'd have to cash in the CD, though, and I'd hate to lose that rate.

Answer Man: Plus they'd probably make you give back the sweatshirt.

Attack of the Chicken Eaters

From the time I was a boy, my father has taken care to teach me the value of living my life according to the principles contained in just four little words, and those words are "all you can eat." When I was a teenage metabolic wonder, my dad would drive me two hours to a fire station pancake-eating contest, beaming in pride as one by one the firefighters would topple onto the floor, comatose on starch and maple syrup, while I motioned for another stack of flapjacks.

Champion eaters often burn out early, and my father was, at that point, in semiretirement, rallying only for fried chicken. When it came to chicken, my father could out-eat even me.

Yet neither one of us could hold a drumstick to my sister. Two years younger and tragically undisciplined (she would often save room for dessert), she possessed such a talent for consuming fried chicken that rumor had it the poultry industry wanted her as their official mascot. With training, my father often remarked sadly, she could have been world-class.

One weekend morning my father woke me, his face grim. "New all-you-can-eat restaurant opens tonight," he informed me.

"Yeah?"

He sighed, gazing out the window, contemplating destiny. I waited patiently. "Fried chicken," he finally said. He looked at me. "This is it. We leave at six tonight."

My sister was at the breakfast table, and we greeted each other with curt nods. My father began shoveling French toast in our direction and we ate methodically, pushing ourselves, stretching our stomachs with resolute purpose.

75

"Do you have to go?" my mother wailed, wringing her hands. None of us looked at her. "Then please, please don't take the baby," she begged, breaking down.

"The baby" was my other sister, the youngest child in the family. She was fourteen.

"She can stay," my father agreed. He pointed at us. "But for you two, six glasses of water every hour, and no more food from now on."

We nodded. We knew the drill. The water would keep our stomachs bloated and flush everything out of our systems to make way for dinner.

When we pushed open the swing doors to the all-you-can-eat chicken restaurant, the room fell silent: People sensed something extraordinary was about to happen, probably because we were already wearing plastic bags over our clothes. We were escorted to a table, and my father shrugged off the offer of menus with one word: "Chicken."

I was starving from an afternoon of nothing to eat but water, and the restaurant attacked my weakness, bringing out fragrant bread and succulent salads, tempting me to bulk up on lesser foods. My dad's calm gaze gave me the courage to stand fast.

Finally, the chicken arrived, and we began the annihilation.

With each empty plate, my father would nod for more. After the sixth or seventh trip to our table, the waiter was replaced by the manager, who pretended to drop a fork so that he could peer under the table for the takeout bags he was convinced we must be hiding. Contemptuously, my father had me rise to my feet: I was so skinny, I couldn't have hidden a gumdrop.

"Folks sure can eat a lot," the manager said nervously. At nearby tables, mothers were urging their children not to watch.

After an hour he switched tactics, smirking as he presented us with an enormous platter of gristly, nearly meatless chicken wings. The room went tense, people holding their breaths.

My sister *loved* chicken wings.

"Free dessert?" the manager blurted as my sister lustily went to work.

"Chicken," my father responded tersely.

"Movie tickets? Vacation in Hawaii?"

"Chicken."

For the next forty minutes, the manager watched helplessly as we ate through his profit margins, one platter at a time. Finally, he made up his mind.

"We're out," he told us.

My father stared in disbelief. People who around us were still being served; this was patently a lie.

"You're an all-you-can-eat chicken restaurant, and you have no more chicken?" Dad demanded.

"All-you-can-eat, yes. But not all *you* can eat," the manager explained. "I won't charge you, but you have to leave—you're scaring everybody."

We didn't know it at the time, but that was the last all-you-can-eat chicken dinner in our family's career. My sister developed a very-unprofessional fixation with how she looked in a bathing suit and decided seven pounds of chicken wings was somehow a factor. I moved on to other interests: hamburger. And as for my father—well, I think he concluded that shutting down a restaurant was sort of the gluttony equivalent of winning the Nobel Prize. How would he ever top that?

From time to time, though, he gets a dreamy look in his eye. "Bruce," he'll say to me, "remember all that chicken?"

Jobs Teenage Girls Should Not Have

One of the most important things a father can do is teach fiscal responsibility to his teenage children, which is sort of like teaching appetite restraint to piranhas. The teen years represent a transitional period of life where people attempt to establish themselves as independent individuals by dressing exactly like their friends. They tend to confuse "need" with "want," believing they *need* the most popular cell phone, they *need* the coolest kind of skateboard, they *need* the same purse everyone else has, when all they really, *really* need is to listen to their fathers.

What fathers will tell them is, "If you really want that stuff, go get a job and earn the money to buy it," to which a teenager will reply, "Okay, I need a new wardrobe for job interviews plus a car."

When my teenage daughters first embarked on what they were disappointed to learn would be a lifelong journey of employment, there were certain jobs I told them they should not even bother to apply for, because there were some professions I would not allow. Jobs where they danced by a pole, for example, were as off-limits as jobs where they drove cars for bank robbers. In fact, I can think of several occupations that are inappropriate for teenage girls:

Flight controller: These people are responsible for jockeying aircraft in the sky, guiding them to safe landings—not a job I would want to assign to a person who cannot avoid collisions even when parking in her own driveway. And I can picture the conversation with the cockpit:

Pilot: Flight 201 to tower.

Tower: I can't talk now, I'm busy.

Pilot: Are we cleared for landing?

Tower: I don't care what you do, I have my own life! God!

Pilot: We're on approach, need approval to land.

Tower: Fine. Whatever.

Secretary of State: Since teenage girls are talking all the time anyway, perhaps they would be more suited for this job. Then again, maybe not.

Ambassador: I regret to inform you that my government has turned down your proposal.

Secretary of State: What? No fair!

Ambassador: We feel that how we manage our currency is our own business.

Secretary of State: That is so tacky. God, all my friends are looking at us, I am so embarrassed. Leave me alone.

Ambassador: On behalf of our government . . .

Secretary of State: Stop talking to me! I hate you, I hate you!

Physician: Currently two of my children are on an educational course to become health care professionals of some kind, which is good because it means when I'm old and prone to illness, I can count on having quick access to student loan debt. As teenagers, though, I would have said they were ill suited for this profession, because teens are not interested in work that requires (a) education or (b) work.

Patient: I have this cut on my leg— I think it might be infected.

Physician: Eww! Sick!

Patient: See? It looks bad.

Physician: I'm going to puke.

Patient: What should I do about it?

Physician: It so doesn't matter. Your skin is all like splotchy and gross anyway. Who cut your hair?

Of course, employers wouldn't hire a teenage girl for any of these occupations unless they live in a situation comedy. The jobs my daughters did get were in restaurants, where, against my dire predictions, they were considered to be hardworking, valuable employees. I stopped in to see how my middle child was managing, maybe give her some fatherly advice she'd appreciate.

Dad: Hi, honey!

Waitress: Dad! Stop!

Dad: Stop what?

Waitress: Don't tell people I'm your daughter. God, this is so embarrassing.

Dad: So what's good to eat here?

Waitress: I don't know, like, the food? Just tell me what you want.

Dad: Look at my little girl, working as a real waitress!

Waitress: Oh God.

Dad: (*To a woman at another table*) She always played waitress when she was a child.

Waitress: Dad!

Woman: That's cute.

Waitress: I want to die.

　　　Of course, there are a lot of jobs that teenage boys shouldn't have either—defined by my son as "any requiring work."

Early-Morning Quake-Up Call

I was in San Francisco last week watching a TV special entitled *Now That You're Here, Let's Talk about Earthquakes!*

According to the documentary, our continents are aimlessly drifting around the planet, sort of like my son when I ask him to do the dishes. In this way, the earth is constantly changing—if you don't want to pay the high price of an airline ticket to Europe, for example, you should just wait awhile because eventually we'll be able to walk there free. In California, a pair of continental plates are rubbing each other the wrong way, and apparently it is San Andreas's fault.

There are two signs you may be experiencing an earthquake: (a) You hear a noise like a train, and (b) you are breathing rubble. Because of dangerous aftershocks, experts recommend you remain where you are at least an hour after the quake before you go outside to start your looting. If you are a guest in a small, "pre-code" hotel like the one where I was staying, you are advised to have a couple days' worth of food in your pockets so the rescue dogs will care about finding you. You should also never venture anywhere in the area without such common-sense supplies as five gallons of drinking water, an emergency power generator, and a llama.

There are some things you can do to increase your likelihood of surviving a California quake, like move to Kansas. Also, it is a good idea to have an earthquake plan all figured out ahead of time, because it is difficult to write down your plan when the room is shaking.

By law, the hotel had to provide an emergency evacuation plan, and I eventually found it in the

"Things to Do in San Francisco" book. In the event of a catastrophic earthquake, I learned, my hotel would be offering its "elevated platinum" members late checkout at no extra cost.

Well, okay, it would be up to me to come up with my own plan because this was only my second stay in the hotel, which made me a "scrap metal" member. As such, I was allowed free elevator rides to and from my room and had to spend only one hour each day helping other guests with their luggage.

After the show ended I lay in the dark, unable to sleep as I reviewed all that I had learned about earthquakes in San Francisco, which I felt could be summed up as "They Want to Crush Bruce Cameron." I decided that upon hearing what sounded like a train, I would leap out of bed, run to the sliding glass door, open it, step out on the balcony, and then jump over the railing onto a grassy hill six feet below, where I would sprain both my ankles. Diane Sawyer, describing my bravery, would abandon any pretense of objectivity and allow a sob to roughen her voice, and I would be invited on stage to sing with Sheryl Crow at the annual Benefit to Raise Money for People with Sprained Ankles.

This seemed like a pretty good plan to me, and I fell asleep wondering which photograph they would pick for the *Time* magazine "Man of the Year" issue.

I awoke with a literal jolt. It was barely morning, and I could hear what sounded like a train approaching my room from down the hallway. Worse, I could *feel* it, the vibration rattling everything in the room.

Okay, I'm Not Panicking—I have a plan! I jumped up, mindful of the fact that when the paramedics found me, I'd be wearing nothing but my boxer shorts, which meant I would experience the humiliation of having to tell my mother she was right about needing good underwear for the ambulance. I sprinted to the sliding glass doors, opened them with a crash, and bounded out onto the balcony in preparation for my big leap.

And there, just a dozen yards away, was—of course—a train, the commuters staring out their windows at me as I stood exposed on my hotel balcony.

I knew what they were thinking: "What's the Man of the Year doing without his llama?"

Diana

Perhaps the first woman to whom I ever felt physically attracted was a beauty named Diana Dietrich. She had long, golden hair and slender legs, which she crossed and recrossed all day in a seductive manner, driving me into a state of fevered yearning. Sometimes she would turn and smile at me, and my heart would send tremors through my entire body—the uncertain grin I forced onto my twitching lips in return probably led her to conclude I was suffering from intestinal bloat. I sat and schemed ways to win Diana's love, carefully constructing fantasies in which I heroically rescued her from man-eating alligators, marauding pirates, and other dangers common to the Kansas City area.

We were in third grade.

Diana was the oldest child of the school principal, so my hidden affections made me feel like I was coveting the camp commandant's daughter. Mr. Dietrich was a stern man who prowled the lunchroom and told kids they should eat their vegetables, which was how we knew he was evil. He would wander up from behind an unsuspecting student and spear him with a malevolent glare. "Aren't you going to finish your lima beans?" he'd demand in a silky whisper, standing still as an ice statue while the poor kid spooned mouthful after mouthful of the loathsome things past a shocked and disbelieving gag reflex.

In one of my fantasies, I rescued Diana from some vicious koala bears on the school bus and from that point forward her grateful father would stop by my table, spy my untouched Brussels sprouts, and then give me an avuncular wink, while the other third graders gasped in amazement and voted me class president.

Toward the end of the school year, my passion still unrevealed, I began to despair of ever making

Diana my girlfriend. To my bitter disappointment, no giant bats had terrorized the children on the playground, nor had floodwaters roared down the hallways, sweeping Diana within range of my manly grasp. I was going to finish out the semester with my first love totally unrequited.

Then fate intervened, and I was put next to Diana in music class. Music was taught by a demented woman who truly believed we would waste our TV-viewing time practicing the flutophones we'd been issued. She would stand in front of us and wave her arms in a violent fashion, forcefully conducting an orchestra capable of emitting only a desultory chorus of thin whistles and peeps. We sounded like a flock of chickens with the bird flu.

Sitting next to Diana in that class, randomly tooting out flutophone notes and nodding patronizingly to the music teacher, I was seized with an impulse of masculine boldness. Moving my foot across the floor, I innocuously touched my shoe against Diana's . . . and left it there.

This sort of rankly overt sexual contact was unheard of in third grade; I half expected Diana to drop her plastic instrument and scream. Instead, though, Diana responded by leaving her foot in place.

I didn't dare look. Taking a shaky breath, I recklessly pushed a little harder, letting her know this was no accident, that I really meant what I was saying with the toe of my sneaker.

And still she didn't move. If anything, she pressed back, and I nearly swooned with passion—all this time, she had been feeling the same way! I closed my eyes and let my soul guide my music, hooting like a lovesick duck.

I stroked her with my foot the entire class, and never once did she move away. At the end of the hour, when the defeated music teacher exhaustedly motioned for us to quit honking our flutophones, I turned and gave Diana a radiant, when-do-you-want-to-announce-our-engagement kind of smile.

Her response was to blink and regard me as if she had no idea why I was acting so knowing, which startled me. Weren't our feet even now locked in intimate embrace? I glanced down to assure myself that her message of affection was not being misunderstood.

My foot was pressed against the *leg of her chair*. I'd spent the whole class declaring my love to a stick of furniture!

And to this day, the haunting notes of a flutophone can instantly take me back to that traumatic day in third grade.

Birth of a Hamster

When I tell people about the time I had to take my son's hamster to the vet, I see them doing the math. A vet visit costs what, $120? A hamster, which is a nocturnal rodent that may or may not ever recognize who you are, can be had for maybe a buck. Surely for the price of a hundred hamsters, a suitable replacement can be found for one that's ill.

But I had to. Here's what happened: Just after dinner one night, my son came up to tell me there was "something wrong" with one of the two hamsters he holds prisoner in his room.

"He's just lying there looking sick," he told me.

"Oldest trick in the book," I informed him. "You go in to see what's wrong with the sick one and the other one sneaks up behind you and bonks you on the head. Then they change into your clothes and escape."

"I'm serious, Dad. Can you help?"

I put a hamster-healer expression on my face and followed him into his bedroom. One of the little rodents was indeed lying on his back, looking distressed. I immediately knew what to do. "Honey," I called to my older daughter, "come look at the hamster!"

"Oh my gosh," my daughter diagnosed after a minute. "She's having babies."

"What?" my son demanded. "But their names are Bert and Ernie!"

I was equally outraged. "Hey, how can that be? When I agreed you could give them to him, I specifically said I didn't want them to reproduce," I accused my daughter.

"Well, what did you want me to do, post a sign in their cage?" she inquired sarcastically.

"No, but you were supposed to get two boys!" I reminded her.

"Yeah, Bert and Ernie!" my son agreed.

"Well, it was a little hard to tell," she informed me.

By now my other daughter had wandered in to see what was going on. I shrugged, deciding to make the best of it. "Kids, this is going to be a wondrous experience," I announced. "We're about to witness the miracle of birth."

"Gross!" they shrieked.

"Great—what are we going to do with a litter of tiny little hamster babies?" my older daughter wanted to know.

"Well, when my parents' dog had puppies, I took them up to the grocery store in a cardboard box and gave them away," I recalled.

"So what are you going to do, go up with a pair of tweezers so people can pick out their hamster?" she asked.

We peered at the patient. After much struggling, what looked like a tiny foot would appear briefly, vanishing a scant second later. "We don't appear to be making much progress," I noted.

"A breech birth," my younger daughter whispered, horrified.

"Do something, Dad!" my son urged.

"Okay, okay." Squeamishly, I reached in and grabbed the foot when it next appeared, giving it a gingerly tug. It disappeared. I tried again, with the same results.

"Should I dial 911?" my older daughter wanted to know. "Maybe they could talk us through it."

"Let's get Ernie to the vet," I said grimly.

We drove to the vet with my son holding the cage in his lap. "Breathe, Ernie, breathe," he urged.

"I don't think hamsters do Lamaze," I told him.

The vet took Ernie back to the examining room and peered at the little animal through a magnifying glass. "What do you think, Doc, an epidural?" I suggested scientifically.

"Oh, very interesting," he murmured. "Mr. Cameron, may I speak to you privately for a moment?"

I gulped. Oh *no*. My older daughter accompanied me out into the hall with the vet. "Is Ernie going to be okay?" my daughter asked.

"Oh, perfectly," the vet assured us. "This hamster is not in labor. In fact, that isn't *ever* going to happen . . . Ernie is a boy."

"What?"

"You see, Ernie is a young male. And occasionally, as they come into maturity, male hamsters will, ah . . ." He blushed, glancing at my daughter. "Well, you know what I'm saying, Mr. Cameron."

We were silent, absorbing this. "So Ernie's just . . . just . . ."

"Horny?" my daughter offered.

"Exactly," the vet replied, relieved that we understood.

More silence. Then my daughter started to giggle. "What's so funny?" I demanded.

Tears were now running down her face. "Just . . . that . . . I'm picturing you pulling on its . . . its . . ." she gasped.

"That's enough," I warned. "We must never speak of this." We thanked the veterinarian and hurriedly bundled the hamsters and the children back into the car. He was glad everything was going to be okay.

"I know Ernie's really grateful," he told me.

My older daughter grinned at him. "Oh, you have *no idea*," she agreed.

Lucky Ticket

I've always felt that buying a lotto ticket gives you the opportunity to daydream about what you would do with all that money that you've blown on lotto tickets. My father, however, who has retired, buys tickets religiously, dreaming of the day when he'll hit the jackpot and can . . . retire.

"That's not why I play the lotto," he snapped when I pointed out that since he does what he feels like all day anyway, a winning ticket wouldn't enhance his life in the slightest.

"You don't 'play' anything," I agreed. "Any more than when I feed a dollar into the slot of a soda dispenser and nothing comes out I am 'playing' the vending machine."

My refusal to consider lotto tickets a wise investment seized my father's imagination. Clearly, if I didn't want to play, I must have a huge payoff coming, my unused luck building up like a savings account compounding interest. When my sister and I went to visit him recently, he thrust a scratch game at me and invited me to cash in on my karma.

I examined the ticket curiously, finding that first you scratched off the amount the ticket was worth, which might be "as much as $500,000" or as little as five bucks, and then the "number to beat," which was the "opposing player's score" (in this case, the opposing player was apparently "the people who printed the lotto ticket"), and finally, the "big scratch number," which was "your score." If the big scratch number—or "BS," as I came to refer to it—was higher than the number to beat, you won the ticket amount.

"You play it, and I'll give you half of what we win," my dad offered.

"Let's see. Half of nothing is . . . nothing. No, sorry, I'd want at least ten times that."

My sister looked up from her book with an expression that said, *Quit messing around and make your dad happy plus I'm the one who stole your baseball glove in fifth grade ha ha ha.*

I scratched off the amount to win, and my dad went crazy. "Five hundred thousand!"

My sister put her book down and came over to join in the excited delusion. "Yippee!" she shouted— I'd never heard anyone actually say that before. "We're going to win half a million bucks!"

"We aren't going to win *anything*," I informed her, paying her back for telling me there was no Santa Claus. "We probably have to beat a score of ten thousand." I rubbed the number to beat and cocked my head. "Well, this is interesting." I showed them what it said.

Zero. The number to beat was *zero*.

After a full half minute of jumping up and down, I asked them to stop because they were making me do it too.

"With my half I'm going to buy a house!" my sister enthused.

My dad and I looked at her. "Your half?" he repeated.

"Well yeah, you wouldn't give all that money to just one of your children—that wouldn't be fair."

"Who said I'm giving any money to Bruce?" he demanded.

My sister and I stared at him. "You said whatever I won, you would give me fifty percent," I reminded him.

"Well yeah, but not of five hundred thousand *dollars*," he objected.

"So what are you saying, you thought it was going to pay out in yen?" I asked.

"You did say you would give us half, Dad," my sister weighed in.

"Us?" I repeated.

"I'll give you each ten thousand dollars," he announced.

We glared at him.

"What? You wouldn't want more than that, it's taxable," he said defensively. "I'm just looking out for your best interests."

"You're probably going to win Father of the Year," I agreed. "But you said fifty-fifty."

"That was before I knew we were going to win half a million dollars!"

"Oh, believe me, I get that," I assured him. "But a deal is a deal."

Grumbling, he agreed. "But a tie is the same as a loss, so you'd better not scratch a zero on the last one," he warned, which I took to mean that if I didn't win, he wouldn't give me half.

I scratched off the remaining number, which was, of course, a zero.

I felt the whole experience was sort of fun, but both my dad and sister were sullenly angry at me all day. "I'm never making that mistake again," my father sniffed. "You don't know how to play."

Squirrel War One

This is the first in a two-part series in which I go man-to-man in a heroic battle of wits with a squirrel.

Now, I know what you're thinking: not exactly a fair fight, my brain against that of a tree-climbing rodent. But don't fret—to even up the odds, I had my dog helping me.

Some time ago I put a bird feeder out on the balcony, because I like to feed birds and not squirrels. Within minutes, however, a small, gray, definitively non-avian squirrel was sitting in it, busily stuffing its mouth with seeds. Two birds sat watching from a tree limb nearby, probably wondering why the man of the house had laid out food for the squirrel and not for them.

I put on a facial expression that communicated a clear message: *I eat small squirrels.* I threw open the door and charged out, yelling as if I were storming a machine-gun nest.

The effect was exactly what I would have hoped for: The squirrel dove off the railing, snared a tree branch like a trapeze artist, and scrambled up the tree trunk. Unfortunately, the birds were alarmed as well, taking frantic wing to escape the howling madman hurtling out of the house.

The squirrel chided me from its perch, saying something like, "You scared me to death! I nearly choked on the food you put out for me!"

"Teach you to mess with the squirrel avenger," I replied smugly. My then-six-year-old daughter was impressed with both the aggressiveness and the effectiveness of my actions, especially when I repeated them every two to three minutes for the next hour. For some reason, the stupid rodent didn't realize I was standing watch at the window, waiting for it to climb into the feeder so I could charge out again. My dog knew it, though, and was barking and running around in circles inside the house, so excited there was no hope of calming him down. When I burst through the doorway like a SWAT team, the dog would charge out with me, usually getting entangled in my legs so that we'd both go sprawling. The squirrel would watch all this and then dive for the tree, though with each repetition its retreat became more leisurely, almost as if it were beginning to believe my dog and did I not pose a mortal threat.

My daughter drew a cardboard sign, "NO SQURELS," but that didn't help either—the thing simply didn't respect the law, even when it was posted. Eventually the squirrel figured out that while my dog and I could rush out yelling, barking, and falling, we couldn't actually touch it, because the feeder was mounted on a post in the yard, eye level with me on the balcony but just out of arm's reach. From that moment forward it just watched us with a bemused expression as I stomped and yelled and screamed and scared off every bird for five square miles. The dog would race into the yard, snarling, and then find a stick and bring it to me because, hey, free stick!

There's a reason why we humans are smart enough to toil long hours at jobs so we can earn money to buy food, while poor dumb squirrels either eat what they find lying on the ground or are forced to wait for people to put out bird feeders filled with free seed: technology. We have *weapons*.

The next time the squirrel showed up for a snack, I had my son's water gun, and was able to stand on the balcony and blast the critter with a long, drenching shot. This offended the squirrel, who thought we'd come to an understanding about our roles: It ate, and my dog and I provided the entertainment. Rodent dinner theater. You're not supposed to spray water on the *audience*.

I sat menacingly in a rocking chair on the balcony, water gun across my lap, the squirrel skittering around in the fir tree overhead, thoroughly defeated.

And then it started pelting me with pinecones.

How I handled this unprovoked escalation from water cannons to sub-ballistic missiles will be the topic of the following essay.

Squirrel War Two

This is the second column in a thought-provoking series about how my dog and I are dumber than a squirrel.

Previously I explained that despite the fact that I had poured (plainly labeled) *bird*seed into a (universally recognizable) *bird* feeder in order to feed (well, duh) *birds*, a lawless squirrel had invaded. This so intimidated the local birds that they weren't landing in the feeder, though I suppose they might also have been put off by the way my dog and I kept noisily charging out the door to curse at the squirrel.

In the face of this injustice, I felt I had no choice but to deploy advanced human weaponry, using my son's squirt gun to hose down the squirrel and send it scampering. I settled into a chair on the porch, water gun in my lap, a study in vigilance.

And then I got hit with a pinecone.

That's right, a pinecone smacked me on the crown of my head. I thought the tree itself had just dealt an improbable blow—pinecones do fall of their own accord, after all. But when the second one stung my scalp, I looked up and there was the squirrel, eyes glinting, hauling himself up the evolutionary ladder from nut gatherer to projectile thrower in one afternoon.

Here's something they should teach you in Special Forces: If you fire a squirt gun straight up at a squirrel who is trying to concuss you, most of the water will cascade back on your face.

The squirrel nearly fell out of the tree, it was laughing so hard. I stomped into the house, yelling at my dog, who despite the battle raging in the front yard was napping in the living room. He seemed offended to be so rudely awakened, but that's what happens in the military: You always pick on someone of lower rank. "Go out there and scare the squirrel away!" I instructed.

He raced outside, his fur an angry ridge on his back, but apparently thought my orders had been, "Go to the garage, knock over the trash can, and eat something from it."

Then I was struck with a brilliant thought: Hey, I was at least as advanced a creature as my rodent adversary, even if it was some sort of ninja squirrel. I went out into the yard and looked up at my enemy, who was now on the flat part of my roof, watching coldly. I picked up a pinecone and tossed it at the squirrel, who immediately withdrew.

"It didn't know I could throw *back*," I explained to the dog, who gazed at me worshipfully—my pet might not be good at executing orders, but he was great at sucking up to the boss.

Then the squirrel reappeared at the edge of the roof, the pinecone in its jaws. With a flick of its head, it pitched the pinecone back down at me. My dog snapped into retriever mode, pouncing on the pinecone, racing over to me, and dropping it at my feet.

"You have got to be kidding me," I said to the squirrel.

I took aim and fired another shot, though I have to say that as weapons go, pinecones lack a certain ferocity, even though they do sting when they crack you on the head. "You are so lucky I don't have a hand grenade," I told the squirrel, which was probably true for me as well.

I tried over and over to hit my target, always missing, and every time, it would disappear for a moment, bringing back the pinecone and pitching it down to my dog.

And then it struck me how extraordinary this interspecies game of catch and fetch truly was, and how I had gotten caught up in trying to toss the pinecone softly and accurately enough for the squirrel to snare it midair, as it had learned to do for the dog. Truth be told, I sort of *liked* the little critter now. The three of us were having fun together.

A few days later, when I picked up more bird feed, I also bought some peanuts for the squirrel.

What the heck—we were on the same team.

Boston

Though normally a courageous person unless the situation involves danger, I do have some of the more common phobias: snakes, heights, and Boston.

Please don't think this means I don't like Boston. I like it a lot, particularly in association with "cream pie." It's just intimidating to me to be in a city where everyone has a grandmother who could beat me up.

The last time I was in Boston, the intimidation started in the taxi line. In Boston, cab drivers bomb around the corner as if fleeing a hit-and-run, squealing to a halt only long enough for people to dive headfirst into the back seat before roaring off again. It's against the local religion to wait for anything except maybe a World Series championship, so when I stood still even for a moment, I was yanked out of place by large, red-faced man with a whistle.

"Fa cryin' out loud, ya holding up the line!" he scolded as people scuttled past me at a dead run.

"Well, I'm sorry, I just—I couldn't figure out where I was supposed to go," I stammered.

His eyes bulged at me, driven by enormous pressure inside his head. "Whaddya mean? Ya go to the taxi! Ya wanna taxi, or not?"

"Well, yes, sure. Yes."

He looked me up and down suspiciously. "Wait a minute. Where ya from?"

For some reason, I named the place of my birth, the tiny village of Petoskey, Michigan, famous for its large sign proclaiming "Not Responsible for W. Bruce Cameron." His face relaxed. "Oh, a small-town kid, huh?"

No one has called me a "kid" in some time, but I agreed that this was accurate.

"Hang on," he told me. He blew his whistle and the bustling people in the taxi line halted like hunting dogs on point. "Wait a minute, folks, this guy's from a wicked small town in Michigan."

"Aww, how cute," the crowd murmured. Several people reached out to tousle my hair as I sheepishly made my way to a waiting cab.

The cabbie leaped out as if the cab were on fire. "Yer socks are down mine too, bottom fort!" he shouted at me, or so it sounded like.

"Mike, hold on," the whistle man warned. "This boy's from a wicked small town in Michigan, he don't unnerstand English so good."

"Oh. Gotcha." Mike took a deep breath. "It's okay, son. Just get in the cab. The Sox are down by two, bottom of the fourth. Just saying hello."

I slid into the cab, and the crowd waved and called after me as if I were Dorothy in the balloon: "Bye! Bye!"

Mike drove with what I suppose you could call restrained death wish, blaring his horn through intersections and veering toward pedestrians with a snarl in order to keep them on the curb. Occasionally he pointed out a historical marker, and I would briefly glance at it before I resumed praying. Several cabs roared past us, the drivers staring at Mike in disbelief. He shrugged his shoulders at each, shouting an explanation through his open window. "Small-town kid in da back, gotta take it easy!"

We pulled up in front of the hotel and stopped, the bellman peering at me curiously, possibly wondering why Mike hadn't sped past and dumped me out like a dead body. The two of them conferred, and then the bellman came over and took me by the arm.

"You'll be okay, little fella," he told me. I paid Mike, who punched me lightly in the shoulder, then looked scared.

"Aw, I'm sorry, did that hurt? Sorry, kid, I forgot."

Mike wanted his picture taken with me, and then the bellman ushered me through the mechanics of checking in, warning the desk clerks to "take it easy on this little guy."

In my room I was shown where to put my bag and how to call the front desk if I "got scared."

"You'll be okay, little buddy," the bellman told me. "Just stay inside and don't talk to nobody."

So you see why I like Boston. The people are wicked nice.

Bruce the Answer Man on College

Having a child in college is the best cure I know for some of the worst symptoms of middle age, such as savings accounts and vacations. It's sort of the financial equivalent of stepping into an elevator shaft—except that in this case, at the end of each semester, the elevator takes you back up to the top floor so you can do it again.

For those parents who believe they might accidentally have given birth to children smart enough to get into college, here's a session of Bruce the Answer Man to address their concern. ("Concern" in this case being the same as "panic.")

Q: I've always meant to establish a college fund for my son, but now he's nineteen. Does this make me a bad parent?
A: No, it makes you a typical parent.

Q: Please explain the meaning of college "nondiscretionary fees."
A: Take tuition, room, and board and subtract it from your net income. The amount left over is what college will cost you in "non-discretionary fees."
Q: But that leaves no money for food, clothing, and shelter!
A: Having a child in college means giving up such luxuries.

Q: What are the steps I should take to obtain a college scholarship for my child?
A: First, be a professional athlete, and second, marry a professional athlete.

Q: At what age should I start saving to send my kid to college?

A: I'd say sixteen.

Q: What? Won't my kid be in high school by then?

A: You misunderstand me: I don't mean when your kid is sixteen, I mean when *you* are sixteen. Any later than that and you might as well forget it.

Q: I'm hoping that my daughter can find employment over the summer to pay at least half of her expenses during the school year. What sort of job would you recommend for this?

A: Neurosurgeon.

Q: Are student loans a good idea?

A: Student loans are very effective at keeping someone broke long after graduation. The theory behind them is that your child borrows money at a low interest rate and then pays it back after he has earned a degree and is unemployed and living with you.

Q: What is the difference between "in-state tuition" and "out-of-state tuition"?

A: Your child will want you to pay "out-of-state tuition."

Q: I'd sacrifice everything I have to enable my child to obtain a college degree.

A: Well, that's not going to be enough.

Q: How can I mentally prepare myself for having my daughter go off to college?

A: First, buy a postcard with a picture of a Cancun resort hotel on it. Write "Wish you were here" on the back of the postcard. Next, open a box of Pop-Tarts and remove one of the pastries and set it out on the table for three days. Then shut down your furnace and turn off all the lights in your house. Sit there in the gloom, shivering, and start eating the stale Pop-Tart. When you are halfway finished chewing your way through the thing, pick up the postcard and pretend your daughter just sent it to you while on spring break.

Q: Now that my son is in college, it seems like the only value I have to him is that I pay the bills.

A: You see much less of your son now, and when he calls, it is very often to ask for more money, so it is understandable that you feel this way. But despite the fact that he doesn't express it, I can assure you, it's not just the money—your son also cares very deeply about the fact that when he comes home to visit, you do his laundry.

Q: I don't get what all the fuss is about: I feel like I have enough money to send my child to college.

A: It's an honor to get a question from Bill Gates. For everybody else, I hope this edition of Bruce the Answer Man has been helpful!

From the Dog about the Cat

To: *Master of the House*
From: *Dog*
Subject: *Cat*

Master:

The cat is despicable. She doesn't do any tricks and never comes when you call and I've been there and I know she can hear you. We need to face facts: It is time to get rid of the cat.

Before the cat's arrival, meals were very festive times. I would sit and stare attentively at your lips, trembling slightly and drooling. You would play the game of pretending to be cross and demand that I leave the area, but whenever you cooked dinner, your children would slip me food under the table.

Now, though, the cat is allowed to jump on the table— actually physically walk on the table! You don't yell at the cat; you just pick her up and put her back on the floor, and I know you don't see it but she always gives me a haughty look as she walks past me.

And speaking of meals, I have always been satisfied to eat the gritty pellets of meat by-products you bring home in the giant bags, right? Have I ever once, ever, failed to finish a meal? But now I find out that the cat is being served lobster and salmon and crab—and she never consumes all of it! This means there are little containers of delectable snacks lying around, and how can I be blamed for making sure they get eaten? Why do you get so mad? As long as the *pet* food is going to the *pets*, isn't that what is important?

Then there is playtime. I think we can clearly see that I am a big dog, descended from a noble line of hunters accustomed to chasing prey and attacking it. Haven't I nearly managed to take down a few cars as they've driven past the house? The cat is about the size of a squirrel and in my view should behave like one, but when I attempt to chase her, she hunches up and spits at me! This cannot be sanitary. And shouldn't she be declawed? I'm very concerned about the potential for damage to the furniture plus my nose.

Speaking of sanitation, do you realize that the cat goes to the bathroom in the house? And not in the drinking basins like you do, but in a sandbox in the basement. What are we going to say if some woman brings her baby over to play in the sandbox and the cat has been using it as a toilet? I used to police the thing for you, but you put it up out of my reach for some reason.

I'm not the only one who feels the cat is an evil person. Here is a note from the hamster:

To: *Master of the House*
From: *Hamster*
Subject: Cat

Please tell cat to stop staring at me while I work.

—Hamster, Department of Rodent Wheels

I also tried to get a note from the fish, but apparently it believes that everything happening outside its bowl is some kind of reality TV show.

I don't understand why the cat is allowed up on the bed and I'm not. I am far more cuddly than any stupid cat. I think her purring sounds unhealthy and may be a sign of tuberculosis. And why doesn't she ever get a bath? She smells like saliva from licking her paws—you'd never catch me licking such ridiculous places. I often smell wonderful from rolling in roadkill, yet you give me baths all the time!

And speaking of sleeping, sometimes I will be taking a nap and she'll come right up and lie down beside me. Usually I'm too tired to do anything about it, but then later the other dogs smell her on me and crack a lot of jokes at my expense.

So, not to exaggerate, but the cat has brought the family to complete ruin. I'm sorry I've got to be the one to bring it to your attention, but now that I have, I think we can all agree that we should go back to the way it was, when I was the number one pet.

Yours truly,

The Dog

Memory Layoff

I have a reputation for being tenacious and dedicated—once I've committed myself to a goal, I won't quit until I'm bored. Thus it should come as no shock to anyone that I'm still focused on trying to improve my memory. (Obviously, I expect you to remember that I am having a problem with forgetfulness. If you don't, well, that's rather ironic, isn't it?)

My biggest problem is in forgetting the names of people, which can be very awkward when you're the best man at their wedding. Under most circumstances, I try to cover up my embarrassing lapse by pretending that I usually call the people in question by pet nicknames—which is how I wound up proposing a toast to "Scuz" and his new wife "Bucky."

The problem is one of overpopulation. Too many people are stored in my brain already, and they treat every attempt I make to retrieve a name as if it were some sort of giant audition, everyone vying for the same part in the play. Who should get the role of the guy who told me I should call him if my cable TV ever went out? Several plausible candidates immediately try out for the job.

"Call me with any problems," booms Mr. McCord, my parents' TV repairman in 1966.

"No, call me," insists Melvin, the mechanic who is using my car as a device for prying money out of my savings account.

"Call me," declares some guy who was once in my house wearing a shirt with the name "Jim" stitched over his breast pocket. Either he or his clothing was named Jim, I suppose, but I can't recall why he was in my house and could easily be convinced that his shirt said something else, like "Tim" or "Kim" or " FedEx."

The solution to my dilemma lies, I've decided, in getting rid of some of these bad actors. This should be simple; it's just a question of going in and telling them their services are no longer needed.

"You're fired," I advise the memory of Bill Huffster, a bully who used to terrorize me on the playground until I finally stood up for myself and had my sister punch him in the stomach. Then I hid in our basement until his family moved to another state.

"You can't fire me," Bill sneers. "You're afraid."

"Ha! I'm not afraid of you. I'm now a mature man, strong and brave, and you're just a third-grade kid," I inform him loftily.

"Oh yeah?" he snarls menacingly.

"Don't hit me!" I blurt.

"See? You're scared. Now give me your lunch money or I'll make you climb up on the monkey bars and sing 'My Name is Nancy' for everyone to hear."

Not that again, I hate that! "I don't get it—how come you always make me sing that stupid song?" I implore.

He shrugs. "I'm in third grade. I sort of lack imagination."

"Well, look, why can't you just leave? Go bother my sister, she's the one who socked you in the stomach," I suggest.

"She's not here to protect you, Nancy boy. It's just you and me."

"Well, I wouldn't say she was protecting me, exactly" I object, miffed. "I just happened to mention that you were making me stand up on the monkey bars and she knows I have a fear of heights, so she sort of took it into her own hands . . ."

"Are you going to stand there all day and whine, or are you going to fight?" he interrupts. (Besides being a bully, he really is very rude.)

"I'm not going to get into a fistfight with a third-grade boy, Bill," I inform him loftily. "It would not be dignified."

"Plus you're afraid I would beat you up," he snickers.

Then I'm seized with a brilliant thought. "Ha!" I shout. "I can't sing the song for you because I can't remember the lyrics."

"Well, that's pretty ironic," he observes.

"So I might as well forget you too," I continue triumphantly. "My weakness is my strength!"

"My name is Nancy," he responds softly. "My pants are fancy . . ."

"Watch me and I'll do a song and dancey," I rejoin, unable to help myself.

Unfortunately, there are some things I seem to be unable to completely forget.

Last Dance

When my son was a toddler, he used to love riding in his car seat because it gave him a stable platform from which to pitch things at the back of my head. His giggly joy when he managed to nail me with a soggy chunk of Pop-Tart was so full of delight, I couldn't find it in my heart to get mad at him, though I hated it when my boss would interrupt a meeting to ask me if I realized I had pastry crumbs in my hair.

When he wasn't filling the air with projectiles, he would be singing out landmarks as we passed them. "Bus bar!" he always cried when we drove by the outbuilding where the county kept the school buses corralled—the "bus barn." In the summer the buses baked under the sun like large beasts napping in a field, but during the school year the buses were sometimes out on their rounds, inspiring a conversation like this:

"No bus, Daddy?"

"No, no buses today."

"No bus?"

"No bus."

"No bus?"

"No bus."

"No bus?"

"Okay, fine. Yes. Yes, there was a bus."

"No bus?"

I'm not sure when it was decided that it was no longer necessary for him to be strapped into a child safety seat whenever we went for a car ride, though I am fairly certain it was before he got his driver's license. And I don't remember the last time he thought the lack of buses at the bus barn was a topic worthy of debate.

What I do remember is the last time he held my hand. We were downtown on a crisp fall afternoon, navigating on foot through the impatient rush-hour traffic on our way to the bookstore. This is a kid who grew up in the mountains and who had always regarded automobiles as solitary hunters; confronted with so many of them on the prowl at once, their tires barking angrily at stoplights, he became very nervous. He might have been aged eight, then—certainly old enough that my instinctive, parental reach for him whenever we crossed a street was always shaken off with a shrug of annoyance. But the very real danger posed by all that hurtling metal caused him to seek reassurance, and I felt his hand curl up into mine as we stepped off the curb.

It was the size of it that struck me, how much his fist had grown since the last time I'd held it. That, in turn, led me to reflect on the fact that we just didn't hold hands anymore.

Safely across the street, he released me, and we left the episode unremarked. For me, though, it was a rare milestone in the otherwise shockingly swift transformation of my little boy into man.

We parents are not often afforded the opportunity to specifically remember and treasure the last time our kids perform some childlike act. I can't recall the final bedtime story I read my children, or the last time any of them needed to be carried anywhere. I didn't notice when it was no longer necessary for me to kiss every one of their dolls good night when I tucked my daughters in, or even the last time I tucked them in. There's no warning that a treasured ritual is having its curtain call; if there were, perhaps we'd do something special to record the occasion, in memory if not on paper or video, so that maybe we could relive that precious moment.

Nowadays whenever I pass the bus barn and the yellow behemoths are out on their routes, I note it for the record. "No buses," I murmur, even if I am by myself. If my son is in the car with me, he gives me a bland look, registering my observation but clearly feeling the matter doesn't call for further conversation. He doesn't remember.

But I do remember, just as clearly as I can remember the wet smack of a partially chewed Pop-Tart catching me behind the right ear, and the last time he held my hand, crossing a busy street on an autumn afternoon.

Ice Fishing with My Father: Very Funny

My dad asks me if I'd like to go ice fishing in his shanty with him. "Why don't we both just crawl into the freezer? It's bigger, warmer, and there are more fish in there," I suggest.

"Very funny," he says to me. This is what my father has said to me after every joke I have ever told him. His lips say it; his face never does.

An ice-fishing shanty is basically a tin outhouse out on a frozen lake, except that in an outhouse the hole has a purpose. In ice fishing, the hole is what you stare at for hours, hoping that at some point you'll break the monotony by falling in.

Outside, the wind whipping the snow around, it feels a hundred degrees below zero. Inside the ice shanty, protected from the elements, it's much colder.

People who love to ice fish usually say the same thing all day long: "Pass the vodka." If they don't like to ice fish, they usually sit around and tell jokes to my father. At least, that's my experience.

Anyway, my father lives in the part of the United States where they consider Canadians to be warmer and more stylish. The lake has already frozen over and is thick enough to support us as we wander out onto what looks like winter in Kansas without cows—at least, we *hope* it is thick enough to support us. If it's not, instead of feeding on fish, we'll be doing the opposite.

My father has placed his shanty in a very secret fishing spot on the ice—so secret the fish have never heard of it. "I have a new auger," he says to me.

"That augurs well," I say gamely. His look says I'll have to improve the level of my jokes if I expect to win the coveted "very funny" award.

The auger is basically a huge drill bit with a wicked point on one end and a retired gynecologist at the other. My father's new toy also has a small engine: He starts it with a few pulls, so that now our ears can be as miserable as the rest of us.

"Wouldn't it be quieter if you just held the auger steady and I spun the lake?" I shout at him.

"What?" he shouts back, meaning "yes."

He braces himself, holding on to what look like bicycle handles on either side of the motor, and hits the throttle. With a roar, the point of the drill bit bites down into the ice and immediately begins spinning my father in circles.

It turns out to be impossible to help a whirling gynecologist when you are laughing so hard you fall down. I lie helpless on the ice as he eventually decides to get off the merry-go-round and kills the motor. Dizzy, he staggers against the metal walls of the shanty and then he, too, is lying on the ice.

Most men have to spend several hours ice fishing and drinking their favorite beverage before they fall down, but my father has deployed new technology.

"Works pretty well," I finally tell him.

"Very funny," he says.

We then discuss the merits of our individual plans of attack. My father thinks we should both grab the auger. I think we should both buy some fish.

Once we've fired that baby up and are holding on to it and are being vibrated by what sounds like a rocket launch inside a steel drum, we grimly brace ourselves on the ice, which gives us very little purchase because—guess what?—it's *ice*. Chunks of the stuff come out of the steadily deepening hole as my father and I, gripping each other, circle like sumo wrestlers. The deeper we go, the faster we seem to be circling.

Finally, with a gush, we hit black water—or rather, the water hits *us*, bathing our legs. My father hits the kill switch and we stand, panting, our feet soaking and our bodies vibrating. I'm pretty sure I could throw up if I wanted and maybe even if I didn't.

"You think any fish heard that racket?" my dad asks.

To which I reply, of course: "Very funny."

Son of Puberty

Gradually it's becoming apparent to me that my son is no longer a little boy. He doesn't sleep with a pacifier anymore, he no longer demands a bedtime story every night, plus he's taller than me and has a learner's permit.

When my daughters hit puberty, they did so with an audible impact. Suddenly the house was filled with a lot of shrieking and sobbing, but I couldn't help myself; their clothing had become so tight it was causing me pain. And they didn't seem to be enjoying themselves very much either, judging by the anguished expressions on their faces, though this didn't mean they were willing to call the whole thing off.

My son, though, seems to be handling the massive changes occurring in his life with the same attitude he employs toward his household chores: complete apathy. He doesn't scream at me that I am the Meanest Man in the World just because I refuse to allow him to go to the movies with his bra straps showing. He doesn't demand that No One Use the Phone Because He's Expecting Like the Most Important Phone Call in His Entire Life Because Brittany Broke Up with Derek!!!! (excessive punctuation actual). He basically just eats, grows, sleeps, and grows.

Despite his apparent lack of interest in the subject, I decided it was time to provide him with some instruction on how to handle the changes he's experiencing, so I wrote him the following letter.

My dear son:

There's a reason you're wearing new pants: You outgrew the old ones during math class. Thanks to you, there is now a contest between the clothing budget and the food bills to see which one will overtake my income first. They're both winning.

What you're going through is called puberty, while what I am going through is called consumer debt.

You know you are different because your voice has changed; you used to sound like a choirboy, now you sound like a prison guard. But here's what you don't know:

- Soon you will have acne. This is a condition that causes unattractive red welts to protrude from your face whenever you speak to a pretty girl. Eventually, adolescent acne goes away of its own accord, and then you'll have rosacea, which is often referred to as "adult acne."
- Recently you may have noticed that you are becoming obsessed with girls. There is no cause for alarm, even though you'll *feel* alarmed—your pulse pounds, you sweat, pant, and grow dizzy whenever a woman enters your field of vision. This feverish mania strikes all males at a certain age and will eventually pass because you'll be dead.
- Currently your metabolism is burning at approximately the same level as a nuclear power plant in meltdown. To keep from starving, you've learned to eat dinners the size of my kitchen. Eventually, your internal fires will cool, and at that time you'll need to learn to eat less, or risk getting fat. When you figure out how to do this, please let me know, because I'm currently going with the "get fat" plan.
- I love you and want you to live through this, which is why I have been so reluctant to teach you to drive. Also, I love me and want me to live through this too.

But I'll teach you if you promise not to drive fast, and then I'll buy an old car with a small engine so you can't. You'll hate it and claim to be embarrassed to be seen in it, so I'll reply that you should feel free to save your own money and buy a Corvette. This is what my father told me when I was your age, and I'm still saving.

Puberty serves an important function: It is a biological process designed to make parents want their children to move out of the house. Without it, parents might be tempted to say things like "Why don't you live with me until you can afford your own place?", which then leads to a conversation about "Don't you think you should move out before you turn fifty?"

So puberty is normal. It isn't a disease.

It just feels like one.

From the Cat about the Dog

To: Large Human Resident of My Home
From: Her Royal Highness, Princess Feline
Subject: The Burdens I Must Bear

You are my most senior staff member, and by "senior" I mean, of course, "oldest," because I hold both of your daughters in much higher regard. This position means you have certain responsibilities—responsibilities you are not living up to.

Naturally, I am speaking about the dog, who has recently written a cowardly memo to you in an attempt to spark a revolt in the household. It was your duty to administer swift and preferably capital punishment to the insubordinate animal, and your dismal failure in the matter has led me to craft this letter. This forces me to do something I am utterly loathe to do: acknowledge your existence. I must warn you that as a result, I am putting a copy of this memo in your personnel file.

This whole matter is most unseemly, as the dog lacks standing to register a complaint of any kind. This is an animal who, when excited, attempts to make love to the sofa—an animal who, when allowed outside, rewards us by defecating in our yard!

How often, I ask you, have we been enjoying a lovely evening of our favorite activity—sitting in front of the television in the family room, everyone taking turns stroking and worshipping me—only to have this mutt release a gaseous emission that brings tears to our eyes and screams of anguish from your children? Of course, you yourself are to blame here for the bad example you set with your own flatulent behavior. In fact, there is such a strong link between your initial discharge and the dog's follow-up volleys that I've come to think of them as "sympathy farts." You'll never catch a cat performing such an indelicacy. In my view, the both of you should be banished to the deck—you can watch television and me through the window.

His tendency to bark at the most routine event—such as the ringing of the doorbell (is this supposed to be some sort of warning? We all heard the doorbell, for goodness sake!) is most perturbing, as it interferes with my hobby— bird-watching. (I've been observing the birds in the feeder for more than a year now, and have determined that most of them can be classified as "edible.")

The only function at which the animal excels is as a pillow for my mid-late afternoon nap, and sometimes for my early late afternoon nap as well. Yet even at this he often fails, falling into a restless state full of leg-twitching and soft yipping. (I know you think he is dreaming of chasing rabbits, but nothing could be further from the truth. You know what he is dreaming of? Running from cats, and well he should. He knows he's in serious trouble with me; you can tell by the way he slinks around in my presence.)

As a species, canines represent a broken rung on the evolutionary ladder. Have you ever seen two or more of them mingle together? They sniff each other in unmentionable places, then race over to lift their legs on the bushes, proudly strutting around as if they've caught a mouse or something, when all they've done is urinate on target.

Even worse: I think the fool canine actually likes me. It's probably because I am so beautiful; but have you ever thought about what it is like to be licked by that tongue? It's like being wiped down with a drooling carpet.

In short, the dog has done nothing but cause trouble ever since I, its replacement as the most beloved animal in the house, arrived to take the throne. This attempt to violate the chain of command and appeal to you to stage some sort of peasant uprising is just the latest affront. We would be much better served if we replaced him with a pet we would all find more enjoyable and fun.

May I suggest a family of free-range gerbils?

Offspring Offsprung

When our family all lived together under one roof, my two daughters despised each other at the molecular level. They would appeal to me almost daily to intervene and inflict massive punishment on the other for (a) always using/borrowing/stealing stuff without permission, and (b) existing.

Whenever it seemed the only peaceful way to resolve their conflict was with some form of homicide, I would weigh in with fatherly diplomacy, noting that if you were going to kill somebody, you should go outside so as not to wreck the furniture, and oh by the way in just a few more years you will both be living somewhere else, in separate dwellings, thus sparing me the cost of blood pressure medication.

Then they both moved out and got their own apartment. With each other.

I was dumbfounded. Wasn't my older daughter the same person who said she couldn't sleep at night because she hated the way her sister *breathed*? Didn't my younger daughter claim her sister was deliberately trying to drive her insane by squeezing the toothpaste tube incorrectly?

"Is this some sort of matter/anti-matter experiment?" I demanded.

"Oh, Dad," they laughed gently, "we're grown up and independent and mature and we need money for food."

What I soon found out is that this living arrangement is much more efficient than if they lived apart. With this system, when one of them borrows my blender, they can both make use of it, and then they can each ask the other to return it to me until I have forgotten I even own a blender. In this way I gradually have gained something everyone needs in the kitchen: more counter space.

"How am I supposed to cook for myself if I don't have any knives?" I asked them.

"A good chef only needs a single high-quality kitchen knife," my older daughter informed me primly.

"Which you borrowed!" I thundered back.

"You need to eat more fruits and vegetables anyway," my younger daughter advised.

This last statement rang in my ears long after I hung up, and I realized my daughter was right: I did need to eat more! I made myself a hamburger, flipping it with a salad fork because my daughters had borrowed my barbecue utensils.

A few hours later, my older daughter phoned back and invited me to their place for dinner. Realizing that they loved me and would probably prepare a healthy, low-fat meal because they were worried about my cholesterol, I enthusiastically declined. However, as a father, there are some things a daughter can say to get me to do just about anything, and those things are "chocolate" and "cake."

When I arrived for dinner at their small apartment—so similar to the one I first lived in when I moved out of my own parents' home—I was reminded of something I hadn't really thought about in a long, long time: my toaster. Also my clock radio, my CDs, my television . . . it's as if their place was the Official Museum of Stuff That Used to Belong to Dad.

Before the cake there was a dinner of rice and beans, peppers, fruit salad, and yogurt—all the sort of food that a man my age should be eating if he wants to go into anaphylactic shock. I received an urgent message from my stomach, wanting to know if we had been captured by the enemy.

Finally dessert was on the table, and we all heartily dug in and watched me eat it. My stomach stopped complaining and started releasing endorphins, and I sat back contentedly and let my daughters lecture me about my diet.

And then something strange happened: Without accusation or argument, my daughters worked together to clear the table and do the dishes, courteously smiling at each other whenever they collided in the tiny kitchen.

Watching them, I remembered a time when nearly every morning one of them would be in shower while the other pounded on the door, murderously screaming to be let in. I always had to intervene to prevent daughter-induced structural damage.

To tell you the truth, I sort of miss those days.

My Father the Dog Trainer

My parents are the kind of people who believe that dogs understand full sentences, like this: "Okay, we're going to the store, we'll be gone a couple of hours, please stay out of the trash and don't lie on my bed, that's off-limits and you know it!"

What the dog thinks: *Bed!*

So my father is perplexed that his two Labradors continue to bark at everyone who comes to the door, even though he's sternly delivered his sermon "Thou Shalt Not Bark at the Person at the Door Unless He Is a Criminal." When it's my dad at the door, the dogs bark even at *him*, though they are always wagging their tails to indicate they know he is not a criminal.

"Stop barking or no dinner!" my father thunders at them.

What the dogs think: *Dinner!*

The dogs are named Nick and Carly—Nick is a large jet-black male, and Carly is a smaller blonde female. Observing them carefully, my father concludes that it is Nick who is the perpetrator—Carly barks only because Nick is barking. To test this theory, he feeds Nick doggie snacks as a neighbor comes to the door, and, sure enough, Nick is distracted by the treats and doesn't bark. Nor does Carly bark, either because Nick didn't bark or because she's focused on the question of whether she'll get a treat herself.

With this proof in hand, my father orders an anti-bark shock collar in Nick's size. When it arrives, the dogs bark at the delivery man. My dad shows them the box, but the mere threat doesn't seem to bother them, and they keep barking until he gives them dog treats.

My father doesn't want to physically harm his dog, so he decides to test the collar on himself first. He puts the collar around his neck and makes a barking sound, then screams. Excited, the dogs bark.

"It hurt!" he complains to me on the phone.

"It's a shock collar; did you think it was going to feel *good*?" I ask him.

"Well, I'm not going to use it on my dog," he says.

He puts the collar away to give to my mom for Mother's Day, and orders a non-painful bark collar.

"It shoots a mist of concentrated lemon juice out of these two nozzles when he barks," he chortles.

It sounds harmless enough, but when my dad tries it out on himself, it squirts lemon juice in his eyes. He staggers around the room, blinded, the dogs barking excitedly.

"It burned my eyes! I'm not going to do that to Nick," he says. "Plus I hate the smell."

"You hate the smell . . . of lemons?" I ask cautiously.

"You would hate it too, if it ever got squirted in your eyes from a bark collar."

Thinking about it, I decide that's not likely to happen.

The next device looks like a small plastic speaker. It emits an annoying, high-pitched sound every time the dogs bark. He sets it up and looks at it expectantly. The dogs decide to take a nap. My dad barks. Nick begins to snore.

"Nothing is happening," he complains. "I've barked and barked."

"Maybe it can tell the difference between a dog bark and a gynecologist bark," I suggest.

My dad goes to the door and opens it, then shuts it. "I'm home!" he shouts. The dogs don't wake up. He stomps his feet. "Hello! I'm a stranger, breaking into your house!"

What the dogs think: *He's really losing it.*

Eventually a neighbor comes over. Now *that,* they react to.

"They started barking and then wouldn't stop," my father bitterly informs me.

"Almost as if they were irritated by an annoying noise," I muse.

"I had to feed them dog biscuits to get them to shut up," he says.

I ask him whether maybe he shouldn't try just giving them dog biscuits when someone comes to the door and they don't bark. He doesn't think it will work but admits there are no more gadgets to buy.

The positive reinforcement is successful: They don't bark when someone is at the door anymore.

However, they do bark whenever he gets out the box of dog biscuits.

Teaching My Son to Drive

I don't mind a lot of personal risk unless I am the person, and then I hate it. As the saying in our family goes, "A real man knows when it is time to face danger, and when it is time to curl up in the fetal position and make whimpering sounds."

I sensed danger a few months ago when my son informed me that the Department of Motor Vehicles thought it would be a good idea if he got behind the wheel of my car and plowed into a few mailboxes. (What he actually said was "learner's permit," but I knew what it meant.) "Dad," he announced with solemn, forced sincerity, "I'd be honored if you taught me."

"I'd be injured if I taught you. Why do you need to drive? Haven't you always been able to find a ride?"

I suppose I have always known that this moment would come, just as I've always known that someday my son would grow up and move out. I guess I had just hoped that the whole learning-to-drive thing would occur *after* he moved out.

Learning is usually a matter of trial and error. In this case, "trial" means "ordeal" and the error was believing I could teach my son to drive in the first place. Positioned in the driver's seat for the very first time, his hands on the wheel, he interrupted my nervous lecture on "keeping your father safe" with one question: "So how fast can this baby go?"

"I suppose we could hit a hundred," I admitted, "but you would never—"

"Only a hundred?" he interrupted scornfully. "A Ferrari can go 180."

That's when I broke it to him: I am not buying a car that costs more than my net worth, and even if I did,

I would never loan it to someone who is less concerned with "how to work the brakes" than "how to pop the clutch."

"But you always said a Ferrari was your dream car!" he protested.

"Yes, but in my dream, you're not the one driving it."

When I taught my daughters to drive, there was a lot of frustration, tears, and anger. I reacted the same way with my son.

His first driving lesson starts off well, if you consider "fast" to be a synonym for "well." Once we are moving, my son and I have the following conversation:

"Okay, son, you're moving too fast, here. Too fast. Slow down. Can you . . . Hey! Slow down!"

"Hang on, that's my cell phone."

"I am hanging on! You can't answer—"

I watch in dismay as he answers his phone with one hand while shifting gears with the other. "I have to go," he tells the person on the other end. "I'm driving, but my dad keeps grabbing the steering wheel for some reason."

"You can't steer with your knees!" I tell him. "We could have had an accident."

"But that's how you do it when you have a phone call," he points out calmly. "Hey!" He honks the horn at a car zooming past us. My teeth click as he stomps on the accelerator.

"What are you doing?"

"He was in a VW!"

"What do you mean?"

"You always say that it's an insult to be passed by a VW. What gear should I be in to take him?"

"We're not 'taking' anybody. Slow down, you're going way too fast."

"But you told me the cops never watch this section of the highway."

"Okay, lesson over for today. Pull over."

"What? Why?"

"Because your driving is interfering with my instinct for survival. Put on your blinker, and slowly ease over to the side of the road. Gently use the brake. Son, slow it down. Stop!"

"Whoa, that was sweet."

"Why did you do that? Why didn't you stop gently? You almost set off the airbags!"

"A slow stop wouldn't have made any skid marks like you always leave in the driveway."

I put my hand over my heart, wondering if it was leaving skid marks on the inside of my rib cage.

It's going to be more difficult than I thought to teach my son to drive. Somewhere he's picked up a few really bad habits!

The Day I Was Floored

I was recently stuck on an elevator, an event made no less dramatic by the fact that the doors were open. Okay, maybe a little less dramatic.

I was by myself on the elevator, having just been to the dentist to have my teeth and my wallet scraped clean. It was descending smoothly when all of a sudden it stopped dead with a loud, slamming jolt similar to what it felt like when I saw the bill for the dentist. There was a grinding noise and then the doors eased open between floors, though there was about two feet of space at the top where I could crawl through if I decided I wanted to be cut in half when the elevator got going again.

I opened the little door on the panel, picked up the phone, and was gratified when someone answered.

"Security," he said.

"Hi. Uh, I'm on the elevator."

"I know."

"What? Oh, you mean you can see me?" I peered around for a camera.

"What? No, who do you think I am, Santa Claus? I can't *see* you. You called on the elevator phone. There's a little light on my switchboard that says 'Elevator.' I can see *it*."

"Oh, right."

"Sir, I must ask you to hang up the telephone immediately. It's to be used only in case of emergency."

"Wait! This is an emergency. The elevator is stuck between floors."

There was a pause. "I'm not sure that qualifies as an actual emergency."

"What?"

"Well, it's not like you are being attacked by vampires or something."

"So wait, they put a phone in the elevator for vampires? It's a vampire phone?"

"It is not a vampire phone," he responded testily. "I was just using that as an example. My daughter reads these books where the kids in high school are all vampires. She drives me crazy. I was just thinking about that when you called."

"Oh. So you weren't seriously suggesting that the reason they put a phone in the elevator was so people would call you if there were vampires."

"Of course not. It's for what I said, emergency use only."

"I think, though, if you were an elevator company, you might consider a stuck elevator to be an elevator emergency."

We compromised: I would concede there were far more urgent situations than being stuck on an elevator and he would look up what to do in his emergency operations manual.

"Okay, first, don't panic."

"I'm not panicking," I responded.

"Me neither. Okay, second, relax."

"I'm relaxed."

"Me too. Third, calm down."

"Okay, that's the same as don't panic and relax! When are you going to work on getting me out of here?"

"You don't sound calm to me."

"I'm calm! What's next?"

"Okay. I'm to ask you to describe the nature of the emergency."

"Okay."

"So . . . what is the risk to life and/or property?"

"You mean you want me to tell you *again*?"

"I'm just doing what it says here, buddy."

"The elevator is stuck between floors! I'm trapped! I could starve to death in here!"

"So would you say the risk to life and/or property is mainly from starvation?"

"No! I mean, eventually, maybe, but not immediately."

"Then it's not an actual emergency, is it?"

"I thought we compromised on that one already."

"Yeah, but now I need to write this down in the log, and I can't write that you're hungry. I'll look like an idiot."

"I'm not *hungry*. I never said I was hungry."

"You said starving."

"I said I was trapped! The elevator is stuck. The doors are open. It's not moving."

"You mean to tell me the doors are *open*?"

"Yes, but between floors!"

"Did you try pushing the 'Door Close' button?"

"That won't work; the elevator is broken."

"Try it."

"It won't work!" I shouted, exasperated. I punched the door close button in frustration and the doors immediately sighed shut. With a jolt, the elevator began descending again, and within a minute I was in the parking garage.

I thought about calling the security guy to tell him that the button worked, but I decided against it.

After all, the phone was for emergency use only.

Meet Your New Granddog

My daughter called me a few weeks ago with what she clearly felt was terrific news. "You're a grandpa!" she gushed. "Isn't it wonderful? Hello?"

My initial reaction to this shocking pronouncement was to wonder when I would stop gasping. Through the haze of my panic (I'm not old enough to be a grandfather yet! I'm still saving money for my midlife crisis!) I puzzled how this bit of news could possibly be true. She might legally be of age to marry, but as far as I knew, my daughter hadn't had a wedding that I'd heard about—I'm pretty sure I would have noticed the bills. And though she was certainly biologically capable of bearing live young, I doubted she could pull it off in a weekend, which is how long it had been since I had seen her last. She accused me all the time of not noticing when she was wearing a new outfit, but I was positive I hadn't seen her wearing maternity clothes at any point during the past nine months.

If you aren't pregnant, you can't have a baby—I'm pretty sure it's a rule. But wait, what if she'd adopted a child?

"Dad?"

"Just a minute, I'm still fibrillating on this."

Would any responsible adoption agency give a baby to a woman who was financially dependent on regular loans from her father and still hadn't returned his blender?

"Her name's Duchess," my daughter advised.

Okay, would any adoption agency give a baby to a woman who would name it "Duchess"?

"Oh, I get it. It's a pretend baby," I said, relieved. "When you were three, you had pretend twins named Peanuts and Pay-Pay. I used to ask you if Peanuts was salted and you always—"

"Dad," she interrupted, "it's a puppy. Her name is Duchess and she's so cute you won't believe it."

I contemplated the fact that my first grandchild was a dog, wondering why I didn't feel more proud. "Hey, how can you manage a puppy? Between work and night school—aren't puppies sort of high-maintenance? They have to be fed, housebroken, trained to bark at three o'clock in the morning . . . oh wait, I think they usually figure that last one out by themselves."

"Well, but *you* work out of the house," she answered.

I was silent for a long moment. "I'm trying to see how that is relevant, here."

"I should have said, 'You work out of the house, *Grandpa.*'"

"Oh, no. No. No no no."

"What does *that* mean?"

"What do you mean, what does that mean? It means no! 'No' as in 'not a puppy,' 'no to a dog,' 'negative on any dukes or duchesses of canine inclination.'"

"Dad—"

"I'm sorry," I told her, "but there's a reason I don't have a puppy, and that reason is called 'carpeting.'"

"Well, it wouldn't be your puppy, it would be my puppy. You'd just be watching her until she got old enough to take care of herself in my apartment," she reasoned.

"Honey, you aren't even old enough to take care of *yourself* in your apartment. Are you forgetting my blender? I think you should wait to adopt a dog until you're old enough to realize you shouldn't have one."

"What do you mean, wait? You mean give up my puppy?" she cried.

"Well, you didn't even ask me," I pointed out.

"Why do I have to ask you? I'm a grown-up! Aren't you always saying I need to be more independent?"

"Yes, that's true."

"Well, how can I be more independent if you won't help me?"

I sighed. "Well, I guess if it is just for a few days . . ."

"They say dogs really calm down after the first year!" she agreed excitedly. "We'll be right over!"

Since then, Duchess has been mostly hanging out at my house—my daughter had to go out of town on business. The two of us get along pretty well, so long as I don't leave anything chewable on the floor, such as a pair of slippers, or a couch.

Taking care of a puppy is a lot of work . . . but it's a lot easier than being a grandpa!

Writers of the Purple Page

I was a very young boy when I realized that my life's purpose—the reason I'd been put on this earth—was to torment my sister Amy.

Amy basically had only two emotional states: She was either in a frenzy, screaming and sobbing and shouting, or she was *really* upset. Anything I did to irritate or anger her would set off such a horrifyingly cataclysmic reaction that I couldn't wait to do it again.

When Amy became a teenager and her unstable condition was enhanced by hormones, it was like going from tornado to hurricane. Like many girls her age, she became weepy and moody, torn apart by foolish romantic crushes, betrayed by shifting alliances among friends, distraught over the slightest insult. My parents warned me that she needed to be left alone, which sounded to my young ears like "You thought antagonizing her was fun before—try it now!"

Amy turned to writing poetry in a top-secret journal that she'd been keeping since she was ten, which was the same year I started reading it. Pink ink flowed across the page in swollen rivers of angst-saturated dreck, each period a meticulously drawn heart, each "i" dotted with a sunflower.

We owned a tape recorder, and Amy read some of this stuff into the microphone, her voice quavering with emotion. Listening to it, I concluded that she was going through a tough time and had turned to making the tape as a way of amusing me.

At this point, Amy had never had a boy call her at the house, so when my mother announced that there was a "Neal" on the phone for her, Amy reacted as if she'd just stuck her finger in a mousetrap. "Nobody say anything!" she screamed, terrified that Neal might hear us talking in the background and conclude that Amy lived with her family and not in a penthouse apartment with some other Playboy bunnies. Everybody froze, listening to a phone call that on Amy's end went like this:

"Hi Neal ha ha ha ha ha you're funny ha ha ha ha you're funny ha ha ha ha."

I did the only thing I could do, under the circumstances: I snuck down to the basement, where I had recently located a hidden phone jack by the furnace, plugged in a phone, picked up the extension, and flipped on the tape recorder. Amy's dramatic, whispery voice wafted out of the tiny speaker:

You stretch my heart like a rubber band
That snaps back into place when you smile
And though I can see me doing many things
I can see me combing the hair of angels
I can see me riding a purple cow
But I can't see me not loving you

At the words "purple cow," Amy came out of her stunned silence and screamed so loudly my skin crawled with goose bumps of joy. She said nothing to Neal, no "Can you hold while I go stab my brother?" Instead, she stomped through the house in a homicidal fury, raging from one phone extension to another. My mother and other sister fled to the grocery store; my father hid under his bed.

Neal remained on the line, respectfully listening to the things Amy could see herself doing, which included living in a kangaroo's pouch and more purple cow rides but never not loving him. I could hear him breathing while Amy kicked in the door to my bedroom and, from the sound of it, pulverized all my belongings.

The poem didn't so much end as run out of drivel. I put the phone to my ear.

"Hey, Neal, are you there?" I whispered.

"Yeah. Who's this?"

"This is Amy's brother. They keep me in the basement. They won't let me out."

"Huh," Neal replied, accepting it.

After an hour or so, I left the basement, and Amy charged me like an angry bull. No, wait—like an angry purple cow. I bravely hid behind my mother.

Because of the structural damage done to the house, my father sternly ordered me never to do anything like that again. And I didn't.

At least, not more than a dozen times.

The Top Dogs

When I die, I want to be reincarnated as one of my mother's dogs.

It was hard for my parents when their three kids grew up and moved out of the house, especially since my older sister did it a total of eight times by the time she turned thirty. Once we were gone, my mom and dad professed to missing us, so yes, they are both having memory issues. What part of having kids did they miss—the work, or the expense? Plus, I'd always understood that they felt they didn't do a very good job of raising their children on the grounds that only one of us became a doctor.

Needing something to shower their attention on, they decided to raise Labradors, only one of which, in my opinion, has even a *shot* at getting into medical school. His name is Nick, and he's bright enough to know how to open the refrigerator and make himself a ham sandwich (though he eats the ingredients separately and assembles the sandwich in his stomach).

What's crazy about Nick's behavior is that if he wants a ham sandwich, all he needs to do is ask—my parents will do anything for their dogs, up to and including donating a kidney. But Nick likes to cook and can often be found in the kitchen, whipping up a delicious meal using nothing more than the few ingredients my mother set out for dinner.

Their other dog, Carly, is beautiful, blonde, and nowhere near smart enough to be a doctor, or to make a ham sandwich, or even to *be* a ham sandwich. Carly will watch in complete bewilderment as Nick places his paw on a lever to raise the garbage-can lid, and will have no idea what he's doing as he carefully sticks his head in and daintily removes some delectable morsel from the trash. Her response will be to knock over the can with a crash, summoning my father, who will yell at Carly while Nick nods wisely from the corner.

"Why did you do that, Carly?" Nick will ask in dog-speak.

"Huh? Do what?" Carly will respond, baffled.

When I telephone, my mother always asks me, "Would you like to talk to Nick?", which is her way of saying, "I need a sanity hearing." After a minute or so of what sounds like a losing wrestling match with the phone, she comes back on.

"He's shy," she tells me.

"He's not going to do very well as a doctor if he refuses to talk to patients," I warn her.

"Here, I'll put Carly on. Carly, say hello! Say hello!" she coaxes.

There's a lot of noise as Carly tries to figure out if the phone is worth eating. "Good girl," my mother praises.

Nick and Carly were on my mind recently when I read that a Japanese company called Medical Life Care Giken has developed a stress test for pets that uses a stick-on patch applied to the animal's feet. Previously, the only way to test a dog was to ask it, "Nick, are you stressed?" (The test didn't work because Nick was too shy to answer.)

I'm going to buy some of these stress-test patches right away for my mother to use on her dogs, who probably find it pretty stressful that they don't know what sort of treat they'll be getting next. They also have a pretty demanding schedule, filled mostly with barking out the window and lying in the sun.

Nick: Hey, Carly, I'm lying here on the carpet, and I noticed the patch of sun isn't where it used to be.

Carly: I'm stressed.

Nick: Me too, that's really stressful.

Carly: Guess I'll go back to sleep.

Nick: I'm also stressed because of these patches on my feet.

Carly: Really? I ate mine.

Nick: What? You're not supposed to eat them, you idiot. Why did you do that?

Carly: Huh? Do what?

Nick: You're making my stress even worse! I think I'll bark out the window!

Carly: Me too!

(Five minutes of barking)

Carly: Hey, Nick!

Nick: Yeah?

Carly: What are we barking at?

Maybe when I visit my parents, I'll put the patches on my own feet.

Looking for Mr. Bunny Coo

When my younger daughter was two years old, she decided she was a fully independent adult. I can remember the exact moment it happened: She was standing in front of a machine that dispensed gumballs of a size designed to make Heimlich a household name, and she wanted one. I told her no, we needed to go, so she wrapped her arms and legs around the thing like it was a runaway horse, threw back her head, and screamed so loudly that everyone in the store stopped what they were doing and ran over to see what sounded like an ongoing ax murder.

Prying her off that gumball machine was like sticking my hands into a basket full of angry cats. Round two of the match took place in the parking lot, where half a dozen people wrote down my license number as I attempted to fold my daughter into her car seat. It was like trying to bend a two-by-four that's kicking you in the face. Finally, tear-stained and sweaty, chest heaving, legs and arms limp with exhaustion, I buckled my own seat belt and drove her home.

Nothing you try on a two-year-old—rewards, threats, exorcisms—will work in the long term, but once you and your toddler have had it out a few times, you'll reach an understanding based on the fact that you're the adult (you're smarter, you're stronger, you provide the food) and she is the child (she has all the power).

I was eventually able to implement a system based on what child psychologists would call "lavish bribes." If she would stop throwing mashed potatoes, for example, I would buy her a castle in Germany.

One of my promises led me to take her out for a day of shopping and lunch, just the two of us. She wore an outfit she picked out herself: a pink ballet tutu, a Kermit the Frog T-shirt, and red cowboy boots. I wore a jacket whose pockets were stuffed with wet wipes. We purchased a small stuffed rabbit she named "Mr. Bunny Coo," a soft, floppy-eared animal, and ate at a fast food restaurant—so named because if the children don't eat their food fast, bored adults will steal all of their french fries.

Somewhere during the afternoon, Mr. Bunny Coo disappeared. My daughter was inconsolable, crying brokenheartedly even after I promised to buy her a living unicorn. Certain this incident would cause a childhood trauma that would wind up costing me thousands of dollars in psychotherapy, I frantically returned to the restaurant and retraced our steps to the park and to the arcade, but the rabbit was nowhere to be found.

Since that time, I suppose I have always been on the lookout for Mr. Bunny Coo. Was that him clutched in a baby's hands, peering out of a child's backpack, driving a bus down Main Street? There were one trillion stuffed rabbits for sale in this country, but none of them were the same.

Then last week I stopped dead in front of a store window, staring openmouthed at a jumble of child's toys. There, on top of the pile, was unmistakably the missing rabbit, his glass eyes unreproachful as they gazed back at me.

I'm not sure what I expected when I handed my daughter the stuffed toy some eighteen years after he first went missing, though I suppose eternal gratitude would have been nice. Always a sucker for anything cute, her face went soft looking at it, but her eyes were puzzled when she regarded me. She hadn't asked for a stuffed animal, so why was I buying her one when she would have preferred an Audi? She clearly had no memory of Mr. Bunny Coo.

For me, though, the reunion held satisfying significance. As a parent, you do some things well, and some things not so well. You accomplish some goals and fail at others. Seeing my daughter sitting on my couch, watching TV, her stuffed rabbit nestled contentedly in the crook of her arm, I felt that I had done something well. For almost two decades, I had been trying to find Mr. Bunny Coo. I could finally cross that one off the list.

A Hole in the Yard

A few years ago I was rather disappointed to learn that I'm not smart enough to dig a hole in my back yard.

My cousin Ken had come over to help me build a deck off the back of the house by doing all the work. My father was there too, and was assisting by watching the basketball game and keeping us informed of the score and complaining that we were low on beer. Ken seemed grateful that I had assembled such a crack team to assist him.

Running short of beer during lunch is against my father's religion. He believes the forces of good and evil in the universe are precariously balanced between sandwiches and beer, and that failure to maintain the correct ratio between the two will result in Total Catastrophic Destruction. He demanded to know what I was planning to do about the looming beer shortage.

"Dad." I spread my arms to indicate the deck-building operation that was under way, which at that point consisted of Ken cutting boards and me watching him do it. "I'm a little busy here."

Muttering darkly about being able to eat "only half a sandwich," he went back to the basketball game.

Eventually Ken asked me to use the posthole digger, which is a gasoline-driven auger that bites into the dirt like a corkscrew and then spins the person holding it in fast circles until he finds the shutoff button or passes out. At least, that's what happened the first time I tried it.

"How's that going?" Ken asked me as I staggered around like Mel Gibson at a sobriety checkpoint.

"Okay, except I think I might throw up now."

Time to give it another go. I seized the handles of the posthole digger—the whole thing resembles a pogo stick with giant drill bit on the end. I started the motor, took a firm stance, and engaged. This time I stood rock still, but the entire planet twirled beneath me. Every half second or so, I would see my father's face at the kitchen window, frowning at me because I was horsing around instead of solving his beverage crisis.

I was thrown to the ground and lay there, the entire universe out of balance.

"We need a rodeo cowboy," I told Ken.

"Just keep your feet still," he advised, as if I'd been using the posthole digger to practice my ballroom dancing.

I grimly took the handles and this time actually managed to dig the hole, the auger going straight and true and my arms coming out of their sockets. Then there was a puff of white smoke from the hole, and the motor died.

"What happened?" I asked Ken, who was sniffing at the burning-rubber smell with suspicion.

My father appeared. "All of your electricity just went off," he announced in a *That's it, I'm getting a new son* tone of voice.

Eventually we decided to call the phone number on the sign that said "Before Digging, Call This Number." It hadn't seemed important before.

The two men who were dispatched by the utility company were very impressed when I explained to them that they could have free sandwiches. They drank iced tea with their lunch, which my dad found so heretical he had to lie down on the couch.

"The thing is," one of them told me, "you have three wires going into your house. Two are hot, and the one in the middle is the ground. You managed to put the tip of that auger right between the ground and one of the hot wires."

"I've been getting pretty good with the thing," I admitted.

"So what I'm saying is, if you had gone a quarter of an inch in either direction, the shortest electrical path to the ground would have been up through you, instead of through the metal auger. We'd be picking pieces of you out of the bushes." He held up a slice of turkey as a visual aid.

Ken's eyes widened. "Whoa," he said finally. "I would have really liked to see that."

So here's the lesson I learned from all this: Even if you are an expert posthole digger like me, and even if you have the universe balanced between lunch and liquid, you really should call that number on the sign before you start screwing with the Earth.

Depending on My Dependents

The one thing I can say about my children is that I know if I really, really need them for something, they'll be there for me unless they're busy.

A few days ago I needed them, because I came down with the stomach flu and my insides were actively becoming my outsides. As a man, I am capable of suffering any illness in stoic silence as long as I know that other people are aware of how miserable I am. My kids seemed like a good choice to be those people, as they love me and owe me money.

My children have caller ID, so I was confident that no matter what they were doing, when they saw who it was, they would immediately put me through to voice mail. I left them each a brief message explaining I had caught a bug, but not to worry, I was sure I was going to be all right.

"So what's this about you dying?" my older daughter asked when she returned my call.

"Did I say dying? I'm sorry, that's wrong. Dying would be an improvement."

"I'm looking up your symptoms on the Internet—this could be food-borne, it says."

"Food-borne, as in born of food? I don't think so. The food has left the building. Now I'm just bringing up pain. Can you come over?"

"Do you want me to take you to the doctor?" she asked.

"No, I'd rather you just stand at the foot of the bed and feel sorry for me."

She rang off with some lame excuse about being at work, though clearly all she was doing was going on the Internet for food-borne illnesses. My younger daughter phoned a few minutes later.

"Your sister says she doesn't care how much pain I'm in, she's not coming over," I advised her.

"I know, I just got a text message from her."

"She has time to send frivolous text messages, but not time to come over to assist her father when he is regurgitating his internal organs," I translated. "I hope you're calling to say that you want to be the *good* daughter."

"No, I want *her* to be the good daughter. I'm at work."

"I don't think you understand. This is, without exaggeration, the most sick any human being has ever been in the history of our species," I told her.

"'Without exaggeration,'" she repeated.

"I need my children here to provide me with sympathy and clean out my garage."

"I *am* providing sympathy," she replied. "I was just sending you an e-mail telling you how sorry I am."

"Oh, honey, you can't get a good feel for how much I am suffering from just e-mail; doctors have known that for hundreds of years. I need my sympathy to be on-site, immediate, and lavish."

"Dad, you know I'm sorry you're sick, but what good would it do for me to just go over to your place so you can see me being sorry? Is that what you really want?"

I thought about it; she did have a point. "Yes, that's what I want."

She told me she had to go because her boss "needed" her—hadn't I just said that *I* needed her? What kind of company did she work for, that put a boss's needs over a father's?

"Wassup, I heard you're sick," my son greeted me on the telephone a few minutes later.

"I just brought up everything I've ever eaten in my entire life," I confirmed. "When are you coming over?"

"Pass," he said.

"Son, I don't think you understand. When a man gets sick, he needs his loved ones there to provide sympathy and do chores. This is a fundamental male characteristic; you need to come over so you can see how it's done."

"I think I can sort of figure it out from a distance. Besides, if I go over there just to offer moral support, I might wind up catching this thing."

I mulled this over. "Worth the risk," I decided.

In the end, none of them came over. Sadly, I wound up suffering in silence, my illness completely unknown to anybody.

Except they are probably reading this and feeling horribly guilty and will be here any moment to try to make amends.

Unless they decide to pass.

To Live and Work in LA

For reasons which are not yet financially clear, I have come to Los Angeles, California. My stated purpose is to "break in" to show business—and thus far that's precisely how I've been treated, like an intruder who has gained unlawful entry into private property and who, under state law, may now be legally shot.

The American Broadcasting Corporation is filming a pilot episode of a television series based on my book, *8 Simple Rules for Dating My Teenage Daughter*. I've been hired to stay out of the way. After six weeks of conferences and script rewrites, the only contribution I've made thus far has been to say, "I thought we were going to have lunch at this meeting."

I blame my lack of involvement on the fact that I don't have an assistant. In LA, everyone has an assistant, which is the person who asks me, "Do you want anything to drink?" every time I enter a room. That's how I know I'm talking to an assistant—they are all concerned I might be thirsty. After fetching water (with a slice of lime) for a couple of years, the "assistants" become "executives," and then someone brings *them* water.

I recently watched a tennis match between two executives, each of whom brought along an assistant. When one executive received a cell phone call, he handed his racquet to his assistant, who stepped in for him. Then the other executive got a call, and the two assistants wound up playing each other.

In LA, cell phones are considered more important than oxygen. After being here for a week, I wrote a professional humor joke:

Q: How can you tell if someone in LA is on a cell phone?

A: His car is moving.

No one has laughed at this, which suggests to me it won't be picked up for the fall season.

I've seen cars pull over to the shoulder of the freeway because their cell phones broke down. Traffic moves so slowly on the freeways that the vehicles stopped on the shoulder actually appear to be going faster.

I don't know where all these people are going all the time, though it might be out to dinner. It's very important to have your assistant book you in a special restaurant every night, where you can be seen by other people or their assistants. I have actually done this a couple of times—gone to a restaurant to spend my children's college fund on a dinner and have the following conversation with the waiter:

Me: I'll have the chicken in the expensive lime sauce.
Waiter: Very good. Bach or Brahms?
Me: Sorry?
Waiter: Do you want the chicken that was raised listening to Bach, or the chicken raised listening to Brahms?
Me: Well . . . what's the difference?
Waiter: The Bach chicken has a Baroque flavor, while the Brahms chicken tastes more Romantic.
Me: I guess I'll go with the Baroque flavor.
Waiter: Very good. And for your potatoes, would you prefer those that were dug up, or those that climbed out of the ground voluntarily?
Me: What's the difference?
Waiter: We don't have any of the voluntary ones.

I go with the indentured potatoes. I'm a bit concerned that the waiter might not think I am an

Important Person, because I don't have an assistant and also they've seated me at a table in the cloakroom. So I push a raincoat out of the way and mention casually that I'm in LA because I'm a screenwriter.

"Really?" the waiter says. I nod modestly.

"He's a screenwriter," the waiter says, pointing to the bartender. "He's a screenwriter," he continues, gesturing to the valet. "So's the gentlemen outside, there, through the window."

The gentleman outside is a man living in a cardboard box.

"I used to be a screenwriter," my waiter confides, "but now I am a producer."

Sitting in the cloak room may not get me much attention during the meal, but I do meet several Important People as they leave, most of whom tip me rather handsomely when I hand them their coats. Adding up the five-dollar bills, I realize I'm actually making pretty good money as a screenwriter in LA!

At this rate, I'll be a producer in no time.

The Best Skin Damage
Money Can Buy

My children tell me I'm too old to worry about sun damage to my skin causing premature aging—they say for me now it's just "aging." And they are too young to worry about it, shrugging off my urging to avoid the sun, which is so dangerous that the government has pledged to eliminate it by the year 2021. Studies have shown that too much sun exposure when you're young can lead, years later, to plastic surgery. As a father it is my job to warn my children of dangers, especially my daughters, who are college-aged and think that just because they no longer live with me, they don't have to pay attention to my curfews.

"By the time my skin gets all wrinkly, I'll be like thirty-five and my life will be over anyway," my twenty-two-year-old daughter scoffs.

"I just don't want you putting on your tiny little bikini and hanging out at the pool where you might get sunburned or pregnant," I admonish.

"I don't, I go to the tanning salon."

"Why would you go to the tanning salon?" I sputter, mindful of the fact that the equipment at such places has been shown to cause young people to borrow money from their fathers.

"Because it's summer and I need a tan," she replies simply.

"Gee, I wonder if there is any other way you could get a tan besides paying a fee for it," I speculate wildly.

"Dad, I'm way too busy for that. Did you TiVo those shows like I asked?"

"Wait a minute, the tanning machine is faster?"

She laughs. "It's not a *machine*, it's a little booth with lights and a timer. Yeah, in fifteen minutes I can get the same tan I would get in an hour and a half of lying in the sun."

"So you drive to the tanning booth, park, go inside, pay, change clothes, wait for a booth, spend fifteen minutes getting tanned, change clothes, and drive home. I can see why it is so efficient."

"No, Dad, of course not. You pay *after*."

"I just don't like the idea of you getting blasted with powerful rays," I complain.

"It's okay. I wear sunscreen."

I have to admit, this one stops me. I literally have trouble finding the right words for my next question. "So you pay money for a tan, but then you wear sunscreen to prevent it?"

"No Dad. I get tanned, I just don't want to get burned. I have fair skin, no thanks to you."

"You have *skin* thanks to me," I point out. "And why don't you just stay in the booth for, say, five minutes with no sunscreen? I thought you were little Miss Efficiency, here."

"Well, because you pay for fifteen minutes. I don't want to waste it."

"I have to ask, has there ever been any study into whether these rays can cause *brain* damage?"

"Besides, I go to the tanning booth to avoid getting tan lines."

I have to think about that one for a minute too. I don't like the image. "And why," I finally ask, "do you need to avoid tan lines?"

"You know how you'll see someone at the pool and right above her top she's all white because that's where her tan line is? I hate that look."

"Wouldn't the solution be a larger swimsuit?"

"Oh, Dad, I'm not a little girl anymore."

I frown because that's exactly the point I thought I was making. "A tan line is a good thing. It tells boys where to stop; it's like police tape."

"Dad. I'm in college. I don't date boys. I date men."

Like that's going to make me feel better. "Honey, would you just read this article? Too much sun is actually unhealthy."

"Oh, Dad, nothing's going to happen."

And that's the point, isn't it? By the time you're old enough to realize bad things *can* happen, you're at the age where they already are. She accepts the magazine I am holding out to her because I'm her father, she respects me, and she needs money.

"I'll read it at the pool," she promises.

"What?" I say incredulously.

"I'm going to show off my tan!"

To The Person Sitting Next to Me.
Yes, You.

The invention of the laptop computer has meant that in all sorts of unlikely situations—on buses, at picnic tables, in school—we can pretend to be working.

"Why don't you go over to your sister's house and help her move her piano?" my mother wants to know.

"Can't," I grunt, showing her my laptop, angling it so the solitaire game is hidden from her view. "Working."

I'm not going over to my sister's to move her piano, because it's fruitless. The unfortunate fact is the furniture in her house doesn't *like* her piano, and objects to its presence in every room by becoming off balance and awkward, like a little boy forced to wear a tie. My sister should give up playing the piano and buy a big-screen TV; then I'd go there all the time.

Right now I am typing this on my laptop as I sit on an airplane. More accurately, I'm *in* the airplane. It's a small "commuter" aircraft, and the designers apparently felt that therefore only small people would fly in it, for the seats are as cramped as my sister's bedroom with her piano in it.

One family has brought a baby so young, the mother probably barely made it through security before becoming fully dilated. This just-out-of-the-oven baby may be shriveled and tiny, but his voice is fully developed. When he shrieks, the noise is so loud that it scares the poor little guy to death, so he shrieks. His mother makes quiet "shhh" sounds so we'll all think she's in control of her baby.

As I write these words, the person sitting next to me watches raptly, not saying much (though he did snort in agreement about how loud the baby is). Now he has come alert, straightening a little, not sure he can believe his eyes.

He's the sort of person who believes that the armrest separating us belongs only to him. Well, wait, now he's shifted a bit, giving me some room. There, he just gave me a little more.

When he came aboard the aircraft, he was speaking into his cell phone, shouting very loudly, "I am an important man with important phone calls, so everyone should pay attention!" He shoved his carry-on bag into the overhead bin, smashing my suit coat the way a wad is tamped down into a musket barrel.

I don't know what he had for lunch; I only know from his breath that it must have been dead for a long time, much of it spent lying in the sun by the side of a road. He gave me a good blast of it when he turned and made several unsolicited remarks about the flight attendant's body. The woman to whom he referred is young—not much older than my daughter—but I resisted the temptation to toss my seatmate through the emergency exit. Instead I said, "Flight attendant?", deliberately twisted in my seat, focused on the *male* flight attendant in the back of the plane, and agreed that while he wasn't my type, the man did, indeed, have a wonderful rear end.

Though my seatmate seems the sort to crave being the center of attention for everything but a public hanging, he's become increasingly agitated as he reads this, and has taken to staring at me in disbelief. It strikes me as being a good time to write that everyone knows he has a toupee, and that, if forced to guess, most people would speculate it is made of squirrel fur. (He's patting his head.)

I suppose that's rude of me to write, but then, it's rude to sit and read other people's computer screens, especially when you have to move your lips to do it. And for all he knows, I'm writing about some other, fictional person who found a dead squirrel by the road, ate some of it for lunch, and made a wig out of the rest.

The plane is mostly empty, and without explanation, my seatmate has snapped open his safety belt and is moving to another place, glaring at me murderously. I'm too busy working to meet his eyes.

I think I'll play some solitaire now.

My First Dog

When I was seven years old, Mr. Shaw's dog had puppies, and I offered to trade him my sister for one. He threw his head back and laughed when I said this, which I interpreted to mean he'd already heard what a terrible sister I had. He told his wife, who also laughed (did *everybody* know about my sister?) and then called my mother, so I figured I was in big trouble—I didn't exactly have the authority to negotiate such a deal, even though in my opinion it would have benefited the whole family.

Half the message must have gotten through to my parents, because a few months later my dad opened the backyard gate and in bounded an eight-week-old Labrador. The puppy and I ran at each other like twins separated at birth, wrestling around in sheer joy. (Only later did I find out that my father had cut a worse deal—paying cash instead of unloading my defective sibling.)

Today people leash their dogs and instantly bag up any messes their pets leave on the grass, which must embarrass the animals to no end. When I was a kid, though, it was generally understood that dogs and children ran through yards as free spirits, and that's what I remember—running, my dog at my heels.

Her name was Cammie. She loved table scraps and car rides and rolling in stinky things, and she was terrified of our neighbor's twelve-ounce kitten. My father took owning a Labrador seriously and spent many weekends in the fields with a duck decoy and a whistle, vainly attempting to teach Cammie hand signals. Cammie just couldn't seem to get the hang of it—the few times she stumbled upon the dummy in the weeds, she'd pick it up and look at my father as if to say, "You want *this*? It's not even real!"

Cammie's interpretations of my father's signals:

Signal: Short blast of whistle, sweep hand to the left.

Reaction: Run back to see if this meant my father had doggy treats.

Signal: Two blasts of whistle, clap hands together.

Reaction: Run back to see if this meant my father had doggy treats.

Signal: Throw whistle on ground in disgust.

Reaction: Run back to see if this meant my father had doggy treats.

Cammie was the only person brave enough to ride on the toboggan with me down Dead Man's Hill, so named because we all swore we knew somebody who knew somebody who had died sledding the steep slope, which terminated in a rocky creek bled dry by winter. I would never have attempted such a suicidal stunt except that Betsy Nelson told me she thought it was "brave." I clutched Cammie and hid my face in her neck, so when she wisely bailed out of the plummeting toboggan, she took me with her, and we wound up in a soft snow bank together, Cammie licking me with her coarse pink tongue.

During my POW phase, Cammie stood guard while I tried to tunnel out of my back yard. When I was lost at sea, Cammie stayed on the square of basement carpet that was my life raft, loyally remaining by my side as long as I had milk bones. Cammie brought my boomerang back when it refused to return on its own, and she panted in the back seat when my father taught me to drive—I took to it the way Cammie took to hand signals.

When I was in high school, Cammie had some relatively minor surgery, but the anesthetic overwhelmed her system, and she died with the whole family gripping her fur in grief.

Despite the fact that we know we will outlive them, we adopt pets like Cammie because of the love they give us, and their unwavering willingness to stand by us even when we stick them on a toboggan, blow whistles at them, or unsuccessfully insist they try to overcome their terror and attack the neighbor's tiny cat.

When I was a boy, Cammie was with me wherever I went, and sometimes even now she shows up in my dreams, ready to chase down boyhood pleasures.

She was my first dog, and I'll never forget her.

A Hypochondriac's Compendium

Because I'm technically over forty, it's been a bad year for me health-wise. I've had a host of ailments, including an appendicitis attack, spleen disruptions, and liver migrations, all made worse by the fact that my doctor doesn't agree that I've had any of them. Instead, he says I have mild hypochondria, which is silly—I have *major* hypochondria! If left untreated, I could die from it!

A hypochondriac is a person who gets a disease by hearing about it. So when, for example, I heard about a rare disease called "cornu cutaneum," in which a four-inch horn grows out of the center of one's forehead, I knew for certain I had it. Panicked because I didn't think I could make a living as a rhinoceros, I phoned my doctor and told him I had all the symptoms of the illness.

"You have a four-inch horn growing from your head?" he demanded.

"All the symptoms except that one," I amended.

"Like?"

"Like, I'm starting to find elephant skin very attractive, and I have an increasing urge to head-butt a Land Rover."

"All right," my doctor said after a lengthy pause, "put sunblock on the affected area."

"And that will cure it?"

"Can't hurt," the doctor said hippocratically.

I've also got the Ebola virus, where one's body basically just falls apart, something that has been happening to me since I turned thirty. There's no known cure, though my doctor has prescribed diet and exercise, which he says can't hurt. I disagree; exercise *does* hurt, and probably makes my Ebola worse to boot.

Probably the worst affliction I've had so far this year is Alien-Hand Syndrome, where my right hand, strictly on its own, tries to kill me via strangulation or donuts. I've watched, mesmerized, as my hand spookily reaches into a box and pulls out a chocolate-covered custard-filled bismarck, which you know has to be even worse for you than a donut because they taste even better. You'll recall that Dr. Strangelove, played by Peter Sellers, had Alien-Hand Syndrome, and that the movie ended with total nuclear annihilation, though my doctor isn't sure that's going to happen in my case.

I call my doctor and the nurse puts me through when I explain that if left untreated, my new disease would lead to the destruction of the planet, plus also she says something about how she doesn't get paid enough to take calls from people like me.

"Your hand has tried to strangle you? Honestly?" he asks skeptically.

"I think it has tried to strangle me *dis*honestly," I correct. "It pretends to be just lying there. I think it's waiting for me to fall asleep."

"How do you know you've got this rare syndrome?"

"Because," I say triumphantly, "the rest of me has akinetic mutism!"

Sufferers of akinetic mutism are awake and conscious, but lie around unmoving and unresponsive, like a man watching golf on television. My problem was that except for my Alien Hand reaching for a donut and occasional trips to the mirror to make sure the sunblock was keeping the rhino horn at bay, I'd pretty much done nothing but nap all weekend, even though I had lots of work to do.

"If you had akinetic mutism, you wouldn't be able to make this phone call—that's where the mutism part comes from," my doctor tells me.

"So I have *talking* mutism?"

"Tell you what. When you suffer from this condition, are you by any chance holding the TV remote?"

"No," I answer defensively. "My Alien Hand is holding the remote. I have no control."

"Try unplugging the television."

"That . . . seems kind of radical," I reply faintly.

"Can't hurt."

I'm not so sure—what would my Alien Hand do to me if I rendered the remote useless?

"You seem to be catching a lot of strange diseases lately. Have you been reading about rare disorders or something?" he asks.

"No, not at all! Well, there is this one book."

"What's it called?"

"Rare Disorders."

"Ah. I'd like you to send it to me," my doctor requested.

"So you can provide better treatment?"

"Sending it to me *is* the treatment."

That's when he explained that I have hypochondria, which I found in the book right next to hyponatremia, whose symptoms include fatigue, listlessness, and apathy.

I decide I'll send him the book later—right now I just don't feel like doing it.

The Great Hoodwinki

When I was thirteen years old, I was a professional escape artist known as "the Great Hoodwinki," except that no one actually knew me as that and I wasn't professional.

I thought that people would admire the clever play on words, since "Hoodwink" means "to fool" and "the Great Hoodwinki" would remind the same people of "the Great Houdini," though who these "people" were supposed to be I had never really defined. Probably the local news anchor, a woman I had such a crush on that when her show came on the television, I couldn't bear to watch.

News Anchor: You're the Great Hoodwinki? That reminds me of the Great Houdini, only more clever!

Me: "Hoodwink" means "to fool."

News Anchor: Will you marry me?

Me: Well, I'm only in eighth grade, but sure.

I would burst in on my father, standing between him and his baseball game. "I," I would thunder, "am the Great Hoodwinki, Escape Artist to the Stars!"

"I," my father would reply, "will pay you a quarter to go away."

In my opinion, "going away" and "escaping" were not the same, entertainment-wise, but collecting a quarter did make me a paid professional, so I took the money.

It's frustrating being an escape artist who has never actually escaped from anything, but I didn't see that as my fault, but rather as an intimidating attribute: *People fear the unknown.*

"Put me in a straitjacket. Tie me up in a gunnysack. Suspend me from a crane! I, the Great Hoodwinki, will escape from them all," I challenged my fourth-grade sister and her friends, feeling fairly confident they couldn't put their hands on any of those items.

The girls were unhappy that I was interrupting their game, which involved a teddy bear named Baby Henry getting married to a stuffed rabbit named Pinky Cuddles in a wedding that had been going on since second grade. They wanted me to leave them alone, but they couldn't come up with the twenty-five cents my father had established as the market price for that particular service, so I continued to pester them until they agreed to tie me up with some old rope that I'd come across that no one was using for anything. (Later my mother went to hang laundry and announced her intention to prosecute the person who took down her clothesline, giving the Great Hoodwinki something else to escape from.)

Once they got into it, my sister and her friends really enjoyed encircling my arms and legs with the thin gray rope, but I just grinned at them, because I was flexing my muscles Houdini-fashion, and when I relaxed, the resulting slack would make it easy to unravel their pathetic little knots. The only problem was that Houdini had muscles to flex, whereas I had only stringy sinew barely thicker than the ropes binding my limbs. The girls stuck me in a closet and closed the door, which was fine by me because I didn't want anyone witnessing my amazing escape techniques that I would employ as soon as I thought of them. When I struggled free of my bonds and burst from the closet, my family would cheer, Baby Henry would call off his wedding, and the News Anchor would pick me up in her Channel Four News van after school so that everyone in eighth grade would know she was my girlfriend.

I had plenty of time to indulge in these and other fantasies, because, as it turned out, little girls are actually pretty good at tying boys up in knots. In fact, I had so much time for contemplation, I finally came to the realization that to be an escape artist required something more than the coolest name ever—something like skill, maybe, or practice.

I was pretty disappointed to realize this, as it had deep implications for my life. To join the Beatles, for example, I would have to do more than master the words to "Hey Jude." To be a movie star, I probably needed more than a list of people to thank in my Oscar speech.

All that lay in the future, though—for now, I just had to figure out how to escape from the closet.

My Edgy Haircut

A man's haircut needs to make a powerful statement about who he is. "I'm a successful businessman," one style will tell the world; "I'm an artist," brags another. My own haircut seems to deliver this message: "I'm a bellhop."

For a long time my barber was a woman who I felt did a really great job because she was attractive. But over the past year or so, I've been traveling a lot, and have stuck my head under scissors in shops all over the country, most of which came to my attention because their employees were carefully trained and certified to be inexpensive. With some important meetings coming up, though, I decided it would be worth the money to get "styled" at a more expensive shop.

"Something trendy," I tell a friend of mine.

"I don't think trendy people use the word 'trendy,'" she objects.

"'Modern'? 'Mod'?" I suggest.

"Oh my."

"Well, what, then?"

"'Edgy.' You want 'edgy.'"

There's nothing in the Yellow Pages under "Edgy," but I do find a "Hair Multiplex" that takes "walk-ins, skate-ins, and bungee-ins." I decide I'll "walk-in" from my "car."

Once there I hesitate on the threshold; the décor of this place leans heavily on rough cement walls and naked lightbulbs, as if my haircut will be preceded by an interrogation. The woman at the receptionist station stares blankly at me, blowing a bubble whose purple color exactly matches the hair on the left side of her head. She blinks, her silver eyelid piercings twinkling, and I realize as I approach her that I am afraid.

"Heph yuf?" she greets me.

"I'm . . . what?"

"Duh yuf haf a appifma?" she asks.

"I'm sorry . . . do I . . . do I have what?"

"A appifma!"

"Do I have an epiphany?" I repeat. Then I brighten because, well, I do. "Oh! 'Appointment'! Did you just go to the dentist or something?"

She shakes her head and sticks her tongue out at me so I can see her stud. "If's neh," she tells me.

I'm spared from coming up with some sort of response to this by the appearance of a thin man who calls himself "Shock." He peers at my head through yellow lenses. "You'd better come back right away," he decides.

"So you'll be cutting my hair?" I ask, hustling to keep up with him.

He shakes his head. "I'm in charge of triage," he explains. We enter what appears to be a Soviet-era bomb shelter. "Sit here. Use the computer."

Shock disappears through a doorway make of parachute silk. A computer program flashes at me, allowing me to customize my haircut. I'm invited to choose a shampoo made from mud, bark, or recycled newspapers. The styles can be "asymmetrical blunt," "random slash," or "sudden trauma." I choose "acupuncture" over "primal scream" and "vegan" over "Vulcan."

The folds of silk whisper and a man enters, holding a computer printout. He is large and bald. "Call me Truck," he offers. "And you are . . . ?"

"Bruce," I suggest.

He shakes his head. "Damaged goods," he corrects. I wonder if this is my new "lodge name." "Hair," he lectures, "is fish, and your head is the ocean."

I absorb this carefully.

"You've been using chemicals on your hair. When the ocean is polluted, the fish die. With no fish, the waters turn toxic, and all life on the planet comes to a tragic end." He gives me a stern glare.

I gulp.

"As is true with love, to save you, we must first destroy you." He pats his bald pate meaningfully.

"This doesn't sound . . ."

"Stop." He holds up a massive hand. "This is more important than just you."

Thankfully, he can't shave my scalp that day. First I must meditate for three weeks, without bathing or eating anything that rhymes with "DiCaprio." At night I must wear a hat made of aluminum foil, and I'm to phone Truck immediately if my dreams have anything to do with chickens.

I pay my $80 for the consultation and leave. In the parking lot, a man tries to hand me his car keys, thinking I am the valet. "Sorry," he apologizes when I correct him. "It was just, you know, the haircut."

I decide this suits me just fine.

My Daughter's Rejectable Boyfriends

As my daughters get older, they are more and more likely to thank me for what a good job I did raising them, so I'm sure that will happen any day now. They will recognize that I protected them from all sorts of dangers, such as serial killers, car crashes, and dating. In fact, I'm still on the job—just because my daughters have both reached the so-called age of consent doesn't mean I have to give it.

My older daughter is currently dating a young man who seems very mature and responsible, so naturally I'm very suspicious of him and feel we'd all best be served if the relationship went on a "cooling-off" period for a few years. "But you've never liked *any* of my boyfriends," my daughter protests.

"That's not true," I inform her. "I liked that one guy who got transferred to Sweden."

"Him? Why him?" she wants to know.

"Because he got transferred to Sweden," I reply logically.

Thinking she was doing something besides proving my point, my daughter compiled the following list of what she considers to be my "unreasonable" objections to her most recent boyfriends.

Ted

My objections: Ted seems too "friendly." He's always smiling, like he's got some terrible secret from his past. What's he got to be so happy about all the time? I do not want boys who are dating my daughter to be happy, I want them to be burdened with concern that they are not measuring up to my standards. Maybe he's on drugs. He's not fooling me; these happy-go-lucky types are always the ones who go crazy and wind up getting arrested for trying to shoot the president.

Billy

Who the heck is named "Billy" anymore? That's a kid's name. By the time someone grows up he should have a man's name, something masculine, like "Bruce." Or "William." Maybe he *isn't* grown up. Have you seen his driver's license? Maybe the reason you haven't is that he's not old enough to drive! Why don't you find someone who's had more experience in life with things like college, earning a living, and shaving?

Charles

Who's he trying to impress with "Charles"? What does he think he is, a British lord? What's wrong with "Charlie"? Now, that's the name of a trustworthy person, not this "Charles" business. He says he's an "engineer," but so's the fellow who loads things into the back of the garbage truck. And would it hurt the guy to smile once in a while? He's always so serious. Those serious guys, they always wind up getting arrested for trying to shoot the president.

Corbin

His parents must have found his name in the List of Baby Names Nobody Uses. I don't even know what a "Corbin" is, though it sounds to me like the sort of thing that is used by plumbers to unplug toilets. Like, "Hey, Charles, would you bring the corbin over here? The basement toilet's stopped up again." And Charles says, "Sure thing, Ted. Hey, those were good drugs you gave me last night; how goes the assassination plot?" and Ted says "Ha ha, Charles, I love being substandard." And Billy says, "I want to be just like you guys when I grow up to be twenty!"

"What this list proves," I tell my daughter, "is that if it weren't for my judicious application of common sense, you'd wind up being known as 'the poor woman who is married to that habitual corbin-user, now serving time in juvenile hall for sending death threats to the White House.'"

When I say stuff like this to her, my daughter usually stares at me in utter silence for several seconds, struck dumb by the sheer wisdom of what I say. After all, she can't deny that I was ultimately proven right about Ted, Billy, Charles, and Corbin—none of those guys are around anymore, ejected from our lives due to my objections (though my daughter implausibly insists that she also had something to do with the decision).

Clearly, then, as long as I'm on the job, my daughters will be protected from dating the wrong sort of men, or any sort of men.

Someday, they'll thank me.

The Dogs I Know

In my neighborhood, it's best to be a dog—but isn't that true of all neighborhoods? I never see dogs out raking leaves or fixing their screen doors. Instead I see them wagging in ecstasy over finding an unclaimed stick: What an amazing world, there's this stick sitting here I can just have for the taking! Want to stop raking leaves and throw it for me? Come on, don't you want to be happy?

Probably the most overjoyed dog on the street is my neighbor Bailey, a four-month-old golden retriever who is always so excited to see me that he tries to jump from the ground to my head. As he levitates, Bailey yips and twists and his tail wags his body all the way to his nose. You don't pet Bailey so much as just thrust a friendly hand into a tornado of joyful fur. After a walk around my block, you will have Bailey hair on your pants, on your shirt, and in your ears.

Then there's Dewey, a Boston terrier who puts his feet on my shins and tries to climb up my legs. Dewey likes to be scratched just above his nonexistent tail. His owner is a woman who models bikinis for a living. None of the men in the neighborhood have been able to summon up the nerve to talk to her.

"I can't believe you stop her on her walks to chat with her and play with her dog all the time," one guy tells me enviously.

"Who?" I ask.

"The hot woman with the little black-and-white dog," he responds.

I realize he must be talking about Dewey. "His owner is a woman?" I reply. I've always been so engaged with Dewey I've never noticed he even *had* an owner. I don't know the person or people who own Bailey either, though I am usually conscious of someone muttering, "Sorry, sorry" as Bailey tackles me in the chest.

I don't feel that I'm missing anything. I doubt the bikini model would ever be as happy to see me as Dewey is, and probably if I tried to scratch her rump, she would have me arrested.

Sometimes I'll see Ben, an old cocker spaniel who slowly walks the neighborhood in quiet dignity. Ben regards Bailey's dervish-like locomotion with thinly disguised contempt: You're supposed to walk with the leash limp, not seize it in your mouth and dance in circles until you become tangled and fall to the ground like a roped calf.

Old Ben knows something about me that the much younger Dewey and Bailey don't: I'm Carly's dad—Carly, an aging female black Labrador with a snout covered in gray. Lately when I run into Ben, he'll sniff me up and down carefully, and then knowingly regard me with sad, rheumy eyes. The scent of Carly has faded from my hands and clothes.

It's been some time since Carly walked with me around the block, but I haven't been able to bring myself to stop writing as if she were still alive, just as it has taken some time to become accustomed to eating a sandwich without her staring intently at every bite. It's far easier to move through the world as if I still had a Lab at my side than to remember the sad fact of her passing.

That's what dogs do—they bring us so much joy that when they're gone, the happy part of you doesn't believe they've really left.

Sometimes I would catch Carly watching me as I sat at my computer, and there seemed to be some concern in her expression, a worry that without her, I'd just sit all day and rattle the keys on the keyboard, my face washed in pale light from the monitor, never having any fun. I might have been imagining it, though—she probably thought I'd be just fine in a world where every yard offered free sticks.

I've been thinking lately that it's time to get another dog. I miss all that joy. So I will, one of these days, but until then, I'll just have to content myself with the dogs of the neighborhood.

John Ritter 9/17/48 – 9/11/03

For a year now I've been telling people "I'm not an actor, but I'm played by one on TV." As the father of the TV family on *8 Simple Rules for Dating My Teenage Daughter*, John Ritter stepped into a role that I created in my book of the same name, a role based rather unimaginatively on myself. And he did a better job at it than I do: As a dad, I lose my temper a lot more. John played his role with gentle and goofy kindness.

And that was John, a kind man who didn't hesitate to help people who needed it. When the audio version of *8 Simple Rules* was produced, John offered to read it at a fee far below what he could command in the market. Interviewed for the media blitz that preceded the premier of the show, he took care to credit the original work as the inspiration for all that followed—which isn't how things are usually done in Hollywood. He did these things as a favor to me. He didn't have to; it wasn't in the contract. It was just in John to do that sort of thing.

At the taping for the pilot of *8 Simple Rules*, the studio audience burst into applause when they first caught sight of John Ritter. Despite three decades as a star, the look on his face almost seemed bewildered, as if he couldn't believe everyone was so excited just to see him. He walked to the foot of the bleacher seats and spread his arms as if giving everyone in the room a hug.

The last time I met with him, he gave *me* a hug. We had lunch, and he wouldn't let me buy—which isn't how things are usually done in Hollywood. He was the talent, you see, so he shouldn't have paid for anything—but it was just in John to do that sort of thing. We talked about fatherhood, how proud he was of his older children, and the joy he took in his little girl Stella.

The last time I saw John he was with Stella, on the pier in Santa Monica, California. He looked just like what he was: a dad out for a weekend stroll with his little girl. Seeing him with her, I was reminded of the day he taped the pilot, how instantly everyone warmed to the idea that John Ritter was a man who loved his children. That's what the show is about, you know—a father who loves his family. And that's what John was about too.

I was crossing the pier to say hello to him that day when I stopped, deciding that I shouldn't interrupt the private moment he was sharing with Stella. I figured that as a celebrity, he rarely was afforded the luxury of an unaccosted afternoon.

Now I regret that I didn't approach him. My instincts were correct—he deserved the privacy—but had I known I would never see him again, I would have wanted to take some moments for myself. I could have used one last hug.

Spelling Boy

When I was in third grade, I was beaten up on the playground for winning the spelling bee.

Back then I thought of myself as a pretty tough kid, but I didn't have a chance in this particular fight: I was at least an inch shorter and ten pounds lighter than she was. Apparently by besting the odds-on favorite—a girl we called "Linda Blotnick" because that was her name, and because when someone has a last name like "Blotnick," you can't *not* say her first and last name every time you mention her—I offended Rhonda. No one considered that it was Linda Blotnick's fault and not mine that I knew how to spell "pachyderm" and she didn't. Nor was it seen as ironic when Linda Blotnick spilled hot tears as the teacher (even he was on her side!) said, "You should know this one, Linda Blotnick," even though "pachyderm" means "thick-skinned" and by crying over such a minor insult, Linda Blotnick demonstrated she was anything but.

Now, Rhonda had a very special affection for Linda Blotnick, and seeing her best friend cry turned Rhonda into an enraged pachydermatous rhinoceros who charged all the way across the playground at me, yelling something that sounded like "Die, Spelling Boy!"

I saw her coming and had enough time to prepare myself for battle by ducking behind my friend Brad Smith and clutching his coat. (Even ancient warriors like the Spartans had shields—in this case, my shield was Brad.) Brad, however, was uninspired by my brave stand, and dodged out of the way so as not to be impaled by rhino horns.

My father never taught me how to fistfight with a girl, though if he'd been there, I suppose he might have been disappointed when I started crying. But

Rhonda, menacing in a pink skirt and Mary Janes, socked me so hard it knocked the spelling right out of me. If Linda Blotnick was going to cry over "pachyderm," it certainly seemed reasonable to sob over being punched by one.

"Linda Blotnick always wins the spelling bee!" Rhonda yelled, which was ridiculous—by third grade, you haven't lived long enough to do *anything* "always."

"So what?" Brad taunted from the safety of the top perch of the monkey bars. Rhonda's face darkened, and I gave Brad a beseeching look: He wasn't helping. "She lost this time over 'butter'!"

Rhonda paused in my beating to give Brad a puzzled look. "'Butter'?"

"Brad's word was 'butter,'" I reminded her. I looked up at Brad. "No, Linda Blotnick lost over 'pachyderm,'" I said. "It was on the list of spelling words."

"Yeah, at the bottom of a list of like five hundred words," Brad shouted back. "Who reads *those*?"

"Now you're mad at me too?" I demanded.

"You need to give Linda Blotnick the prize back," Rhonda decided, raising her fist to explain what would happen if I didn't.

"It's not a prize, it's a certificate, and it's got my name on it. What good will it do for her to have it? And Brad, you stupid idiot, the last ones on the list are the only ones to read, because they're the hardest; you know when it gets down to the final people, those are the ones they're going to use."

"Hey! Don't call me stupid!" shouted the boy who had painstakingly sounded out "B-U-D-U-R."

"What does pach . . . pack . . . What does that word mean?" Rhonda snarled.

"'Pachyderm'? I don't even know!"

"Now who's stupid?" Brad challenged.

"Spell it," Rhonda ordered. She shoved my shoulder.

"What?"

"Spell it," she repeated. "But this time, do it wrong."

I blinked. Clearly there was some sort of principle at work here: Brad hooting at me from the monkey bars, Rhonda the Rhino literally beating me into stupidity—if I caved on this, I would be following the example of all the people in history who held their tongues while despots burned books and trampled intellectual thought.

Of course, I didn't know about those despots; couldn't even spell the word because it hadn't been on the list—I was only in third grade!

"B-U-D-U-R-B-U-T-T," I said quickly.

Rhonda nodded, satisfied. "Linda Blotnick won," she pronounced smugly.

And, by third-grade logic, I guess she did.

Here Comes Tucker

October is National Sarcastic Awareness Month. Right, I'll be sure to celebrate that. It's also National Caffeine Addiction Recovery Month, but I don't know what events the organizers are planning because I've slept through the meetings.

Some people celebrate October as Bat Appreciation Month, which I can, well, appreciate, but I am not sure what to make of the declaration that it's also National Window Covering Safety Month. I guess one should cover one's windows with drapes and not with something less safe, like explosives.

Most significant for me is that October is National Adopt a Shelter Dog Month, which my fiancée and I celebrated by adopting a shelter dog named Tucker. As if this writing, he's been alive eleven weeks, but he's been chewing my shoes only one of them. Before he came to live with us, he was sheltered by Life Is Better Rescue, a Denver-based animal rescue group of which my daughter is founder. Dumped into a box within scant hours of his birth, Tucker and his siblings found their way to LIBR by a kind person who realized that without immediate intervention, the newborns would die.

As to the person who so heartlessly abandoned the newborns, could I just say that I hope that he winds up on the receiving end of Bat Appreciation Month? (If it is "bat" as in flying mammal as opposed to "bat" as in baseball, I just hope they are flying mammals who *bite*.)

Of course, I'm a forgiving person who can find it in my heart to truly wish no actual harm comes to the callous, pitiless dog dumper. There, I'm celebrating National Sarcastic Awareness Month after all.

Tucker and his brothers and sisters were taken to a German shepherd rescue dog named Belinda who had just hours before weaned her litter of pups. Belinda looked at the shelter workers with a *You've got to be kidding me!* expression, but ultimately took the pups in and nursed them as her own. Perhaps Belinda believed she had had a wild night at the Sigma Chi house. The puppies were tiny—probably born of an unspayed spaniel, by the look of Tucker's features, though there is really no way to know.

I've got a book out right now called *A Dog's Purpose*, so the question I'm asked most often is "What kind of dog do you own?" I'm proud to be able to honestly say, "I don't know." But by rescuing Tucker, I actually saved two dogs who might otherwise have been euthanized—Tucker, of course, plus the death-row dog who was rescued and took his place at LIBR.

Tucker may be of dubious heritage, but he is a genius, I promise you. He has a demonstrated ability to reach up onto a coffee table, dig into a pile of mail, and locate and shred a check. All the credit card bills and solicitations that he could have destroyed to my complete apathy, and he finds the only item that I care about. That's what he shreds. A bookshelf full of paperbacks I've forgotten I even own, and Tucker can locate the signed first edition of *The Caine Mutiny* and eat out the signature page while I'm taking a shower.

After a stern lecture on why I need my sleep, Tucker woke me up at three in the morning to further discuss the issue. He also needed to go outside, though once there it took him fifteen minutes for him to find the exact right spot for him to do his business. He seemed pretty disgusted that I immediately bagged and removed his work of art without taking any time at all to admire it.

He is, of course, adorable. I've abandoned all attempts at work and pretty much spend my days on the floor wrestling with him. He weighs only about seven pounds, so I pin him a lot more than he pins me. It's tiring, though—his energy seems limitless, while I'm both sleep deprived and exhausted by all the unaccustomed crawling and dog fighting.

I guess you could say I'm all Tuckered out.

Party Bruce

I am currently going through that socially awkward stage of life known as adulthood. I'm not very good at it.

I guess I was sick the day they taught the class on "How to Go to a Party and Be Witty and Enjoy Meeting New People and Not Get All Sweaty." Instead, I was attending the seminar on "Why You Should Have Stayed a Fetus." I am, and have always been, terminally shy.

When I get to a party, I immediately notice that I want to go home. It's not that I don't enjoy parties, I just think they are more fun when I can experience them on DVD. Being there in person means I must I circulate, nodding pleasantly, avoiding people's eyes until suddenly I find myself face-to-face with the one person with whom I can instantly bond: the dog.

It was a lot easier when I was a kid. Whenever I met someone new on the playground, we'd head over to what we called "the kinderfuge"—this thing that spun around and around until we got dizzy and threw up. In college we'd head over to the keg machine, but the rest of the experience stayed the same. Now, though, I'm supposed to make adult conversation, and throwing up is generally frowned upon, even though I'm so nervous that's what I feel like doing.

I don't know why I'm so socially awkward. Generally when I meet people for the first time, they smile at me and laugh at my jokes before they take my order. I know many words of the English language and can align them in my brain so that they come out of my mouth in sensible sequence. For some reason, though, I've just never been comfortable having conversations with people with whom I don't share something in common, like DNA.

Part of it's the sweat thing. My skin believes that if I'm being introduced to people, especially female people, they will be happier if they can see that my capillaries are capable of delivering so much blood to my cheeks, it sets off my sprinkler system. Years and years of being literally steamed has given me Poached Traumatic Stress Disorder.

But mostly it's just a general lack of faith in my ability to engage some stranger in a conversation that won't have them thinking to themselves, *I'm so bored I want to drown myself in the spaghetti sauce.* This is despite the fact that nobody has ever actually done that—tried to submerge themselves in Italian food, that is—though several times I've seen people overdose on the hors d'oeuvres. That's the problem with being shy—it's a reaction that defies the accumulated evidence of lifelong experience.

A drama coach once told me, "Bruce, every great comic is afflicted with some sort of self-esteem problem. You're just not a great comic." He told me that I should just picture everyone in their underwear— oh, like *that's* not going to make me nervous?

"Just go up to people and start talking, say whatever's on your mind," my more social friends urge me. So I do, interrupting a group of strangers. "Excuse me," I say politely, "has anyone seen the dog?"

A lot of people are surprised that I can give speeches and appear on television shows and not experience any anxiety, because public speaking is one of the most common fears, along with gum surgery and having Michael Moore show up for dinner.

"Maybe you should get some therapy for this and all of your other issues," my youngest sister tells me kindly.

"It's because no one likes you because when you were in high school you never let me listen to your records and Dad and Mom didn't care about it," says my other sister, proving I'm not the only one who needs therapy.

Maybe being a writer means that every time I say something, I know I could have said it better. I wind up feeling stupid for having uttered anything at all.

Or maybe I just prefer the company of dogs.

Dog vs. Man

Announcer: Welcome, ladies and gentlemen to today's wrestling match, between Tucker, a mixed-breed dog, aged ten months and weighing 22 pounds, who must take a pill, and current champion Bruce, an aging guy of Scottish extraction at 160 pounds.

Commentator: That can't be right. He's heavier than that.

Announcer: Well, that's what it says on his driver's license.

Commentator: He's a real oinker. A pork platter.

Announcer: And Tucker is doing some bows and stretches, getting ready for today's match.

Commentator: Pretty small to be competing with such a sumo.

Announcer: And there's the bell! Bruce is moving in with his right hand extended . . .

Commentator: He's got a treat!

Announcer: Yes, he's hiding the pill in a treat and he's calling for Tucker to take it, and it look like . . . it looks like . . . He took it!

Commentator: This one's over before it started!

Announcer: Ladies and gentlemen, just ten seconds into the match, it looks as if the champ has put down the challenge from the scruffy upstart!

Commentator: Wait! What's that?

Announcer: He spit it out! Round one is over, and Tucker has swallowed the food but not the medication. Let's get over to the champ's corner. Bruce, what happened?

Bruce: I really thought he'd go for the treat, but he somehow sensed the pill was in there and spat it out at the last second.

Commentator: Champ, care to comment on the rumor that you're much heavier than your stated weight?

Bruce: What? No, that's wrong.

Commentator: Whatever you say, Fat Boy.

Announcer: There's the bell! Bruce has another treat, but it doesn't look like Tucker is going to go for it. A move left, a move right, Tucker's on the couch, he's across the floor, he's trapped in the corner . . . And Bruce has him and is forcing the pill and the treat into his mouth! This is exciting folks, Bruce is stroking his throat, holding Tucker's mouth shut . . . and at the bell . . . at the bell . . .

Commentator: It's out!

Announcer: Tucker spat the food right in Bruce's face! Champ, what can you tell us?

Bruce: I thought the combination of the food and the pill, with me holding the mouth shut and stroking his throat, would get his instincts going. Now I've got dog food all over my face.

Commentator: I'm surprised you didn't eat it, oh Heavy One.

Announcer: Can you give us a hint what you're going to try next?

Bruce: I've crushed the pill and wrapped the powder in a bacon-and-cheese treat.

Commentator: Bacon and cheese, that explains the spare tire around your middle.

Announcer: The vet has said Tucker must take this pill . . . What are you going to do if he won't?

Bruce: Defeat is not an option.

Commentator: Neither is dieting, apparently.

Announcer: Okay, folks, here we are for the third and final round. Bruce has the treat.

Commentator: He's got Tucker mesmerized, waving that food around.

Announcer: Poor little fellow is just intellectually outmatched. Bruce is moving closer. Tucker's eyes are on the treat. This one looks like it's over. Wait! The dog is on the move!

Commentator: Lard Boy is trying to catch him!

Announcer: They're running and there goes a kitchen chair!

Commentator: Chairs are flying and the dog is leaping over the coffee table where the cheese and bacon was prepared and this little guy has outsmarted the fat champ! The dog has snatched cheese and bacon on the fly!

Announcer: The champ is yelling for the dog to drop the cheese and bacon from the coffee table, but here's the thing: He's trying to *feed the dog cheese and bacon*! What's the difference?

Commentator: The dog is not only skinnier than the champ, he's smarter. Plus better looking.

Announcer: The champ lunges . . . whoa! Just missed, knocking into a bookshelf and toppling some books! The dog's running, the champ is chasing . . . and there's the bell! We have a new world champion!

Commentator: Naturally, the heavy, out-of-shape champ is breathless, his huge gut heaving.

Announcer: Bruce, what happened out there?

Bruce: I shouldn't have left the treats out where he could get them. Tactical error.

Announcer: What now, champ?

Bruce: Well, here's the thing: He still needs to take this pill.

Guitar-Mad

I've always thought that the purpose of musical instruments was to produce music, but my new neighbor—a twenty-something young man with an electric guitar—doesn't seem to agree. When he plays his instrument, it sounds like he is doing something really awful over there, like peeling an electric cat.

Not that I'm against electric guitar music—I'm a baby boomer, so I believe my generation invented that plus everything else.

He doesn't seem to be taking lessons; he's entirely self-deluded. But what he lacks in skill, he makes up for in amplification: Every night around dinnertime, the entire neighborhood vibrates as if under attack from a giant dental drill.

Gradually, the wail and hum of his efforts has organized itself into a recognizable pattern, to which my neighbor has added his voice in a song entitled "I Can't Sing, Either." This is his opening number every evening, and also his closer. The rest of the time it sounds like he is systematically destroying his guitar with a hacksaw.

I've called the police to ask them if they could please come over and dispense Vicodin. When I described my problem, they sent a patrolman to my house to explain why they couldn't just have the cops discuss the situation with the young musician using bullets.

"I'm sorry, Mr. Cameron, but I'm not willing to go over there and shoot your neighbor's kid," the officer apologized.

"That's because you haven't heard him play yet," I responded.

The officer seemed to consider this, and then he pointed out something that hadn't occurred to me because since the arrival of the guitar, I hadn't been capable of thought. "When neighbors start calling the law on each other, it always escalates," he said. "Do you want that?"

If by "escalates" he meant "the SWAT team opens fire," then sure, of course I wanted that. But I saw what he was getting at—people shouldn't turn to the police to solve their problems if there's a possibility that they can sit down, neighbor-to-neighbor, and agree to throw the guitar out the window. I decided to put on earmuffs and go over there.

When I knocked on the front door of my neighbor's home, I don't know who I expected to answer it—Satan, probably. Needles would be hanging from his arms, and his skin would be covered with tattoos of vile creatures attacking schoolchildren. He'd listen contemptuously, spit on me, and slam the door.

But the young man who responded looked less like an evil demon and more like the counter clerk in a donut shop, his pale face timid and shy. I introduced myself, and he said his name was Darth.

"If I'd been a girl, it was going to be Leia," he explained. "Or Yoda."

I told him I was there because several of the neighbors were hoping that when he practiced the guitar, he would shut his windows and stop playing. He was shocked.

"You can hear me?" he moaned, his whole body quivering with shame. "I'm sorry, I'm not used to such a quiet neighborhood."

I wondered were he lived before that he could make such a racket and no one would hear him—the Chicago airport? He told me he was saving up for lessons, but right now he was just teaching himself. "No, really?" I responded.

As we chatted, I realized I had misjudged the young man. Darth was just a boy trying desperately to master a skill that looked easy on YouTube: You swung a guitar around, colored lights flashed, and girls threw their underwear at you. He hadn't considered that he was making every dog in the neighborhood want to run away. He was so apologetic he was almost weeping, and it made me feel bad that I had fantasized about setting him on fire.

Darth agreed that he would keep his windows shut, his amplifier turned down, and hold off giving a Live Earth concert until he was sure it wouldn't damage the planet.

And I learned you can't judge a Darth by his music.

Football Hero

I saw some high school boys at football practice yesterday, and it reminded me of when I was an All-State high school football player, which happened early in my imagination. (I probably could have been All-State and won a full-ride scholarship to a Division I school, except that the coach, clearly jealous of my athletic abilities, didn't send me in for any plays because I technically was not an actual member of the team, since I hadn't specifically tried out.)

I did play in junior high school, on a team so hideously inept that opposing coaches were said to groan aloud when they saw who they were scheduled to go up against. Enfranchised as the "Giants," our team was composed of a twitchy group of boys not yet ready to make a firm go at adolescence, "giant" in no modern sense of the word.

So hapless were the Giants that in twelve games, we did not win the coin toss a single time, unable to turn in a respectable performance even at a contest of pure chance. This meant every afternoon started the same, with our squad dribbling a faltering kick downfield with so little force that one might suppose the kicker was missing an ankle. As the ball rolled into the arms of a runner, we would woefully spread ourselves apart on the field, leaving a clear alley toward the goal line like a wedding party lined up to throw rice.

Once we gained possession of the football, we generally handed it back to the opposing side as quickly as possible, like a neighbor returning mail that had been misdirected. By halftime the scorekeeper's arms were tired from changing the numbers on the board, and the winning players would be yawning and scratching themselves.

I played wide receiver because I was skinny. Before every snap, I would confidently stare out at the opposite goal, though in truth I had never actually been near the place. Usually the only sound would be a couple of my teammates crying. I would give the player opposite a hard, mean look, as if I were going to slam into him on my way downfield, but he'd usually just wink back because we had an understanding.

Then, with a clash of helmets and the thud of the Giants falling to the ground, thc ball was snapped! The starting quarterback for the Giants was a wispy lad whose sole aim in life was to prevent any damage to his expensive orthodontia and who released the football whenever it appeared one of the defenders was close to making a tackle, which was every play since the Giants' offensive line was no more impediment to the pass rush than a light summer breeze. I'd trot out my pattern, yelling "I'm open!" so the girls within earshot would know I was a hero, and watch as the football went in some completely random direction.

And one day, without warning or plan, the ball dropped into my arms. I could not have been more shocked if I'd caught a dead goose falling from the sky. Embarrassed, I started running for the goal line. No one stood in my way: The opposing players had stopped covering the pass because it was more fun to rush the quarterback and recover fumbles.

Hey! This could work! I glanced at our team's bench to see what they thought of this unexpected development: They all looked sick with dread. And then I poured it on, running at the speed of, say, a four-year-old girl. Behind me the opposing players were gaining on me like an avalanche, and it occurred to me I might actually die soon.

With just a few yards to go, I was hit; it was like being slammed from behind by my father's Oldsmobile.

The impact drove me forward, and, though I had certainly been willing to fail, the momentum carried me over the line for the only touchdown of my football career. I grinned at where my girlfriend would be sitting if I'd had one, while my teammates celebrated like we had just won the Super Bowl.

So my high school coach's decision not to play me? His loss.

Puppy IQ Test

If I were to submit my sixteen-week-old puppy to an IQ test, I'm pretty sure this is how it would turn out.

Question #1: Your owner screams "No!" whenever you squat and urinate on the carpet. He picks you up in midstream (literally) and races out the door with you. When you recover from the trauma of it all and squat in the grass, he praises you and gives you a treat. He takes you for long walks, the whole point of which seems to be for you to squat in the grass. What can you conclude from this bizarre behavior?

Puppy Answer: He wants me to pee on the carpet.

Question #2: Your owner was eating delicious salty things from a bag when the phone rang. He left the bag on the couch. What should you do?

Puppy Answer: Eat everything in the bag and then eat the bag. Wait until he's back and looking under the couch cushions and just starting to get suspicious before throwing up on the carpet.

Question #3: Your owner says he's just going to the mailbox for a moment and will be right back. It appears you're going to be alone in the house for less than two minutes. What should you do?

Puppy Answer: Chew and swallow the last two pages of the mystery novel he is reading. Wait until he's discovered what I've done before throwing up on the carpet.

Question #4: How often should you bark for no apparent reason?

Puppy Answer: It depends when you're talking about. If it is night and my owner is asleep, every fifteen minutes is appropriate. During the day, random barking is not necessary because he doesn't sleep during the day.

Question #5: While on a walk, you come across, in this order, the following items: a cigarette butt, a half-eaten hot dog, and a really disgusting small black thing about the size of an almond. What should you do with these items?

Puppy Answer: Cigarette butt: Eat it. Hot dog: Eat it. The really disgusting black thing: Eat it. Wait until we're back home on the carpet before throwing up.

Question #6: You're at the park, running off leash. Your owner calls you. What should you do?

Puppy Answer: Go to him immediately! Unless there is someone nearby you haven't met, then go to that person immediately! Unless there is a dog nearby, then go to the dog immediately! Or, attack a dandelion immediately! Or run in the opposite direction immediately! Just don't ever do the same thing twice— we don't want to encourage him to do a bunch of "training."

Question #7: Identify the function of each of these items: Shoes. Socks. Electrical cord. Your owner's nose.

Puppy Answer: Chew toy. Chew toy. Chew toy. Chew toy.

Question #8: Your owner has just thrown a ball about a dozen yards away and is now saying, "Get the ball! Get the ball!" What does he want you to do, and what will happen when you do it?

Puppy Answer: He wants me to watch him get the ball. When he gets the ball, he will throw it again and say, "Get the ball!" again. He'll repeat the process until he gets bored, and then we'll go inside so I can pee on the carpet.

Question #9: Your owner just brought in a box of expensive dog toys. There's a big rat with a squeaker in it, a tennis ball with a squeaker in it, and a dragon with a squeaker in it. What should you play with?
Puppy Answer: The box.

Question #10: What is the one thing your owner is doing a lot more now that you live in the house with him?

Puppy Answer: Using the carpet cleaner.

Question #11: Your owner seems to be having a bad day. His mood is gloomy and his back is bothering him. What should you do?

Puppy Answer: I should run to him and play with him. His mood will get better immediately, and before long he will have forgotten all of his problems and will be rolling around on the floor with me, laughing. It's the whole purpose of a puppy.

Attack of the Marshmallow-Eating Alligator

Back in the 1980s, my grandparents, Dick and Emily, moved to Florida because they wanted a better climate to argue in. They had one of those relationships where they fought so much, they couldn't even agree on what they disagreed on.

Their little home in Florida was a few dozen yards from a boggy pond that kept trying to evolve into a swamp. Dick liked to go down to the water's edge and feed marshmallows to the small alligator who lived there, probably hoping that one day it would grow large enough that he could feed it Emily. Emily would stand at the screen door and yell at him that he was going to be sent to prison for feeding wildlife, but when she called the DA's office, they refused to run a sting operation on her husband even though she promised to testify.

I saw the alligator one time: It looked like a half-submerged suitcase. My grandfather would toss the marshmallow into the water and the thing would swim over to it so slowly the water never rippled, opening and closing its mouth without drama, then sit in the water and regard Dick with an unwinking lack of gratitude.

Dick named the alligator "Blanche."

Then one day Emily showed Dick a newspaper article claiming that when alligators lunged, they could move "as fast as a horse," which I suppose might be true for the first half foot. To my grandfather, though, it implied that one day Blanche would gallop after him and take him down before he could make it to the house, where Emily, seeing what was happening, would lock the back door.

So he stopped feeding Blanche. Then he became concerned about *that*. What was the alligator thinking, out there in those dark, marshmallow-less waters? What was Blanche *plotting*? Whom would the alligator blame for the sudden loss of its primary food supply? Why, Dick, of course; how could it know it was Emily's fault for finding that article?

My grandfather became afraid to get the newspaper from his driveway. So Dick told Emily that if she wanted the paper, she'd have to get it herself. As she headed out the front door, Dick would scurry to the back screen and yell in the direction of the swamp, "I see that you're getting the newspaper from out in the front of the house!", but Blanche never took the hint.

On his birthday he had an idea: He could drive to the pond! His Cadillac could outrun a horse any day. Once he fed Blanche a few marshmallows, he would be back in the reptile's good graces and could resume going to the grocery store without fear of being followed. Dick grabbed a bag of marshmallows and got in his car.

Once he was at the pond, Dick had a problem: To throw the marshmallows, he would have to roll the window down, and then Blanche could easily climb in. Well, not easily—Blanche was an *alligator*. But any animal who could run as fast as a horse could probably jump as high as one.

The solution was to drive down even closer to the water, lower the window just enough for a marshmallow, and throw the alligator treats from inside the car through the crack in the window out onto the pond.

This proved impossible: The marshmallows kept bouncing off the glass. Worse, Blanche had seen the activity and was headed over to check it out; Dick could see the thing's evil eyes. Panicked, he decided to pull the car forward and just dump the whole bag out the window, but in his excited state he stomped on the accelerator and shot into the water!

He yelled at Emily to call a tow truck, but she refused on the grounds that he deserved to drown. Fortunately, at about that time, my mom called to wish her dad a happy birthday, and Emily was forced to admit that Dick couldn't come to the phone because he was busy sinking his Cadillac in the swamp and being attacked by Blanche. So my mom called the tow truck, from 1,300 miles away.

It was the last time Blanche got any marshmallows.

My Dinner-Guest Questionnaire

My insurance company loves to stick little informational pamphlets in with its bill so I won't notice that I'm writing them a check. The topics usually boil down to "how to avoid doing something that might cause you to file a claim which we would then reject because you're supposed to be paying us money not the other way around."

The most recent mailing was a little flyer cheerfully entitled "How to Keep Your Dinner Guests from Suing You!" Apparently my insurance company has heard about my cooking. At any rate, the advice was broken down into three parts: (a) Don't invite anyone to dinner without asking them a series of questions, (b) don't invite anyone to dinner who is known to file a lot of lawsuits, and (c) don't invite anyone to dinner.

I've always thought it was a good idea to ask potential dinner guests questions about their eating habits, in case they turn out to be, say, cannibals. But my insurance company alerted me to the idea of probing for other issues, such as alektorophobia, which is a fear of chicken.

Me: Dinner tonight is poorly prepared chicken!

Guest: I'm afraid!

My (patent pending) Dinner-Guest Questionnaire, which I plan to release soon as an e-book, is currently in "beta" stage, which is what software companies call products that don't work. I'm willing to take (paid) suggestions for additional questions; please send them to me, along with a check for $10, which is what makes them "paid."

Dear Potential Dinner Guest:

My insurance company and I are looking forward to the pleasure of your company!

You may have heard the old expression "Never arrive at a person's house empty-handed." A gift for the host, in other words. Of course, we're old friends, so this is more applicable than ever.

I'm cooking one of my specialties tonight, a French dish called *Que diable l'est?* (loosely translated as "What the heck is it?") Dinner will be served at 7:30— arrive earlier if you want to enjoy the smoke.

I want to avoid any incidents like what happened the last time I cooked, when it turned out my guests were allergic to E. coli. So:

Are you able to eat red meat? What about meat that *used* to be red?

Are you on any medication that would induce side effects we might find amusing?

Are you vegan, or is there some other reason why you're so angry?

Can you explain why anyone would be afraid of chickens?

Are you allergic to (a) shellfish, (b) peanuts, or (c) penicillin? Because the dish I'm making has all three.

Are you known to gamble foolishly and without regard to the odds of losing? If so, please bring a large amount of cash.

If you start choking, do you want me to perform the Heimlich maneuver? What if you are *not* choking?

(*Men only*) You're not going to bring that same bimbo you brought last time, are you? (Disregard this question if you married her.)

(*Women only*) Can we not talk about (a) how hard it is to meet nice men and (b) all the cats you have, unless (c) you're willing to admit a causal link between the two?

You know how a good host will tell a guest who has had a little too much to drink that it's better for the guest to spend the night than to drive? Wouldn't you say it's easier if the guest just doesn't drink too much?

I've been told that I tend to tell long, boring stories at dinner, tales so excruciatingly dull that it gets embarrassing for everyone. If you hear me getting started on one of these, please, for my sake and everyone else's, listen politely.

If my dog stares at you during dinner, take it as a sign that *somebody* would like what I cooked.

Would it be awkward for you if you arrive and I'm not there? If this happens, please feel free to help yourselves and make dinner. You may need to buy some groceries—there's a list on the refrigerator. Also, while you're out shopping, I need a new pair of pants and plane tickets to Hawaii.

Aren't you glad that I invited you to dinner?

Best in Show

I suppose it is a sign that I am finally being taken seriously by the literary community—have, in fact, risen to the pinnacle of my profession—that several months ago I was asked to judge a Halloween-costume contest for dogs.

To be entirely accurate, I wasn't an actual judge; apparently I'm not qualified to render a decision on matters such as which miniature poodle looks most like Batman. Instead, I manned a microphone during the competition and made announcements like "Please be reminded that contestants are not allowed to pee inside the contest arena."

I'll bet you that's not the sort of thing you hear at a Miss America Pageant.

The contest itself was held to benefit a charitable organization called Life Is Better Rescue, which provides training for pets being adopted from animal shelters—abandoned animals often have behavioral issues that need attention before they are suitable for placement in people's homes. Unfortunately, LIBR does not address behavioral issues in teenagers, so don't try dropping them off.

Some of the costumes were very elaborate— three wiener dogs, as an example, came dressed as wieners. They could barely walk because they each were laughing so hard at how the other two were dressed. The contestants were supposed to parade in a circle, stopping in front of me so I could interview them about world peace, but a lot of the dogs veered off because they were distracted by the need to chew on their costumes. A Labrador I talked to had no comment about international politics, but his expression clearly communicated, *I wish I weren't dressed like a chicken.*

Other animals were more enthusiastic. A white German shepherd dressed as Pegasus happily pranced into the ring, as if to say, *Look at me! I have wings plus I just passed the snack table and swiped some cupcakes!* A golden retriever dressed as Britney Spears looked thrilled to be out of rehab. And a pug in a lobster costume glared at people as if saying, *You think pugs are ugly? Not compared to lobsters, we're not!*

An animal psychic was on hand to look into the minds of the dogs and translate their feelings into words for the humans, such as *Hey, how come Pegasus got to have cupcakes?* She reported that the Labrador would rather eat chickens than dress like them, which anyone could tell since the dog was lying on the floor with its eyes closed so it wouldn't have to look at itself. She also predicted that my career as a writer would go better next year, because how could you do worse than hosting a dog costume party?

Actually, despite the fact that I didn't see how this was going to get me short-listed for a Pulitzer, I enjoyed being the master of ceremonies for the event and also eating the cupcakes that Pegasus couldn't reach.

When the time came to announce winners, everyone was really excited except the contestants. Some of the categories seemed suspiciously as if they had been created on the spot—the mixed breed dressed as a chili pepper, for example, really didn't have any competition for Spiciest Costume, unless maybe you counted the basset hound in a bikini. Two shelties were dressed as weary travelers—to make their costumes more realistic, they lost their suitcases in Cleveland. Best Depiction of Creatures Not Found in Nature was a three-way tie between a unicorn, a dragon, and Pamela Anderson. And when the chicken-garbed Labrador won for "Best Food-Themed Costume" it groaned aloud at the humiliation. *Even the wiener dogs are laughing at me,* its mournful face seemed to say.

The judges—who had apparently undergone special training so that they were more qualified than I to award prizes for Most Nautical and for Best Costume with a Biblical Theme (Old Testament)—decided to give the grand prize to the Britney Spears dog, on the condition that it not be allowed to drive home.

I sang the customary "Here She Comes, Miss Ameridog" song, while the dog, tears in its eyes, strolled down the runway and lifted its leg on my podium.

When I left the stage, the wiener dogs were still laughing.

You'll Never Guess
Who My Mother Saw

I recently had a conversation with my mother (no relation).

Okay, I suppose I'm technically incorrect—about the "no relation" part, not that I had a conversation. But by the time I'd finished talking to her, I was pretty convinced my mother was switched at birth.

"You'll never guess who I saw *in person* the other day," she gushed on the telephone.

"Who?" I asked politely.

"Guess."

This gave me pause. Didn't she already say I would never guess? "Um, Dad."

"What? No."

"You haven't seen Dad? You should call Missing Persons!"

"No, here's a hint." With that, she proceeded to hum in a fashion that sounded like her telephone was out of order. "Duh-duh-duh-duh," she intoned. "It's from that movie!"

"What movie, *Invasion of the Metronomes*?"

"No, is that a good one?"

"Mom. Okay, what movie?"

"Well, guess."

I sigh. "What's the movie about?"

"I don't remember. Give up?"

"When I'm so close to guessing? Yes, I give up."

"Okay, the movie was *Jaws*."

"The movie was *Jaws* and you *don't remember what it was about*? That's like saying you can't remember what *Apollo 13* was about. Mom, *Jaws* is about a shark; what else would it be about, dentists?"

"Well, I know that," she said. "I just didn't want to give it away."

"So you saw one of the actors from *Jaws*?"

"Yes!"

"Okay. So . . . Roy Scheider?"

"Who?"

"He played the police chief in *Jaws*."

"The police chief? There was a police chief?"

"How about Richard Dreyfuss?" I responded, ignoring the question.

"Didn't you already guess him?"

"So if it wasn't Richard Dreyfuss or Roy Scheider, who was it?"

"Give up?"

"Yes, please, I very much give up. Totally and completely."

"Al Pacino!"

I closed my eyes.

"They were filming a commercial for a local restaurant, and I was walking past, and I saw Al Pacino, and I said to him that he used to be one of my favorite actors, and he said thank you so much but we're filming a commercial right now, and I said, right now? And he said, yes ma'am, he was very polite you know, and a nice young man came over and showed me where to stand so I wouldn't be in the commercial."

I thought about hanging up and moving out of the country, but instead felt duty-bound to try to understand what had actually happened. "You sort of lost me at duh-duh-duh-duh," I admitted. "You're saying Al Pacino, Oscar winner, was in a commercial for a restaurant, in your town of what, fifteen thousand people?"

"I think the restaurant is called Sparkles. Or Bubbles. Or something."

"I'm sure you're right," I agreed. "And it was Al Pacino. The actor from *The Godfather. Scent of a Woman. Scarface.*"

"*The Scarred ... Woman?*" she repeated uncertainly. "I don't know, but my favorite was when he played Captain Kirk."

"Captain . . . Kirk? From *Star Trek?*"

"No no no, from the one we were just talking about."

"Mom, are you taking all the medication you're supposed to be taking? Captain Kirk is from *Star Trek.*"

"Did I say Captain Kirk? I meant Captain Queeg," she apologized.

"Captain Queeg," I mused. "Wait, *The Caine Mutiny?* That was Humphrey Bogart! Mom, I promise you that for many, many reasons, Humphrey Bogart was not in Traverse City, Michigan, doing a commercial for a new restaurant called Bubbles. Though I suppose you could say he does look a little like Al Pacino. Who, I'm so, so sad to report, was not there doing that either."

"Well then, who was it?" she demanded.

"You're asking me? Wait a minute ... the captain. You mean Captain Quint? The captain on the boat in *Jaws?*"

"Yes!" she said delightedly. "You guessed it! Though as an actor, Humphrey Bogart was no slouch, let me tell you that."

"But Mom, Captain Quint was played by Robert Shaw. He died when I was in college."

"He did?"

"Yes, Mom."

"Then I wonder who it was . . ."

216

I'm sure my mother saw somebody when she wandered on camera while they were shooting a commercial for a restaurant called Sparkles or Bubbles or something.

We'll just never know who.

A Letter to My New Puppy

Dear Puppy,

I am leaving you this note as I depart this morning for a meeting, hoping that you'll read it instead of barking frantically, as the neighbors report you always do. There are a number of what I will charitably call "misconceptions" on your part that I think I can clear up for you, leading to a more pleasurable pet experience for both of us.

You have been alive for nine months now—in human age, that makes you more than five years old. Now, when I was five years old, I already had a paper route, was reading at a college level, and was pretty much regarded by everyone in the neighborhood as the greatest kid ever. (That's how I remember it. My mother, however, remembers that I crammed tomatoes into the dryer vent, turned on the hose and flooded my father's Buick, and stuffed my baby sister into a wagon and tried to shove her out into traffic. Funny how when you're a little kid, your parents remember things so incorrectly.)

At any rate, you're not a puppy anymore, you're a dog now, with dog responsibilities. Certain dog truths should be apparent to you. For example, I got up at 5:00 a.m. *one time*. One time does not make a routine that you need to ensure I follow every morning! Stop barking at me! And then once I'm up, groaning, protesting, and shushing you, you act as if your job is done and settle down to go back to sleep. No! If I'm up to greet the dawn, I want you, my loyal dog, there by my side.

Speaking of things dawning, surely by now it has dawned on you that you cannot catch birds. When you lunge at the end of your leash to try to get a mouthful of sparrow, all you do is dislocate my shoulder. My right arm is now three inches longer than the left. Birds fly— that's what the whole wing situation is about. Dogs do not fly. You can look it up.

(I realize penguins are birds and don't fly. If we're ever on a walk and we see a penguin, I promise I will let you off the leash.)

Also, I have invested a considerable amount of money in buying you some pretty disgusting-looking chew toys. Apparently the parts of the cow so revolting that people can't eat them can be dried, shipped to my house, and given to you so that you can wait for a party and then walk up and spit them into people's laps. I invested in these body parts not so that my friends will conclude that I'm a serial killer with bodies you've dug up from the basement, but because I don't want you chewing on *my* stuff. If it looks more like, say, a stereo speaker than a cow trachea, don't chew it! The same goes for my cell phone—cell phones are not made from cows; you can look it up. Neither are my shoes, my books, or my couch.

When I'm in the bathroom, I really like to be alone—is that so much to ask? I realize I don't give you privacy, but you aren't required by law to follow me around with a plastic bag. It's pretty disconcerting for you to bang the door open like the SWAT team calling on a drug lord and then stand there staring at me when I'm in that position. There is nothing I am doing that can be improved upon with the addition of a dog. I am not holding the magazine because I want to play tug-on-a-magazine!

And there are certain times I would like you to stop barking, such as always. If you see a squirrel out the window, stop barking. If I brush my teeth, stop barking. And when I leave you at home for a little while, surrounded by chew toys and with plenty of food and water, stop barking! I always come back, don't I? I never leave you alone for more than an hour, do I? Don't be so anxious.

I would never abandon you, you know.

You're my puppy.

Right Turn on Red

It is a damp spring morning, and the mushrooms are popping up like Starbucks. I am running late for an appointment with my dental hygienist, a charming woman who is always ordering me to brush the back of my tongue, causing great upheaval in my life. No matter how many times I've tried to follow her instructions, it still gives me bulimia.

"My gag reflex doesn't like it," I complain. "Couldn't I brush something else? My knees, maybe?"

"Your tongue is like a shag carpet. If you don't brush it, things get stuck in it," she lectures. I picture paper clips and doll shoes—the types of things that used to wind up lost in my parents' shag carpet all the time—and tell her I don't think that's going to be a problem.

My lateness is therefore a result of trying, after six months of neglecting my mouth's shag carpet, to please my hygienist with at least one scrubbing, so I've been in the bathroom, clutching the sink and drooling and doing everything in my power to keep from retching. It's an awful way to start the morning. How do we ever convince women to become pregnant?

In the car, I confirm that my radio is still not working. (I keep hoping my vehicle will forget.) Traffic is light but cautious because of the wet streets, so I am surprised, as I sail through an intersection with the green, to find that I am suddenly sharing the interior of my automobile with a Toyota. I've been hit!

The force of the collision cures my radio, which comes on loudly with the voice of one of those political talk-show hosts—my car probably figures it's the next best thing to an air bag.

I gingerly climb out of the front seat, carefully checking my body for any signs of serious lawsuit. The young man who has had such impact on my morning is wearing very stylish clothing—jeans with very expensive holes in them—and a scowl. His car is expensive too, especially since it is now sporting mine as a hood ornament.

"Hey!" he shouts at me. "I have right turn on red!"

He is so vehement that for a moment I'm convinced he's right: What was I doing, so thoughtlessly driving through the intersection when the light was green? I could have hurt someone, or at the very least caused additional holes in his pants.

"I saw the whole thing," offers an elderly gentleman who has wandered up to join us. He points an accusatory finger at the scowling young man. "You ran the red light."

"I have right turn on red!" the young man yells again. He shakes his cell phone at us. "I'm calling my attorney!"

"Yeah? I'm calling my dentist," I counter. I leave a message that I won't be making my appointment after all, but to please tell my hygienist that I brushed my tongue and didn't like it.

"My lawyer says to call the *police*," the young man hisses at me in a *Boy, are you in trouble* tone. He furiously punches the buttons on his phone, which is nicer than mine by the same measure that his automobile is nicer than my car.

"I ought to ram your teeth right down your throat," he mutters at me.

"You'd never get past my gag reflex," I respond.

He pales a bit—he obviously didn't think I could hear him, possibly because I'd had my radio up so loud.

The older man appears to be enjoying himself—he's already witnessed an accident, and as if that weren't entertaining enough, if he's lucky it will evolve into a fistfight.

When the police arrive, they listen patiently as the young man asserts his constitutional rights, including right on red. "Right on red *after stop*," one of them says. "And you always yield to the car with the green."

"That's me," I offer helpfully.

The other cop hands him a citation, and the young man glances from it to me, realization sinking in. I have to admit, I can't hide a small smile of satisfaction at the expression on his face.

He looks like he's going to gag.

The New New Orleans

As a writer, I have always felt that I have something pretty important to say, and from the time I was a college student, that something has usually been "Send money."

I also try to be fair and objective in my writing, unless it's difficult to do. My editor holds me to these high standards, saying, "We don't care what you write, just get it in on deadline." When I point out that it is more important that a column be well written than on time, she agrees, saying, "Okay, but you don't do that either."

I'm not even going to try to be objective in this column, however, because (a) my editor is on vacation, and (b) I'm writing to you from, and about, New Orleans, Louisiana.

I'm down here to help open some of the schools that were hardest hit by Katrina more than a year ago, specifically by providing teachers and students with basic supplies like paper, notebooks, and pens. Thousands of dollars' worth of materials has been collected for the students by an organization called "Friends and Helpers," though after watching me work the past week, they've decided that I'm more of a "Friend" than a "Helper."

There are more than two dozen of us involved in this effort, many of them recognizable celebrities, a group in which I include myself even though they don't. Some rock band I've never heard of is here— they can't be very good, though, because people keep talking about their "platinum albums" and everyone knows nobody uses albums anymore. I won't tell you who they are, and not just because I can't remember their names—this is about the children, not about publicity, though I did volunteer to go on national television and talk about myself.

I have to say, if I were of school age and was told that a bunch of people had flown into New Orleans to make it possible to end my summer vacation, I would be more than a little surly about it, but the reaction of these children has been wonderfully enthusiastic. They went crazy when I walked into the auditorium with the rock band, though how they recognized me I'll never know.

As I handed out high-end backpacks to children who were literally carrying their books in shopping bags, I realized I'm at the age where everything I do makes my back hurt. But I kept at it—their smiles made it all worthwhile.

Now, if you've been following the news about this city, you've probably concluded that the smartest thing a visitor can do is stay away. Apparently the local politicians have taken the money intended for rebuilding and invested it in something more useful to them: corruption. As a result, the area is still basically destroyed, like a room occupied by teenagers.

The charges and countercharges of bureaucratic inefficiency make for great newsprint, but as I stated, I'm not here as a journalist. (In fact, I've never been *anywhere* as a journalist.) I'm here as a normal person hanging out with a rock band. And what I see is that while it might be true that (shockingly) some government money has been misspent or misplaced, it is also true that New Orleans is open for visitors. Restaurants, bars, and hotels offer amazing deals in hopes we'll all come back and enjoy this city's famous hospitality.

There are still blighted areas, such as the Ninth Ward—if you want, you can take a tour bus and see what twenty feet of water can do to a neighborhood.

But the parts of New Orleans most people visit when they come here have dried out and are serving cocktails.

I'm really happy I'm here handing out backpacks full of school supplies and lending this rock group some of my fame. And the good works of many charitable organizations are visible throughout New Orleans, which will probably take many years to rebuild. But full recovery will be possible only when the local economy is humming, and a large section of that economy depends on tourists coming here and acting crazy.

My message, then, is not "send money," but "spend money." Spend it here in New Orleans. They need it.

Dinner with My Niece and Nephew

As an adult, I prefer to sit at the kids' table. The conversation is always more interesting, tending to focus on what food people can, under the right circumstances, shove up their noses. Over at the adults' table, the discussion usually winds up being political and one person yells at the others that they can take their ideas and shove them somewhere *other* than their noses.

"I once stuck a whole chicken up my left nostril," I tell my eight-year-old nephew. His eyes go bright with the possibilities. "No way," he finally announces—though clearly it says something my nose that he had to think about it.

There's no separate kids' table tonight: My nephew Ethan is across from me, his parents are at either end of the table, and my wife and our thirteen-year-old niece sit on my side.

Their father clears his throat. "Maya," he says, addressing the thirteen-year-old, "who was that boy who called earlier?"

Maya's face freezes into an expression of horror. Ethan's jaw drops. "A *boy*?" he shrieks.

"Ethan," his mother warns.

"Oh my gosh. So now Maya has a boyfriend, she's gonna marry him, uh huh," Ethan sings. He starts gyrating in dance, his eyes closed to signify that his sister's in love.

"I think you're a little young to have boys calling," I observe sternly.

"Bruce," my wife warns. She thinks I'm overly protective, which is, of course, absurd.

"It had to do with a science project," Maya mutters into her dinner.

"Have you kissed him yet? I bet you *loooove* him," Ethan says. He begins making exaggerated smooching expressions, which are in no way improved by the guacamole in his mouth.

"Ethan," his mother warns.

"Boys are like snakes. They're not all poisonous, but why take a chance?" I say.

"Bruce," my wife warns.

"Hey, Uncle Bruce, look at me," Ethan calls. He has eaten eye holes into his tortilla and put it on his face, like the Texas Chainsaw Nephew.

"Ethan, stop playing with your food," his father says.

"You need to make a mouth hole," I agree.

"Can I be excused?" Maya asks.

My niece is at the age where you just want to give her a hug and then inject her with something so she doesn't wake up until she's about twenty-two years old. Signs of encroaching teenhood are everywhere if you know where to look, from the earrings that no longer sport tiny pictures of American Girl dolls but instead display jewels, to the fingernail polish that darkens with every layer. Her parents are still blissfully unaware of the transformation about to explode upon them, werewolf-style, when their daughter hits the full-moon onslaught of hormones awaiting her.

"Maya, let's go to the store tomorrow and buy a monkey," I say a bit desperately. This used to be a running gag between us, but now the look she gives me is steady and a bit pitying.

"Yeah, a gorilla!" Ethan shouts. He jumps up from the table and begins phantom-boxing with something in the corner. None of us know what in the world he is doing.

"Ethan," his mother says.

"Fire in the hole!" he replies, giggling.

Maya sighs, and there it is: the eye roll, maybe her very first. I'm sad that I was here to see it. "Ethan, don't be such a . . ." she winds down, cutting her eyes at her parents, unable to think of a safe word.

Ethan eats like a hummingbird, alighting at the table for only a moment to grab something before zipping off to another part of the room. Now, though, he's back long enough to press his face into a pile of shredded cheese, much of which clings to his cheeks. "Whiskers!" he announces.

"Ethan," his mother warns.

We're all trying to look stern, but it's just too funny. Okay, I'm not looking stern, I'm laughing out loud.

"Bruce," my wife warns.

Even Maya is grinning, her thirteen-year-old sullenness breaking down in face of her brother's antics.

"Sit!" their father commands.

"Can we get an orangutan?" Maya asks, unexpectedly playing the game.

"Yes!" I exult.

It's so much fun to have one last dinner at the kids' table.

Without a Dog

As part of his ongoing home improvement project, my dog recently chewed the little tassels off the throw pillows on the couch. He was just ripping up the last one when I walked into the living room, and he was so proud to show off his industriousness that he took the pillow and shook it like a rat. "See?" his expression seemed to be saying. "Where would you be without me?"

Without a dog, I would have tassels on my throw pillows instead of little stubs of yarn that look like small worms. The pillows seem to function just fine without the tassels, so perhaps it isn't a problem. Though they are called throw pillows, I never actually throw them, but I'm sure if I did, my dog would approve. Maybe without tassels, they'll go farther when I throw them.

The question is an interesting one to contemplate, though. Have you ever asked yourself where would you be without a dog?

Without a dog, any time you accidently dropped a piece of food on the floor, you'd have to bend over to pick it up.

Without a dog, squirrels won't have any reason to come into your yard to taunt.

Without a dog, you'd never have anyone in your life who thinks you invented bacon.

Without a dog, a lot of people will know you by your name instead of knowing you as your dog's parent.

Without a dog, you'd have to hump the neighbor's leg yourself.

Without a dog, you'd never have anyone demonstrate how important it is to stop every day and smell the roses . . . and then lift your leg on them.

Without a dog, no one will listen to your opinions for more than a few minutes without interrupting to tell you their opinions, which you won't find nearly as interesting. A dog, on the other hand, thinks everything you have to say is absolutely brilliant and fascinating, especially if you're holding a piece of food while you're talking. Try this with your spouse and you'll see what I mean—a wife will give you maybe five minutes, tops, and it doesn't seem to matter whether you're waving a piece of chicken in front of her nose. There's also an inverse relationship between the number of years you've been married and the number of minutes she'll listen to your big fat opinions. A dog, though, will always pay attention (unless you drop that chicken).

Without a dog, you might eventually forget what roadkill smells like.

Without a dog, there's no one in the house who thinks driving with you to the store is one of the most fun things in the world. No one who is excited to the point of ecstasy to see you come back to the car with your bag of groceries. No one who thinks the drive back home with you is every bit as fun. In short, no one who can turn every mundane thing you do into a joyous occasion.

Without a dog, you'll be without at least one creature who thinks you are the smartest, most decent and heroic human being on the planet.

Without a dog, you might never know the joy of owning custom-chewed shoes.

Without a dog, some of your tennis balls might get really dry.

Without a dog, no one will think you are the most amazing cook in the world just because you can open a can.

Without a dog, you'd have to figure out what to do with your spare income. (With a dog, your *vet* figures out what to do with your spare income.)

Without a dog, you'll probably not take walks every day, and you'll probably never carry little bags for dog poo either. Studies show that just adding those dog walks to your schedule can help you lose weight, live longer, and battle stress (though no one has ever claimed that picking up dog poo does any of these things). Having a dog in your life lowers blood pressure and wards off depression. In short, without a dog, you won't live as long or as happily.

So why would you want to be without a dog?

W. BRUCE CAMERON

Hugs and Kisses

My father is taller than I am. I take after my mother, who is descended from a long line of tiny people who were bred by German royalty to climb into tunnels to hunt rodents. This means it's awkward to hug my father, but it was *always* awkward, because we're from the part of the country where men can show affection only by insulting each other's snowmobiles.

When greeting each other, my father and I first exchange stiff handshakes, as if we've just negotiated a government bailout. Then I pull on his hand to bring him closer, his eyes growing large in alarm, like maybe I'm going to flip him over my shoulder. We seize each other's shoulders like Greco-Roman wrestlers, reluctant to close the distance between our two bodies. Finally he stoops, I gouge him painfully in the shoulder with my chin, and we break apart with a gasp of relief.

My son thankfully passed up the shortness genes when he was selecting his DNA, so that he's even taller than my dad. Hugging him means I need to stand on tiptoes as I give him a quick embrace, like a prom date saying good night to her escort in a Norman Rockwell painting.

It's not that I mind hugging people; I actually sort of like it. It's just that I was never trained in it, never had the rules of engagement explained to me. Look, I'm sure I'd enjoy flying an airplane too, but I've never taken a lesson and doubt anyone on board wants me landing the next jet to Miami. I'm not sure what people expect from me: Do they want a simple hug, a hug and a kiss, maybe a hug, kiss, and a triple axel?

To me, kissing is even more incomprehensible. Take the "air kiss," where one completely misses connecting with the other person's face and winds up smacking at the air like a carp in low water. What's the message of such a thing? "I'd kiss you, but I can't steer my own lips"? No one has ever instructed me on when to use the air kiss, though I'm pretty sure I wouldn't deploy it if it were the first time I was meeting my tax auditor.

Actually, pressing my lips onto another person's face seems shockingly intimate. I remember watching Carter and Brezhnev negotiate a nuclear arms treaty: At the end of it, Carter had to endure a big smooch from the Soviet leader. As a teenage boy, I was so grossed out I decided that if it had been me, I would have opted for nuclear war.

Women are easier—I *like* kissing women, though, again, I've had very little on-the-job training in this arena. If I understand what is expected of me, I'm more than willing to kiss the cheeks of ladies, so long as they aren't too much taller than me.

A few years ago I was on the set of the TV show *8 Simple Rules*, where an episode I'd written was being filmed. At the end of it, the actress Katey Sagal came over to chat with me, and as the conversation grew to a close, she leaned in, obviously expecting some sort of personal contact between us.

I was utterly baffled. She was a star, while I had come to understand that my social stature, as a writer, was roughly the same as the vermin my ancestors used to hunt for in tunnels. What should I do? Air-kiss her? Squeeze her shoulder? Pick up her dry cleaning?

I settled for a rigid handshake, followed by a jerky hug and a kiss on the unexplored area southwest of her right ear. It could not have been more awkward if I'd patted her on the fanny and called her "Toots."

Then there's the European greeting, which somehow involves *both* cheeks, and grabbing hold of the other person's hand as if getting ready for a do-sido. Good Lord! Try to figure that one out; it'd be easier to pass the LSATs.

Isn't there a school I can go to where they teach this stuff?

You can tell I'm upset, here.

I need a hug.

The Church Play

This past Christmas Eve, I was proud to see my ten-year-old niece and four-year-old nephew participate in their church's annual production of the story of Jesus, Mary, Joseph, and Batman.

My nephew, you see, has Batman body armor that he refuses to take off, even in the bathtub. I don't blame him: It gives his little-boy body the rippled abs of a dancer at Chippendales.

My niece has long coveted the role of Mary, but the appointment is strictly political. Her parents just haven't had enough clout on the Christmas pageant committee to muscle the nomination out of the smoke-filled room and onto the floor. The part has always been played by a little girl named Aubrey, whose mother secured the position of play director by plying the corruptible elders with an apple pie so succulent that in most states it would be classified a controlled substance. After fair and impartial tryouts, Aubrey's mother always gave careful consideration to my niece and the other actresses before picking her own daughter.

This year, though, Aubrey's mom was outflanked when my sister-in-law got the church to approve a policy whereby any child with perfect attendance in Sunday School could have the starring role in the play. The elders were too addled with apple pie to think it through, but Aubrey's family always took two weeks off to go traveling in the summer, and would be disqualified.

Aubrey's mom resigned, saying, "You won't have Aubrey to kick around anymore."

The new director, a man, decided the key players should have body microphones, which he didn't hand out until right before the performance because they were expensive and he didn't want to risk them being broken in rehearsal and anyway they were uncomplicated and what could go wrong?

The first line of the play occurs when Mary mounts the stairs, stumbling in her long robes. "Stop pushing me!" she hisses at Joseph, a skinny boy with a sagging beard that looks like it used to be the carpet in a college dormitory.

Joseph announces they will be spending the night in the manger, along with goats, mules, what looks to be about two dozen shepherds sent over from preschool, and Batman. Unable to restrain himself, Batman takes his staff and smacks a papier-mâché goat like it's a piñata. The shepherds begin giggling helplessly.

"I hope my baby comes soon," my niece says sweetly. Five hundred video cameras capture her performance.

The lights dim discreetly as the couple lies down, though we are still able to see Mary struggling to pull the pillow out of her shirt. Over the body mic, it sounds like Michael Moore trying to wrestle himself into the back seat of a Prius. A bright light pops on to signify the North Star, and a trio of eight-year-old wise men troop onto the stage, gazing at my nephew, who in his headscarf looks like what you'd get if Batman had a baby with Yasser Arafat. My nephew, grinning, takes his staff and pokes one of the wise men in the rear end.

"Hey!" shouts the offended wise man, his amplified voice ringing in the church.

"We've come to see the new king," intones the wise man in the lead.

"Not yet!" my niece snaps. She has a line: Tenderly picking up what she has been referring to as her "live prop" (the baby playing Jesus), she says "Behold, Joseph, our son, Jesus." The baby's biological mother stands anxiously by, apparently invisible, while the baby frowns at all of us in disgust. My nephew is astounded; in rehearsal, it was always a doll.

"Hey, Mom, it's a real baby!" he shouts.

Someone with a body mic has something else to report. "Brandon just farted," he says. This is such wonderful news to the giggling shepherds that fully a third of them lie down.

The Little Drummer Boy takes the stage for the musical number, displaying no drumming ability but plenty of noisemaking talent. No one questions whether a drum solo is an appropriate gift for a newborn whose exhausted mother just wishes he'd go to sleep. Batman, bored, begins teaching the papier-mâché goats what position to use if they want to reproduce. The shepherds laugh.

Everyone later agrees it was the best show ever.

Up for Debate

In a little less than a year, Americans will do what they've been doing every four years since the birth of this nation, which is to laugh at the voters in West Palm Beach, Florida.

Before that, each political party must nominate a candidate, so they conduct a series of presidential debates, though most viewers would agree that they aren't really debates, they aren't really presidential, and nobody in them looks like they are at a party. Americans enjoy televised presidential debates because after the one between Kennedy and Nixon in 1960, we wound up with a really hot-looking president and First Lady. In a debate, questions are tossed at the candidates by journalists who appear to be trying to convince the public that it is they, not the people up on stage, who should be elected to office. Clearly, the journalists think being president is like being a contestant on a quiz show, with the secretary of state as host:

Secretary of State: Mr. President, Russia is threatening to cut off natural gas to Western Europe. Quick! Who is the minister of agriculture for Micronesia?

President: Um . . . .

Secretary of State: You don't *know*? Great, now the world will end.

I'm sort of hoping that the people elected to president have advisors to keep track of who is running Micronesia and, more important, where the place *is*. At any rate, after watching several debates over the past few months, I have (a) discerned a pattern, which I will reveal here, and (b) become somewhat pessimistic about the future of the world. This, in general, is how the debates go.

Journalist: Our first question concerns China. In view of global warming, how would your administration handle the threat to the environment from that nation's fast-growing economy?

Senator Q: That is why I introduced my bill, the "Every Child Is Happy" Act, which requires every child to be happy.

Governor Z: This problem, like all problems, would be solved by my administration but would only get worse under Senator Q's administration.

Congressperson A: Wait, which one is China?

Mister X: I have had experience with that sort of thing because of all the money I inherited. You talk about being a happy child!

Journalist: All over the world, people seem to be fighting with each other. How would your administration fix that within the first thirty days of being elected to office, plus ensure large pay raises for journalists like everybody wants?

Senator Q: They are called "earmarks," like the fifty million dollars I appropriated to build a rest area where it is desperately needed, or will be desperately needed as soon as I appropriate the money to build a highway next to it.

Governor Z: Obviously it would be preferable if, instead of killing each other, people would kill only journalists. Under Senator Q, that would never happen.

Congressperson A: I don't think we should be even discussing this until we figure out where we can find China.

Mister X: In my experience, if there are people fighting, you just change the channel. Same with journalism.

Journalist: If you could sum up your administration in one word, what would that word be?

Senator Q: Peace, Prosperity, an End to Bad, and If You Want Children to Be Happy.

Governor Z: Not Senator Q.

Congressperson A: I'm not sure a word would be appropriate.

Mister X: I have lived in bigger houses, I have managed larger personal staffs, and I have always gotten what I want. So a vote for me is a vote for what I want.

Congressperson A: Wait, can I change my answer to "What I Want" too?

Governor Z: How about "Senator Q Is Unattractive. For America."

Congressperson A: Yeah, add that part too.

Journalist: That concludes our debate. I want to thank the small handpicked audience for supporting their candidates no matter how inane their answers, and to remind everyone that tomorrow, on news shows everywhere, the candidates will be attempting to reposition and rewrite the things they said here.

Congressperson A: Like that thing on China, that was sort of a trick question.

Journalist: Until then, I wish everyone watching would explain why they are doing so. Good night.

(And good luck.)

Some Relationships Are No Accident

I am not a mechanic, but I do know that if your automobile suddenly shudders and bucks, you may have a problem, especially if these symptoms are accompanied by the unexpected appearance of a Cadillac bumper in your back seat. When this happened to me a few days ago, I quickly realized I'd been rear-ended in the rear end!

I'm a pretty good driver, but I find a car crash to be something of a distraction. Deciding not to proceed through the intersection with a Cadillac in tow, I put my vehicle in park and turned on my emergency flashers to let other drivers know I knew how to turn on my emergency flashers. Within seconds, traffic virtually halted, drivers gawking because there is nothing more fascinating than a Dodge with an Eldorado in its trunk.

The car that struck me was built pre-OPEC, a brontosaurus of a machine with a front hood large enough to land a small plane on. It was meticulously maintained and polished, its gleaming metal scratch-free with the exception of the part that was now residing inside the Dodge. The woman sitting behind the wheel of this monster appeared to be in shock, staring at me with round, amazed eyes—she'd apparently never seen a professional humorist before. She looked to be in her sixties, a birdlike woman so tiny that it was hard to believe she could possibly control her gigantic automobile. (And, if you think about it, she couldn't.) I opened the Cadillac's enormous driver's-side door, blocking two lanes of traffic with the huge thing.

Her skin was so pale I immediately worried that she might be injured. I tried to recall my first aid training, but unfortunately all I could remember at that moment was how to deliver a baby. Somehow I didn't think that particular skill was going to be needed here.

"Hi, I'm Bruce; I'll be your accident victim today," I joked.

The expression on her face indicated she felt she *still* hadn't met a professional humorist. "Are you okay?" I asked in a medically diagnostic tone, feeling it was a more appropriate question than "How far apart are your contractions?"

"I'm dead," she responded dully.

"Well, no, you're not," I responded, feeling fairly confident on this issue. "Breathe," I advised her, still stuck in my first aid training.

She shook her head. "This car is his pride and joy. My husband's going to kill me when he finds out I ruined it."

I tried to explain that she didn't so much ruin it as give it a Dodge hood ornament, but she was unconvinced. Soon we had police on the scene, proving endlessly mesmerizing to the gawkers.

"Look at that," I could imagine them saying to each other, "parked police cars! It's the most exciting day of my life!"

The woman was named Audrey, and she readily admitted the accident was her fault. I suggested if she was going to drive a car that big, there should be someone riding lookout on the front of it.

"Failure to stop," the officer explained to Audrey as he wrote out a ticket. This was hardly accurate—she had *stopped*, after all, just a bit later than circumstances warranted.

"My husband's going to kill me," Audrey lamented.

I found myself growing angry. Who was this bully, this jerk who would get mad at his wife for having an accident? Who valued his battleship-sized automobile so much that he'd yell at a tiny person like Audrey, a woman who probably weighed less than the Cadillac's antenna?

Audrey's husband soon arrived, a scowling, jowly fellow who looked like what you'd get if you crossed Winston Churchill with a bulldog. She began weeping.

"Oh, honey," she wailed. "Your car!"

His cold eyes surveyed the damage. I drew myself up, ready to defend Audrey against this monster.

He turned to his wife, his face softening. "Forget the car, darling," he murmured. "Are *you* okay? That's all I care about." He wrapped her in his arms.

I realized I'd misjudged him as much as his wife had misjudged her stopping distance. The gawkers might be interested in sheet metal, but as far as he was concerned, only one thing mattered.

Audrey.

Today Ice Stop Ice Skating

As frequent readers of this column know, I am a natural athlete who enjoys participating in a wide variety of sports as long as I don't have to be there in person. This is especially true during winter, so when my nephew informs me he wants to go ice skating, I'm only too happy to tell him he's wrong.

Here's a little history: Ice skating was first invented sometime around 3,000 BC to make the game of hockey more dangerous. It was introduced to North America by the Swedes, who fled the frozen terrain of their native Scandinavia and moved to sunny, balmy Minnesota.

Many Swedes insist it was the Vikings, not Columbus, who first discovered America. This is shocking news to the people who were already here in the first place, many of whom felt they didn't *need* to be discovered.

More history: The Vikings were explorers, famous for wearing silly helmets and never winning a Super Bowl.

The people of Minnesota have many different words to describe the hard blue ice that covers their land, words such as "outside," and "Interstate 90," and "I lost a tooth."

My nephew is descended from both Swedes and Minnesotans, so he is genetically predisposed to dangerous activities such as skating on ice and shopping at IKEA. I, on the other hand, am descended from retired people, and am therefore genetically predisposed to no activities whatsoever. But after observing my nephew's brokenhearted expression, I change my mind and agree to take him skating because he says he'll buy me hot dogs.

Like most men, I've long watched male Olympic skaters grab the body parts of scantily clad women skaters and thought to myself, *I could do that.* In reality, though, ice skating is extremely difficult, because the rink doesn't automatically supply you with a young woman to grapple.

The problem starts with the skates themselves, which are outfitted with sharp metal runners that refuse to stay steady on the ice while you eat your hot dog. Then there's the ice, which, when you drop your head on it, turns out to be both flat and unreasonably *hard.* It's as if you've fallen down on a parking lot in the state of Kansas, only in this parking lot, everyone else runs over and tries to step on you with razor blades. I lie there wondering how the people who built the Volvo could invent a sport like this and not supply air bags.

"Are you okay, Uncle Bruce?" my nephew asks anxiously.

"I've probably got a skull fracture and could use another hot dog," I admit.

After a few minutes, the rink manager skates up to me and demands to know what I'm doing, lying there on the ice when I should be on my feet falling down. I tell him I'm figure skating, and in this case I'm doing the figure of a man who needs an ambulance.

"Get up, and also you can't have hot dogs out here," he tells me.

What? How can ice skating even be considered a sport if you can't eat hot dogs while doing it?

I'm able to struggle to a standing position by clutching the rink manager a handful at a time. "Okay," he coaches, "now push off with your left foot while simultaneously letting go of my pants."

I do as he says, gracefully gliding across the ice and onto my rear end. It feels a little like being tackled by the Minnesota Vikings—I've broken bones I didn't even know I *had*.

At the first aid station, the paramedic cares for my ice injury by *pressing ice against it*. Since when is irony considered a legitimate medical treatment? "You must be from Sweden," I tell him.

"No, Denmark," he corrects loftily. More irony: I'm American—I thought Denmark *was* Sweden.

The paramedic hands me an inflatable pillow—*now* they give me an air bag!—and I sit in the bleachers to watch my nephew, waving my hot dog encouragingly every time he coasts by.

This is, I reflect, a perfect way to spend the day, him ice skating, me eating fatty foods, each of us fulfilling our genetic destiny.

A Whole Lotta Nerve

I've decided to donate my body to science, as long as they'll come pick it up this afternoon.

A couple of weeks ago, I experienced what medical experts commonly refer to as The Most Awful Pain a Human Being Has Ever Suffered in the History of Earth. Starting at the base of my spine, my legs suddenly became shooting fireballs of agony—it was as if all the pain I'd ever had in my life decided to come back for a high school reunion. My thighs spasmed so severely I was pretty sure they were both giving birth to triplets. *Elephant* triplets.

Now, most people would agree that I'm the strong, silent type, the type who never lets anyone know he's suffering. The only people who would not agree are those who were within earshot of me when the pain hit, and I'm sorry it was in such a quiet place, but I'm sure the bride will agree that my symptoms were more important than her wedding.

When I got home, I discovered that the only position that gave me any comfort at all was lying on the couch holding a glass of wine. The pains were still strong and consistent, and my throat was getting sore from all the screaming.

I looked online to determine the cause of my agony, and was able to determine that, according to the Internet, I must have stepped into a bear trap. Recommended treatments included morphine and gnawing off my own leg.

I called my doctor, Dr. Ennui, who told me it sounded as if I had a condition known as sciatica. He observed that it normally went away on its own after a few days, but that if it didn't get better, I should call him back but without all the weeping.

Sciatica, I learned, is a symptom where the big nerves in your body turn into deadly snakes and start biting you. At least, this is what I concluded from the hopelessly technical documents I read on the subject, which seemed to imply that the best treatments are diet and exercise.

Exercise? How do they expect me to exercise when I can barely crawl to the kitchen for more wine?

Dr. Ennui asked me if I would consider nontraditional treatments. "Hey," I told him, "if I thought it would help, I'd suckle a baby weasel."

That one was maybe a little too nontraditional, but the one he did suggest—acupuncture—struck me as being reasonable because I didn't know some lady was going to stick needles in my body.

I've never really been interested in Eastern medicine, so the fact that I even made the appointment should be proof to you that I was running out of wine. My father is a surgeon, so I was more or less raised with the belief that if you had a pain, somebody should go in with a scalpel and cut it out. Western medicine, however, was really letting me down with this whole diet-and-exercise thing, which in my opinion is ludicrously overrated.

I crawled onto the acupuncture bench and lay there while a woman starting pushing pins into my body, idly wondering if out there somewhere a voodoo doll that looked like me was starting to have pains where she was sticking me. She asked me whether I did yoga, and I told her I did once, but that it didn't take. She suggested that perhaps my internal organs were unhappy, and gave me some herbs to drink in a tea that tasted like it was made from the seats of a 1956 Chrysler station wagon.

After an hour of literally being on pins and needles, I did feel somewhat better. The pain in my legs went from shark attack to something closer to piranha. Dr. Ennui seemed pleased that I had done something to make myself feel better beside call him every five minutes, and then he, like my acupuncturist, brought up this yoga idea.

I said I'd do yoga when it came out in pill form. Meanwhile, I'm scheduled for an MRI to see whether there's anything in my body that can be removed.

I'll let you know what happens.

Hounded into Office

Now that the election campaign has officially begun, I'd like to publicly endorse the one candidate I believe has the character to be president: my dog.

My dog has never told a lie. When he gets into the trash can, he meets me at the front door with such a guilty expression, I half expect to discover he has eaten the neighbors. He follows me into the kitchen with his head down, blinking and wincing when I see the mess.

"Did you do this?" I demand. *Yes*, his expression replies. *I did it. I am a bad, bad dog.* And that's it—he doesn't try to spin the story (some studies suggest coffee grounds are actually good for the carpet!) or dull the impact (mistakes were made) or shift the blame (I have asked for the cat's resignation). He faces me in humble misery: The trash can was just too tempting. He made an error in judgment. Isn't this what we want from our leaders, the ability to admit they made an error without piling on a lot of excuses?

And if protecting the citizens of this country from enemies is the number one job of the president, then I can promise you, my dog will faithfully execute the task, so long as the enemies are squirrels. In fact, I can personally attest that in fulfillment of his duties, my dog is more than willing to knock over lamps and grandmothers, and will even plunge headlong through a closed screen door, so eager is he to protect us from all squirrels, foreign and domestic. He'll also sit at the foot of the tree and bark for, oh, seven hours, if you let him. Honestly, can you see any of our current candidates doing this?

Diplomacy is crucial in this dangerous world of ours, and my dog can make friends with anyone. A man could walk into my house carrying a saber, and my dog would try to leap up and lick his face. If the intruder got down on his hands and knees to steal my ﬤ would joyously embrace him and simulat to him. You think when foreign leaders a David, the president is going to be as frien

My dog does not waver from his positions, which are usually on the floor, taking a nap. In fact, he can go all day without changing his position, to the point where I sometimes go over to see if he's still breathing. He does not waffle on the issues, he *eats* the waffle, often right out of the trash can. (*Yes, I am a bad, bad dog.*) So consistent and reliable is he that even after more than a thousand nights of being told he cannot sleep on the bed with me, he still cautiously puts a paw on the mattress and starts to slide up onto the blankets when I lie down, thinking that maybe this time things will be different. I believe such consistency is a real plus in a world leader.

And don't we want the president of the United States to be optimistic? No matter how great things are, my dog always assumes that if we go someplace else, they'll be even better. You think anybody running for high office ever says, "Yes, I want to go for a car ride! I do! Yes! I do! I do! Yes! Yes! Yes!"?

With so many things going on in the world today, it is easy for a world leader to lose focus. I defy any of the presidential candidates to pay attention to a given situation the way my dog can concentrate on me eating dinner. With an unblinking, almost scary stare, he'll watch every forkful of food making the trip to my mouth, ready to lunge at the slightest hint that I might be dropping something edible on the floor. In the past, we've had presidents who have seemed to be, well, a little distracted. I promise you, make a dog biscuit part of the equation and my canine will pay attention until the end of time.

So this election, let's put a dog into office.

It wouldn't be the first time.

Dealing with the Pain

One of the most aggravating things about my painful battle with sciatica is that my back has joined the other side. My left leg is apparently sending to my brain signals like this: "Hey, we're fine down here, except that maybe we're a little hairy and pale. Also, your foot stinks." But when the signal gets to my back, it intercepts it and changes the message to "Hi, this is your leg, we're being gnawed on by a beaver. A beaver with a chainsaw. It really *hurts*."

As twelve years' worth of public school teachers will attest, my brain isn't very bright, so even though we can plainly see with our own eyes that there is no beaver building a dam out of my shins, it accepts the message from my back and announces, "Okay, we'll crank up the agony and see whether we can make this sucker squeal."

To counter this cowardly attack, I've tried a variety of methods. Lamaze breathing, for example, which turns out to be less than completely effective because guess what, it's just *breathing*. I was already doing that. I shut my eyes, counted, breathed in an out, and noticed absolutely no change whatsoever except that after a couple of hours I delivered a baby.

Me, I'm the baby. I admit it, I'm just not that into pain, you know? I would not be much good on the battlefield.

Commanding Officer: Okay, we're going to storm that hill and take out that machine-gun nest!

Me: You know, I just . . . I'm sorry, but that sounds kind of painful. Maybe I should stay behind and just, um, pet kittens or something. I could put smiley stickers on the mortar shells, would that help?

I am far, far better at taking narcotics. Now, the thing about taking painkillers is that you still hurt, but you don't care.

Legs: We're being gnawed to pieces by giant beavers.

Me: Really? How *cute*! Can I pet them?

One downside is that when I'm taking narcotics, I become a little emotional, and tend to burst into tears at commercials with puppies in them, postcards with sunsets on them, and pretzels with salt on them. Yesterday I stopped using a sponge because I felt sorry for it. I have a bunch of bananas slowly turning brown—I'm unable to eat one because it would mean breaking up a family.

I also am pretty effusively affectionate with people I care about.

Me: I just want to say, you've always been there for me. I . . . I really love you, man.

Him: Uh . . . would you like paper or plastic?

And I don't dare drive on the things.

Officer: I pulled you over for driving erratically while listening to Joni Mitchell and sobbing.

Me: Really? That's so *cute*. Want a smiley sticker?

As far as work goes, the drugs make me pretty productive with the TV remote. I watched an entire episode of a Spanish-language soap opera without understanding a word, though I sobbed through the whole thing anyway. I also ordered a box of

ShamWows so my sponge would have some friends to play with.

My editor called to discuss my latest column.

"It *is* sort of a departure from my usual style," I admitted.

"It's a drawing of a penguin," she observed with a disappointing lack of admiration.

"I know. Isn't it *cute*?" I asked, dangerously close to crying.

"Perhaps if you wrote some words," my editor suggested calmly. She's a professional editor with lots of experience, which is why she can make such incredibly insightful suggestions.

"But I did write words," I protested.

"You wrote, 'Eeek. Eeeek.'"

"Right, I wrote them in *penguin*."

"We don't have as many penguin subscribers as you might suppose. Could you try it again in some other language?"

"I really love you," I told her.

My supply of narcotics is, alas, limited and dwindling—my doctor warned me he would not renew my prescription because I'm not a celebrity. I have mixed feelings about it: I don't really like being so absolutely worthless, but I do have to admit, it's kind of nice to feel so loved by an entire family of bananas.

They're so *cute*.

The Head Elf

You may think of me as a newspaper columnist and probably also as someone you'd like to get to know or remember in a big way in your will, but once a year, I become a snarling, cruel, despotic monster.

That's right: I become an elf.

Why don't you keep on changing your will while I explain myself. Once a year I participate in a charity that hosts a holiday party for children who find themselves suddenly homeless due to domestic violence. They and usually their mothers are brought together in a huge gathering for a festive meal and fun activities. The culmination of the party is Santa handing out gifts to every single girl and boy at the party—gifts that have to be collected and identified in a large, chaotic space known by the deceptively joyous name as the Elf Room.

No, don't leave me your piano—that should go to your children, or to someone who wants a piano. Just cash, thanks.

While the children are eating brownies and making Styrofoam snowmen, the elves in the Elf Room are frantically checking lists, trying to account for hundreds of items. Sometimes children have arrived that we didn't know were coming (you can't exactly plan homelessness). Sometimes the adults who agreed to donate a specific gift for a specific child got "too busy" and changed their minds on the whole think-I'll-help-a-homeless-child thing. Some of the gifts are inappropriate—like DVDs, because most of these kids don't have home-theater systems. One year a well-meaning couple, despite our urgings, donated a bicycle: Can you imagine the bedlam if we wheeled a bike into a room full of children who were receiving nice but less exciting gifts? We had to disassemble the thing and rewrap it so that it looked like the poor kid was getting a collection of crushed lawn chairs.

The idea is to have a smoothly flowing stream of gifts out of the Elf Room and into Santa's arms, who will ho-ho-ho his way through hundreds of presents. In practice, the elves in the Elf Room couldn't be more stressed if there were people shooting at us with pellet guns.

Santa, by the way, is assisted by his "wife," a gorgeous woman in an outfit she made herself out of fishnet stockings, go-go boots, and too little cloth to cover much of Mrs. Claus. She looks as though she just finished a shift at the local men's club and has swung by to help hand out presents. No wonder Santa leaves home only one night a year.

Nothing like that is happening in the Elf Room, where for the sake of speed and discipline there's one person in charge of the whole operation: the grizzled, battle-weary Head Elf.

For the past several years, the Head Elf has been me, the person you are remembering so generously in your will.

Not long ago, we had *three entire busloads* of children arrive without forewarning, and our scramble to find gifts for them was comical and frightening. We opened gifts to cannibalize sets of dolls so every child could have one, we stripped the supply closet in the Elf Room (a box of colored pens! Perfect!), we emptied our wallets. The last gift we delivered that day was a candy bar with a ten-dollar bill wrapped around it.

Every child received a present, though. In the Elf Army, we speak of that year as our Vietnam—*you had to be there, man.*

There's almost no joy in being the Head Elf. Some donors understandably want to personally hand over the gift they bought, and I have to turn them away:

This is about Santa and his go-go-dancer wife. I don't get to see the children's excitement or the gratitude of parents and older siblings. Mrs. Claus doesn't meet me later for drinks.

But I'm doing it again this year anyway, and I know I don't have to explain why. Tell you what, instead of leaving me money in your will, why don't you consider donating a gift to Toys for Tots, or e-mail me and I can hook you directly into my charity.

Because of recent economic developments, it looks like it's going to be an especially tough day in the Elf Room this year.

Meet the Sting-Rays

You wouldn't know it to look at me, but I was raised on the rough-and-tumble streets of Shawnee Mission, Kansas.

The day we moved in I was a fourth grader, stomping my feet in puddles of water in the street because, well, I was a fourth grader. Suddenly three boys my age rode up on Sting-Ray bicycles, skidding to a stop in front of me with a triple shriek of rubber. They wore sunglasses, white jeans, and white slip-on tennis shoes. That's right: They were gangsters.

The gang leader folded his arms. "We're the Sting-Rays," he informed me with a sneer so pronounced it looked like he needed lip surgery. He nodded toward the moving van in our driveway. "You moving in or something?"

These Sting-Rays were sharp boys. "Yeah," I replied in a voice tough as marshmallows.

"My name's Ricky," he spat, "but my fighting name's Gearshift because I have a gearshift."

Ricky did, indeed, have a gearshift, a ten-inch lever with a silver knob on it that was mounted just forward of his banana seat. It had no cables running into it and thus served no purpose whatsoever. "Groovy," I said enviously.

"Groovy!" Ricky the Gearshift snorted. His friends snickered. "Nobody says 'groovy' anymore. What are you, the Mamas and the Papas?"

"He's a mama," laughed one of the boys, intimidating me because he wore a real football jersey that, bereft of shoulder-pad equipment, hung on him like a deflated hot-air balloon.

"I meant . . . mud," I said, pulling out a word that as far as I knew was nothing like the word "groovy."

"Mud?" Gearshift repeated uncertainly.

"Yeah, that's what we say where I'm from. Something that's cool is, you know, mud, or dirt or dust. If it's really cool we say, uh, scum."

"Huh," Gearshift replied. He nodded toward the boy in the huge jersey. "His name is Chuck, but we call him Sprocket. It's his fighting name 'cause his bike has a sprocket."

"That's dirt," I said admiringly, hating the ridiculous sound of it in my mouth. Couldn't I have come up with anything better?

Ricky pointed toward the third boy. "And his name's John, but we call him John 'cause his mom won't let him have a fighting name."

"My mom couldn't stop *me* from having a fighting name. All the fights I've been in," I observed. I experimented a little with a sneer, deciding I liked it.

"You been in a lot of fights?" Gearshift wanted to know. "How many?"

"Oh, uh, 557," I said.

The boys registered this as if they somehow found it implausible. Gearshift grabbed his gearshift and shifted into a higher gear with an impressive clicking sound. "Yeah? You ever kill anybody?"

I wasn't sure how to answer this. I really wanted to join the gang and wear white pants and white shoes and be named after a bicycle part, but not if they were going to actually kill people. I decided on tough evasiveness. "Who wants to know?" I responded, though I was sneering so hard it sounded more like "Who wanfs the snow?" I had to repeat it a couple of times, and then Gearshift looked puzzled.

"Me," he answered. "That's why I asked."

"Oh. No, not yet. But my dad has," I advised the Sting-Rays, in case they decided I must be a softy due to my lack of any personal homicides.

I wondered if my father would be okay with me telling the neighborhood that he'd killed people. It might have some impact on his gynecology business.

"I'm going to do a wheelie," Gearshift announced. He expertly turned his bike and began peddling, yanking the handlebars so that his front wheel rose off the ground for a fraction of a second. I was about to yell "scum!" in appreciation when Gearshift's off-center landing turned him into the curb, stopping him so abruptly that he slid forward and hit his gearshift in such a fashion that the rest of us clutched our hands between our legs in instant sympathy.

The next time I saw the Sting-Rays, Ricky had removed the gearshift from his bike.

I never did find out what his new fighting name was.

The Eight Simple Rules for Marrying My Daughter

Having a teenage daughter is a bit like living in the middle of a zombie movie. There will be a knock on the door, and when you open it, you'll find standing there a smelly, unwashed, slack-faced male wearing ill-fitting clothes and wanting to take your daughter on a date. When she appears from where she has been shoveling on her makeup, he'll regard her with that zombie hunger in his eyes.

Your natural impulse is to get rid of this one, but doing so doesn't improve things: There are others out there, a whole zombie army, shambling and moaning toward your home.

And what's really discouraging is that this is just the opening skirmish. As time passes, the zombies become more cunning. They learn how to penetrate your defenses, offering to help you around the house, disarming you with their seeming willingness to respect you. And then suddenly, one of them wants to marry your daughter, and you realize that you were lulled into a false sense of security.

Before this happens to you, I suggest you post these Eight Simple Rules to your front door, for all the zombies to read and heed.

Rule #1: If you neglected to ask my permission before you proposed to my daughter, don't worry about it. You can make it up to me by making sure your wedding is both beautiful and to a different woman.

Rule #2: There are many, many men your age in this world, but there is only one woman who is my daughter. She is unique. You, on the other hand, can be replaced at any time.

Rule #3: It has been my job all my life to make my daughter happy. Now it will be your job. My job will be to make sure you do your job. And don't think that just because my daughter has picked you, it means you meet my personal standards for what is good for her. I haven't made up my mind yet, and will be evaluating you over a time period known as "forever."

Rule #4: You may be wondering how to address me: "Dad"? "Bruce"? "Mr. Cameron"? Let's end the awkwardness: For the time being, I suggest you stick with "sir." Sample phrases to help you become accustomed to this term: "May I wash your car for you today, sir?" "Are there any tasks that I can do around the house while you watch the ball game, sir?" "Is there anything I can do to make your life better, sir?"

Rule #5: Call me old-fashioned, but I believe that any man who wishes to marry my daughter should have a good job and a successful career. I'm not saying you need to be the sole source of income, but I am saying if you don't take care of my daughter, *I* will take care of *you.*

Rule #6: You do not have a legal contract with my daughter; she can break off the engagement if she wants and there is nothing you can do about it except change your name and move out of the country. The same goes for you: I would not want you marrying my daughter if you do not truly feel you are the right man for her, nor, if you break it off, would I want you marrying anybody else. Ever.

Rule #7: You may, in a very male episode of last-minute panic, decide that you need to sow some wild oats right before the wedding. Let's define our roles: If you are the sower, I will be your reaper.

Rule #8: The vows you will be taking commit you to be faithful to my daughter "'til death do you part." Be advised if you break your vows, I'll immediately exercise the second part of the contract.

Naturally, there's more to the whole equation than just what I've got here. These rules are excerpted from my book *8 Simple Rules for Marrying My Daughter* (Fireside, 2008). If you've got a daughter, I suggest you pick up a copy before the zombies breach your defenses.

Middle-Aged Owner's Manual

Welcome to your middle-aged body! This is your owner's manual.

Delivery
You will note that your middle-aged body arrived far earlier than you anticipated. No need to thank us. If you feel you have received this body in error, too bad.

New and Improved
Your middle-aged body is more roomy and better cushioned than your old body. We've added padding to areas where it is most visible so that other people will be envious. And you know how teenage girls wear their pants really tight? With your new body, all your clothes will fit like that! Think how stylish you'll be! How constrained! How unable to sit down!

Fun and Exciting
You may notice that you have started to experience the following: sleeplessness, hot flashes, cold sweats. These are all symptoms of a medical condition known as "parenthood." Nothing can help you enjoy the sensation of being older than to have children tell you that your clothing, music, hair style, and opinions are out of date. If you've avoided being a parent up until now, please know that medical science is working feverishly to extend the years of fertility, and, of course, you can always adopt someone, like Angelina Jolie and Brad Pitt. (Actually, you probably *can't* adopt someone like Angelina and Brad—they're grown people. But think how great it would be if you could. Talk about fun and exciting! Probably make middle age a lot easier to deal with too.)

Revised Operating Instructions
A middle-aged body is like a finely tuned racing machine—a machine in desperate need of repair. Your doctor will have many pills for you to swallow and will provide you with a list of activities separated into two categories: those you cannot do, and those you shouldn't do. Your joints have probably already begun to talk about the things you can't do, and the things you shouldn't do are restricted to those activities that you really want to do.

Random-Access Memory
Recent improvements in data storage means you will be able to remember with utter clarity a picnic you took when you were fourteen years old, but will spend two hours looking for your car keys. You'll find yourself starting a sentence with a declaration like "There are three things we must keep in mind," and then find yourself wondering what in the world the third one was, or whether you even got the second one right. You'll pick up a book and halfway into it realize you've read it before, though by the end of the thing you'll no longer be sure. We've made additional improvements to your memory, but let's be frank: You're probably not going to remember the ones we've already listed.

Brand-New Package
Remember when people used to say to you, "You're so young"? You're never going to hear that anymore unless you go to Florida and join a bridge club. Instead you'll hear, "You look really good for your age," which is so exactly the opposite, it makes you want to grit your teeth, except that doing so might damage your new bridgework. Inside, though, you'll feel absolutely no different, especially if you're a man and you take one of the new little pills available today—you'll feel like a

teenager again, which your wife will find really annoying.

Known Bugs

While we've had your whole life to develop your middle-aged body, there are some known deficiencies we are still working on at the time of release. The worst of these is "version skew" between your brain's perceptions and your body's aptitudes. You still think you can play a game of backyard football and be tackled and get back up without two people helping you. You still think you can travel coast to coast without taking a three-day nap. You still think you can sneeze—sneeze!—without your back muscles sinking their fangs into your spine and paralyzing you for a week.

We're working on these problems and expect to have them fixed when we deliver the next model: your "senior" body. Until then, please enjoy your middle-aged body, because what other choice do you have?

Chinook Come-Home

While the young and single life is certainly exciting, eventually a man wants to settle down, to have someone there to greet him when he comes home, someone to love him and care for him always, which is why we have dogs.

When I was in my early twenties and decided to buy a dog, I carefully researched the most suitable breed by going to my neighbor's house and picking a puppy from the litter in his garage. As it turned out, they were all huskies, a breed of dog about as easy to train as velociraptors. I named my puppy Chinook, and after six months of training I had managed to teach it the following tricks:

1. Tear up the couch
2. Eat my socks
3. Run away when called

Of these three, "run away" was the most annoying, because the couch was from my old room at the fraternity house and smelled like it needed an autopsy, and my socks smelled like the couch. When Chinook ran off, though, it implied she thought she was the boss, which was especially vexing because I couldn't think of a way to prove she was wrong. I lived in northern Michigan at the time, working for General Motors, and, let's face it, huskies are better at running through snow than guys wearing ties and loafers. Lacking a better idea, though, I'd pursue her until finally I'd tackle her and then be too exhausted to do anything but lie there with my arms around her.

This is what you wanted? her look said to me. *A big hug?*

Eventually we reached a compromise: She'd stop running away if I built a fence.

In my defense, I was just doing what many pet owners do, which is to be dumber than my dog. If I'd had any sense, I would have realized that Huskies are bred to drag things across long distances, and that instead of driving to work on the highway, I should have been taking the Iditarod.

"Chinook," I asked her, "why don't you like me?"

I'm hungry, her look said to me. *Pass the socks.*

After a few years I had a family and Chinook decided that sticking around suited her just fine. The children were always willing to sit in the wagon or sled and have Chinook pull them. She was finally doing what she craved: She was *working*.

We moved to a country house in southern Michigan, which is much warmer than northern Michigan by one degree Fahrenheit. Chinook never ran away unless there was a thunderstorm, of which she was terrified. At the first rumble from the sky, I made sure she was safely locked in the basement.

One day when the family was out, a storm came, and by the time we returned home, Chinook had climbed the fence and had fled the thunder. I drove around yelling out my car window (making me very popular with my neighbors), posted signs, and took out newspaper ads.

After a week of searching, I had to face it: I'd lost Chinook. Heartbroken, I saw this as just another in a series of failures in pet ownership, and vowed not to get another dog until I was smart enough to take care of one.

And then a farmer called me, responding to my advertisement. Though it had been nine days and though his farm was more than twenty-five miles from my home, the stray he'd found sounded enough like my dog for me to drive up there to take a look.

When I pulled into his driveway, a big husky was lying out in the field, fifty yards away. As I stood up, that dog raised her head and then streaked across the field in a flash, tackling me to the ground. It was Chinook, yipping excitedly, licking me, jumping on me, crying. I grabbed her and she gave me a look that said, *This is what I wanted. A great big hug.*

That was a long time ago, and I still think I wasn't cut out to be a husky owner—but that day, seeing how happy Chinook was to see me, I realized this:

I must have done *something* right.

No Wake for the Waking Dead

I have no moral or ethical qualms about autopsies, though I do hope to wait awhile before I have one. For a man in Venezuela last month, however, the wait was cut short (no pun intended) when he literally woke up during his own autopsy.

It seems that the victim, Carlos Camejo, was in a fatal car accident, declared dead at the scene, and taken off to the hospital for dissection. Let's just say that Carlos has had better days. He awoke while doctors were making an incision in his face, saying something along the lines of "ow."

The doctors, not accustomed to having their patients discuss this procedure with them during the actual operation, decided they might be better off stitching Carlos back up. An autopsy is conducted to determine the cause of death—it's not supposed to *be* the cause of death.

Carlo's wife, summoned to the hospital to identify the corpse, said, "Yes, that's Carlos, he can't do anything right."

Reconstructing events, it appears the doctors were puzzled over what had killed Carlos, given that he was still breathing. They decided to figure out the reason for his demise, since the only thing the police report said was "fatal car accident," and who dies of something like that? Their first incision, in Carlos's face, was designed to rule out acne as the primary cause of death. At that moment, Carlos's brain registered a lot more postmortem pain than it was accustomed to, and decided to reboot.

Medically speaking, brain activity is considered a sign of life, though as Paris Hilton has proven over and over, the reverse is not necessarily true. Another sign of life is when someone asks you to stop cutting him because it hurts. (I'm speculating on this last item—I've never been to Venezuela, and perhaps the med schools there are different.)

Venezuela is a democratic country where the president, Hugo Chávez, rules by decree. He is a wildly popular leader among those few citizens who are allowed to express their opinion. Some people point to the story of Carlos's visit to the hospital as being proof of how well the health care system is working in that country—in America, Carlos would have had to take a seat in the waiting room and provide proof of insurance before being given an autopsy. Other people may disagree with this sunny perspective, and in Venezuela they have freedom of speech as long as it isn't via the opposition TV station, which President Chávez shut down in May 2007 for having low ratings of 40%.

Interestingly, one of the top television shows currently airing in the United States is the *CSI* family of programs, which regularly score a rating of around 6%. These shows—*CSI: New York*, *CSI: Miami*, *CSI: Sesame Street*—are about autopsies, and maybe would attract a higher audience if the actors playing the victims were allowed to talk during the procedures the way they are in Venezuela. It would be a good opportunity for product placement.

Autopsy Doctor: Though the victim has multiple gunshot wounds to the chest, I suspect his death has more to do with his face. Let's make an incision.

Murder Victim: Now that I'm dead, I sure could use an ice-cold can of cola!

This Carlos-inspired take on autopsies gives *CSI* the opportunity to break new ground as a television show where the murder victim is a recurring character. Even better, Carlos himself could do a cameo! (Provide a little autopsy humor—audiences love that.) He could even say something negative about President Chávez, which apparently 40% of the people in Venezuela would tune in for.

Please note that no one is claiming that a full 40% of the Venezuelan populace is against their president—after all, Chavez is backed by 100% of the Venezuelan legislature, with the remaining 0% of lawmakers alleging election fraud. It's just that in most democratic countries, the government isn't allowed to determine what the citizens may and may not watch— in America, that freedom is expressly reserved to television executives. And what those executives have decided is that we need more *CSI* shows.

Because, as Carlos himself will tell you, it is much better to watch autopsies than to experience them.

Fly Me to the Moon Pie

When it comes to flying, I believe in pampering myself, always picking the best of America's bankrupt airlines. Recently I flew across the country and couldn't decide between first class or business class, since I couldn't afford either one of them. I wound up sitting in coach, so named because you need someone to shout, "Come on, you can do it!" as you try to wedge yourself into your seat.

Many airlines have started adding surcharges to their ticket prices to help defray the cost of items such as fuel and bad management. For example, you can no longer bring two pieces of luggage on the flight—it costs an extra $25 for the airlines to lose that second bag.

"Of course," the flight attendant purrs as I squeeze between the two professional wrestlers to sit in my seat, "meals in our first class and business cabins are complementary and prepared by our first-class chef, Emeril. In the coach cabin, meals cost ten dollars and are prepared by our coach-class chef, Boyardee. Coach passengers may pay an additional five dollars to upgrade lunch to 'edible.'

"In the event of sudden decompression, little orange masks will drop from the ceiling to dispense air. In the coach cabin, the air costs ten dollars, though coach passengers may pay an additional five dollars to upgrade to 'oxygen.'

"For entertainment, passengers in the first two cabins may choose from a wide variety of movies to watch on their personal electronic devices, or, if they prefer, Chris Rock will sit next to them and tell jokes. In coach, our movie today is *Alive*, the uplifting story of a plane crash in the Andes wherein a handful of frolicking survivors indulge in cannibalism."

I eye the large men on either side of me, deciding that if we go down in the Andes, I'm good for a couple of months. Otherwise, I'm not paying all that money for airline food, even if it does look more appetizing than what they're eating in the movie.

After a couple of hours aloft, my nose twitches at an unmistakable smell: They're baking chocolate chip cookies in first class! My stomach comes alive, begging me to eat one before it has to resort to cannibalism. I reach up for the flight attendant button, paying the dollar surcharge to ring the bell.

"How much," I plead, "to buy one of those cookies?"

She tells me $5 and, when I pull out my wallet, hands me a small package.

"What's this?" I sputter.

"Moon pie," she responds.

Now, a moon pie is every bit as delicious as a smear of marshmallow packed between two dry graham crackers and coated in chocolate can be, but my heart is set on an upgrade. "No," I hiss, being careful not to wake the man seated next to me, whose head is resting on my shoulder. "I mean a fresh-baked chocolate chip cookie!"

The flight attendant snatches the moon pie out of my hand. "Those are only for our upgraded travelers," she tells me, marching off.

I sit there, fuming, wondering whether I could storm into first class and swallow a cookie before the air marshal shot me. Then I spot a business-class passenger stretching his legs.

"Hey buddy!" I whisper. I slide out of my seat, earning me a snarl from the professional wrestler guy. I offer the business-class person $10 if he will go get me a cookie. "Or two," I amend.

"Two would be twenty dollars," he replies—must be why he's in business class, because he can do math like that. I tell him fine, whatever, and he leaves.

A few minutes later, he's back. I have my money out, but there's no cookie. "I decided it just wouldn't be right," he advises me sadly. "Those cookies are meant for just the people in front. It would be immoral."

"*What?*" I demand. "What kind of businessperson are you?"

Looking insulted, he turns on his heel and retreats to the safety of his cabin, where coach passengers are not allowed to go. Heartbroken, despondent, I go to find the flight attendant, but I'm too late.

They're out of moon pies.

You Win Some, You Lose Some

My children believe they are more athletic than I am simply because they are better at sports. "No, athletic ability is ninety percent mental," I inform them archly.

"Yes, Dad, as an athlete, you are mental," they agree.

My older daughter's volleyball team participates in—and *wins*—national tournaments. I mentally picture myself doing what she does, and realize I'd be pretty good at it if I tried. "See, your sports genes had to come from somewhere," I inform her.

"That's what I keep hoping," she replies.

Then there is James, my son-in-law-to-be, who is an Olympic-class runner. He is so fast that if I jumped out of a second-story window, he could take the stairs and beat me to the ground. "If you do anything to hurt my daughter, I'll hunt you down," I've told him. "I may have to use a small airplane to do it, but I'll catch up with you."

I suppose "Olympic-class" is a bit vague; I, for example, have always felt that I was an Olympic-class pole vaulter, utilizing my superior mental skills to get myself 90% there. (I mean, it looks so easy: You just run down a track, stick a pole in the ground, and *boing*, you're catapulted into the air! Once you are at the top, you just fall back down, which I figure is the other 10%.) No, when I speak of my future son-in-law as being "Olympic-class," I mean as in "going to the Olympics to compete in the 800-meter run."

I probably would have been pretty good in the 800-meter run myself, except for the fact that when I was his age, they didn't have the metric system.

But there's a catch: To go the Olympics, you have to compete in a series of trials—otherwise, you'd probably see me out there doing the pole vault, if I felt like it. At these Olympic trials, you face the very best this nation has to offer in nonmental athletes, and a few tenths of a second is all it takes to cut you from the team.

Just a couple of weeks ago, James was ranked the fastest man in the country in his event, well on the way to accomplishing his life's dream of representing our nation at the Olympic games. Just a few track meets stood in his way, and one of them, in Eugene, Oregon, had him worried.

James had raced in Eugene before and hadn't done well. He is allergic to certain pollens, the kind released by the tons into the air in Eugene by the local sod farms. He didn't even know about this allergy until he ran in a Eugene event several years ago, when he was nearly struck down by aching, asthmatic lungs. His hope for this year was that a special diet and other precautions would prevent a repeat of the debilitating allergies, and allow him to move beyond the Eugene races and on to the pursuit for Olympic gold.

It was not to be. About fifteen days ago, in the final two laps of the race, James couldn't get enough oxygen to keep his finely muscled legs working at their peak, and he fell too far back to advance to the next trial.

And so, that's it: a life's dream, over in the time it takes to dash a few hundred meters.

I hate the end to this story, and wish I could use my mental powers to fix it. It seems wrong and unfair that he was bested not by the competition, but by the air itself.

In the end, though, this was a contest of strengths, and weaknesses, in human bodies. James trains in Boulder—it wouldn't have been fair to flatland runners to hold the event there. Some athletes may have trouble with the air in China. Maybe it's "unfair" that those of us who are mental athletes could never be in the Olympics except for the pole vault—which, as I said, looks pretty easy.

James tackled his training with determination and showed tremendous courage and optimism in going to Eugene. He's a man to be admired, and I'll be proud to call him my son-in-law.

Shopping with My Mom

When people ask me if my parents are still mentally all together, I explain that they retired fifteen years ago to northern Michigan "for the weather," so actually they were *never* mentally all together.

I am visiting them this August: Temperatures have ranged from the high 40s to the high 80s, and we've had hail, rain, tornados, power outages, and pirate attacks.

Right now my mother is making her grocery list. "What are some of your favorite things to eat?"

"I like broccoli," I say.

"Broccoli!" she exclaims, as if I just asked her to bring home a live polar bear.

"I don't like broccoli," my father says over his newspaper.

"Your father doesn't like broccoli," my mother interprets for me.

"Okay," I say reasonably. "What does he like?"

"I want to get what *you* like," my mother says. "What do *you* like?"

"Not broccoli," my father warns.

"He can have broccoli if he wants," my mother snaps at him.

"What are we going to do with a bunch of broccoli? I don't like broccoli," Dad complains.

"Your father doesn't really care all that much for broccoli," my mother says, whispering so my father won't hear this slander.

"What does he like?" I whisper back.

"What are you two whispering about? I said I don't like broccoli!" my father bellows.

"His hearing is getting really bad," my mother informs me. Then she says loudly, "We're not getting broccoli, for heaven's sake!" She looks at me. "What do you like to eat?"

Her smile is open and innocent, as if this is the first time she's raised the subject. I'm tempted to say "broccoli" again just to see if we'll have the exact same conversation, but I am worried that we will.

"Donuts," my father announces. "Get donuts."

"Donuts?" my mother asks me, the way people will look at a dog and say, "Car ride?"

"I don't really eat donuts," I say almost truthfully.

"What kind of man doesn't eat donuts?" my father demands, outraged.

"You always loved donuts when you were a child," my mother informs me, looking hurt.

"Okay, but I don't eat them now." I pat my stomach.

"All right, I won't get donuts," she says sadly.

"What?" my father says, rattling his paper.

"Your son doesn't like donuts," my mother says.

"What does that have to do with anything?" my father wants to know.

She gives me a *What are you going to do?* shrug. "Would it be okay with you if we got donuts?"

"Well, of course, Mom. I just don't want to eat any."

"But I want to get food you like. What do *you* like?"

"Do you mean to tell me," my father interrupts, setting his paper down, "that you don't *like* donuts?"

"I like them, Dad. I just don't want to eat them."

"If he doesn't like them, he shouldn't have to eat them," my mother tells him.

"I do like them, though," I protest.

"You do? What kind would you like me to get for you?" she asks me.

I can't see any way out of this. "I don't know. The powdered-sugar kind, I guess."

My father makes a face. "Powdered *sugar?*"

"Your father doesn't like powdered-sugar donuts," my mother informs me, a bit unnecessarily.

"Those aren't even real donuts," he says. "Powdered sugar."

"When I was a little girl, we called them fried cakes," my mother affirms.

"No, we didn't," my father objects.

"We didn't? What did we call them?"

My dad shakes his head. "I don't know, I never liked them."

"But your son wants fried cakes," my mother responds.

"Actually, I don't."

"That's not what they're called!" my father yells.

"Your father would rather we not get any," my mother apologizes. Then she leans forward, a conspiratorial look on her face. "I'll buy some and hide them above the bread box," she whispers.

"I heard that!" my dad tells her.

She shakes her head at me. "No he didn't," she whispers.

"There's glazed. There's crème filled. There's buttermilk," my father says, listing all the reasons why I shouldn't like powdered-sugar donuts.

"Would you like any of those?" my mother asks innocently. I wait for it . . .

"I want to get what *you* like."

I Can Wait

Whenever someone taps me on the shoulder and asks, "Is this the right line?" I can always be confident when I answer no. If it were the right line, I wouldn't be standing in it.

My ability to find the slowest-moving line wherever I go is so extraordinary, it's practically a superpower.

When I'm in the grocery store, I inevitably wind up behind a woman attempting to use more than a hundred coupons to purchase a dozen items. Every time a coupon is rejected for, say, being both expired and from Bolivia, she appeals to the Ninth Circuit Court. If the coupon is actually valid, she wants to discuss where she found the thing, like a big-game hunter bragging about bringing down a charging rhino. My vanilla ice cream turns to vanilla ice soup, my lettuce wilts into a green film, my eggs hatch and start peeping.

"Do you still have double-coupon day?" the woman negotiating for her groceries asks.

"Yes, but only on Wednesday," the cashier informs her. "Day after tomorrow."

"Wednesday," the woman murmurs thoughtfully. At this rate, she's going to make it.

Another cashier approaches the man behind me. "I can take you at register 5," she says to him. "But not you," she tells me. "You have to stand there like someone buying shoes in the Soviet Union."

Actually, she doesn't say anything to me. That's another one of my superpowers: When I'm standing in line, I'm invisible. I've confidently stridden up to the counter at the post office, only to have the "This Window Closed" sign placed in front of me when I arrive. The postal clerk didn't see me, so I'm forced to return to the long line, where I've lost my place and, since I'm invisible, no one seems to remember I was next. I have to go to the back of the line and start over.

The man in front of me has a lot of boxes. "I'm mailing everything I own to seven different countries," he boasts proudly.

At the bank, I invariably find myself behind the man who heaves a huge bag up on the counter. "Been saving pennies for eighteen years," he explains to the teller.

"Our coin counter is broken, so we'll have to roll these by hand," the teller replies.

"Oh, well," he winks, "I don't have anything better to do."

When my son was in high school, I spent most of my mornings waiting for him to wake up. Sometimes I would gently try to rouse him by screaming, "Bears are attacking!" or "Your sister's on fire!" while pouring milk on his pajamas, but most of the time I was pretty aggressive. My son, though, could sleep through a waterboarding.

"If you're late to school every day," I'd warn him as he shambled out the door a full hour behind schedule, "you'll flunk out."

"So?" he'd sneer maturely.

"So you won't graduate. You won't be able to get a good job."

"So?"

"So you'll be broke, living in your father's basement, with no friends and no life."

"So?"

The other day I found myself at an intersection where a left turn is legal only during a solar eclipse. I waited so long for my little green arrow, I began to accumulate parking tickets.

As I sat, an old man with a walker began to make his slow, careful way through the intersection.

Naturally, I was able to use my superpowers to have him positioned directly in front of my car when the left-turn arrow made its rare appearance. Cars behind me honked furiously, apparently okay with the idea of running over the guy.

My cell phone rang: It was my son, and I described the situation to him as my arrow winked out. "This guy moves at like a half mile an hour! I missed my turn completely!" I fumed.

"So?" my son observed sympathetically. "And which one of you has it worse?"

My son, who couldn't be bothered with punctuality or even waking up during high school, now holds down a 4.0 GPA in college and has accumulated enough perspective to impart worldly wisdom to his own father.

It was worth the wait.

Too Young for Any of This

I know what you're thinking: I'm too young to have a daughter getting married tomorrow. (That's what *I'm* thinking, anyway!)

Wasn't it just last week that my little girl, all decked out in shiny new shoes, bows in her hair, frilly dress all clean, arched her back and screamed so loud and long that the people sitting next to us had nosebleeds?

If she does that during her nuptials, I'm calling off the wedding.

Maybe it wasn't last week, because my daughter was two years old at the time and had decided to devote her life to embarrassing me in public. We were in church, I recall, and she screamed because she was reaching for a Bible she wanted to "color" in. Thinking that allowing a child to scribble all over a Holy Bible might be sort of out of step with the message of that morning's sermon, I gently and firmly removed the book from her little fingers before she could do any damage to it.

Remember that scene in the movie *Psycho*, where Janet Leigh is screaming because Anthony Perkins makes her drop the soap? Compared to the shriek coming out of my daughter, Janet Leigh was singing "Happy Birthday." When she was done, the minister called off the rest of the service as unnecessary—the devil had been scared clear out of the county.

The protocol for dealing with what was euphemistically referred to as "restless children" was to stand, murmuring politely, and ease out of the crowded pews to a small enclosure in the basement that I called the Screaming Room. (You weren't supposed to let your child kick people in the face as you struggled past; that was my own variation on the procedure.)

The Screaming Room had a loudspeaker so you could hear the minister, but he thankfully could not hear you as you alternately bribed and threatened your child:

"Stop that right now, do you hear me? You stop that, or I won't let you play after church. Come on, honey, stop. Please? I'll buy you a pony. Would you like that? I'll take you to Hawaii. Honey, you have to stop screaming. Stop screaming this instant! Do you want a spanking? Stop slapping me and listen. If I have to spank you, I will. That's it, I'm counting to three. One . . . two . . . three. You hear me? That's three. I'm not bluffing here. I counted to three. Want some cake?"

I didn't really spank my daughter, because if I did, she would somehow summon up even more lung power and really let me have it. Seismographs would tremble as far away as Japan, and the local airport would have to cancel flights because the pilots couldn't hear themselves land.

Sometimes other parents would have their own children in the Screaming Room. They always thanked me later, because once their kids had spent a few minutes with my daughter, they were humbled into silence.

And then there would be silence, as abrupt as a power outage in the middle of a Led Zeppelin concert. Exhausted from the effort of shredding my eardrums, my little girl would reach for me as if nothing had happened, as if right then the congregation weren't upstairs excommunicating us. I'd gather her into my arms and she'd plop her head on my shoulder and wink out, falling asleep with a long, shuddering sigh.

I could have taken her back upstairs at that point except I was pretty sure I would be greeted with pepper spray. Besides, the Screaming Room was comfortable and spiritually located right down the hallway from the church donuts.

More to the point, my daughter's soft head was nestled on my shoulder, totally relaxed and trusting, relying on me to keep her safe and warm while she slept.

So clear is that memory of her sleeping on my shoulder, it seems it must have happened just last month—last week, even. So you see what I mean? We can't possibly be old enough for her to be getting married. She still needs a shoulder to lean on, a father to keep her safe.

That's how I feel, anyway.

I Saw Most Clearly When There Was Nothing to See

Before I went to college, I made a little money painting houses part time, but after I became a college-educated man, I got serious about a career and began painting houses full time.

I was contemplating this complete-circle process one hot day in southwest Kansas, a piece of real estate that completely disproves the theory of roundness as a property of the planet Earth. Show a resident of this flat place a pancake and he'd ask, "What's that incredibly round and mountainous thing you have there?"

There's nothing to stop the wind in this part of the world: If a kid in Denver blows out his birthday candles, someone in Kansas will smell smoke. The hot, flat ironing board that is the land heats this wind, so that as I stood on my ladder, industriously applying a coat of Sears Outdoor White to the parched, weather-coarsened eaves of the house I'd been hired to paint, it felt as if someone were blow-drying my face.

A ladder in Kansas seemed a good place from which to view the future, because in every direction I could see nothing but a complete lack of direction. No trees blocked my path or my vision, no hills promised an arduous climb toward the peak of my efforts, the foliage cowered near the ground or was windblown completely flat like Donald Trump's comb-over. No slate could be more blank, no piece of paper more devoid of résumé. If something were coming, I'd see it from a hundred miles away. But nothing was coming.

So there I was, a twenty-two-year-old college man whose English major qualified him to apply paint to houses. I couldn't wait to run into a popular girl from my high school.

Popular Girl: Bruce! I remember when you painted houses as a job in high school. What do you do now?

Me: I paint houses.

Popular Girl: Oh, I am so going to marry you!

Not that there's anything wrong with painting houses—it certainly seems a more honorable profession than designing Synthetic Toxic Financial Derivative Death Bombs, or whatever are those things that the geniuses at our best banks came up with to generate huge bonuses for themselves as compensation for destroying the world economy. But I'd just spent a lot of time and my father's money at a school of higher learning. The ladder of my career was supposed to be something other than the same one I'd leaned against the houses I painted in high school. Hadn't I learned anything to make the world a better place?

President: The earth will be destroyed if we can't find someone who learned in college how to tap a keg!

Me: I can do it, sir!

Popular Girl: Oh, I am so marrying him!

To keep me company, I'd brought my parents' two dogs with me, young black Labradors who'd never dreamed of a place like this, where the hot wind carried scents from half a continent away and where they could run unimpeded by fences or leashes or dog catchers.

I could see them from my perch, two black rockets joyously crisscrossing the flatlands, their tongues a flash of pink.

From time to time they'd get so far away, they looked as if they were going to cut themselves on the edge of the horizon, and then their heads would snap around and they'd race back to make sure I was still there, panting and dancing at the foot of my ladder, their expressions saying, *Isn't this the best place ever?*

Where I saw a depressing lack of opportunity, they saw nothing but free possibility. There was room to run and they were making the most of it, finding delightful occasion to explore and discover because nothing was stopping them. They could do whatever they wanted, so they were doing it.

I think about that day sometimes, whenever my plans go awry and the future seems drained of promise. The lesson from my dogs is simple: When times are tough, you can see yourself as having no place to go, or you can see yourself as completely free to explore opportunity, and be joyful at the prospect.

When possible, I try to live like the dogs.

Falling for It

You've probably heard the expression "I've fallen and I can't get up," which would be a very appropriate official motto for my 401(k). It's often heard in old TV commercials, in which an elderly woman summons medical assistance via a transmitter in a necklace medallion that looks a little like something Mr. T would wear.

"I've fallen and I can't get up, though I am smiling and cheerful because I'm not exactly the world's best actor," she says.

This commercial speaks to me because I am a member of what is sometimes called the "sandwich generation," stuck between having children who need financial support and parents who want me to make them a sandwich.

My parents don't think they need my assistance, of course, even though my tiny mother has a dog that weighs a hundred pounds, which means it outweighs her by roughly a hundred pounds. The dog is gentle and loving, but when it sees a squirrel, it takes off with a force that could pull a truck out of a ditch, and I know that if my Mom fell and screamed for help, my dad would jump right up to rescue her as soon as it was halftime.

So I tried to talk my mother into getting one of those "I've fallen" transmitters.

"No, Beatrice has one of those, it's silly, it looks like she won the Olympics," my mother said dismissively.

When I asked her what would happen if she fell in the yard, she replied that she wasn't planning to fall. "I don't think anyone *plans* to fall, Mom," I told her.

My father wasn't much help either. "What happens if Mom falls outside and yells for you—would you hear her and be able to go help her?" I asked him.

"Depends who's playing," he responded.

But then something interesting happened: Beatrice, she of the Olympic-medal transmitter, did fall at her house. My mother was there at the time, as were several other women from her church, and I don't know what they were doing at the time, but I don't think it was karate or anything; Beatrice just fell down.

Now, these women are all very nice, but when it comes to trying to help a fallen comrade—well, let's just say that my diminutive mother is the big one of the group. They wisely decided that if they tried to lift Beatrice, they would one by one injure themselves until all the ladies wound up lying there in a pile. Besides, Beatrice had been wearing a medical transmitter around her neck for a couple of months and was eager to try it out, so she pushed the button.

The ladies decided to sit back down at the table and look casual in case the police arrived and suspected them of pushing Beatrice over on purpose. But it wasn't the police who responded, it was the fire department, in the form of a man named Jerry, who, as my mom later described him to me, was apparently built entirely of biceps.

Jerry tenderly reached down and scooped up Beatrice, who put her arms around Jerry's neck and lay her head on his chest. He carried her over to a chair and gently set her down, which took a few minutes (Beatrice wouldn't let go). Finally he told her that he thought she had a bad sprain, though how anything could be considered "bad" when Beatrice was giggling so much is difficult to say.

My mother volunteered to take Beatrice to the ER for an X-ray, which earned her a dirty look from

Beatrice, who wanted to go in Jerry's car and then maybe later drive up to Make-Out Point. Jerry left, after politely refusing offers of coffee, a slice of pie, and a muscle rub.

So naturally now my mother is buying a medical transmitter (what she calls a "dial-a-hunk necklace") and for all I know is out in the yard setting up trip wires. Until it arrives from the mail-order company, she's spending a lot of time over at Beatrice's house, probably making Beatrice run obstacle courses.

So it looks like I was wrong: Sometimes, people do plan to fall.

The Best Dog Movie Ever

The publication of my new novel, *Emory's Gift*, gets me a meeting with a Hollywood producer who professes to be a "big fan" of my work, though in his e-mail he confesses he hasn't yet read any of it.

He's a man in his thirties with black hair so perfectly arranged on his head, it would make a Ken doll jealous. His office is adorned with movie posters and photographs of him with famous actors and other people—I ask him what it was like to meet the governor of California and he responds, "Well, but he's back to being an actor," which is an answer I think I'll save to enjoy later.

We sit down on some couches. "Your book's for sure a movie, I totally see it," he says.

"Thanks!" I say brightly, picturing myself in a new car.

"Dog movies are really hot right now."

That stops me. "Well, okay, but it's about a bear," I say slowly.

"What?" He picks up the cover of my book and frowns at it. I get the feeling it's the first time he's seen it. "A bear?"

"A grizzly bear."

"A . . . Well, okay, but I don't think very many people keep bears as pets. Maybe in Kansas or something, but it's not something anyone who lives in the city can relate to. So we'll make it a dog in the movie—trust me, it will click."

"But . . ." My new car vanishes in a puff of smoke. "It's the story of a boy and his father trying to save a wild bear who lives in the woods."

"Love it! We'll have the dog live in the woods."

"But part of the story is the danger of dealing with a grizzly."

"Perfect. Alex!" he yells at his assistant in the other room. "Look up what's the most dangerous dog." He grins at me. "This will work. Trust me."

"Here's a blog that says dachshunds bite people most often," Alex reports.

The producer gives me a triumphant look.

"I don't think that's right," I say.

"Doesn't matter," he replies.

"But . . . a dachshund living in the woods?" I ask cautiously.

"That's why he needs to be saved," the producer says.

"I don't think the boy's life would be endangered by a dachshund," I object.

"A really big dachshund," the producer suggests.

"It's got to be a bear," I say.

"You're sticking to your guns," the producer says.

"Yes, I guess so."

"Good. I admire that."

"Thank you."

"We can settle the breed of dog later. Okay, we've got the kid, he gets this gift of special powers from Emory the dog, and then what, he can fly? He can . . . Alex, what do dachshunds do?"

"They were bred to go after badgers," Alex replies after a brief pause.

"Okay, love it. He can dig these huge tunnels."

"No, it's not . . . the boy doesn't have any special powers."

"Sure, but that's in the book. People go to a movie, they want to see Dog-boy dig tunnels and fight the evil mole aliens in an underground city."

"I thought it was badgers."

"People hate moles. They dig up your garden. Wow! That's it, the moles are eating all the crops, you got food riots, but they don't want Dog-boy's help because . . . wait, is Emory conflicted, like, he wants to be a good dog but his brain is being controlled by the mole people? That could be why he bit the kid in the first place. Gary Busey."

"Sorry?"

"That's who Emory the dog gives the gift to, Gary Busey. We just signed a deal with him, he's hot again."

"The boy is thirteen years old . . ." I say.

"You're right! It's Dog-*man*. I hate working with kids, this is perfect."

"So, the movie Emory's Gift is the story of Gary Busey being bitten by a giant magic dachshund who enables him to fight the evil mole aliens who are destroying the world's food supply," I summarize despairingly.

"Right. Well, but I hate the name Emory, we'll make it something more vicious-sounding. Like, like, 'Kill-dog.' Or, or, 'Blood-hound.'"

"Blood-hound the dachshund?"

"I knew I was smart to take this meeting with you . . . your ideas are brilliant!"

My Father's Lifelong Diet

My Dad insists an occasional fried pastry never hurt anybody, using the word "occasional" to mean "daily."

"Everything I eat is good for me," he insists, and I have to agree that his diet is certainly healthier than, say, gunfire. Otherwise, the high-fat food he consumes, rich in cholesterol and carbohydrates, is exactly what doctors tell us we should never eat if we want to live a long life.

My father is eighty-four years old.

Oh, and he's also a doctor.

True, his heart has more bypasses than the Los Angeles freeway system. True, he has hearing aids in both ears, which he forgets to turn on when my mother is talking to him. But he's hardly frail—if you don't believe me, try wrestling the remote control out of his hand.

We are out to eat at his favorite restaurant, where he orders the "shrimp in white sauce appetizer," a delicacy so rich with a heavy cream that when the waiter serves it to you, he shouts, "Clear!" and presses two paddles to your chest. I decide it would be rude not to accept a cream shrimp from my father when he offers it to me, which he doesn't.

My wife orders some sort of vegetable hors d'oeuvres for the both of us to share. My dad regards it snidely. "Are you enjoying your broccoli in water sauce?" he asks. It seems he enjoys his food more if we enjoy ours less.

"I want your son to live a long and healthy life," my wife informs him loftily.

He thinks about this. "Been there, done that," he pronounces. He orders a porterhouse steak with garlic butter on it. My wife tells the waiter that she and I will both have poached salmon, romantically entwining her fingers in mine just as I was reaching out to steal a creamed shrimp.

There are apparently three factors that lead to longevity: heredity, habits, and what your wife will let you get away with. When it comes to heredity, I've obviously done as well as I could, and take full credit for that. "If my dad is having a delicious steak soaked in delicious sauce," I reason, "shouldn't I have the same thing?"

"You are having the same thing, only it's salmon," my wife replies. Okay, she doesn't actually say this, but I think she believes it. To her, eating provides fuel for the body, so you should pick the cleanest, purest fuel possible so your engine will run well. To me, you should floor it, and if you blow a cylinder, you'll just have to buy a new motor.

And okay, I don't actually ask my wife if I can have the porterhouse steak, because I don't want to look like some wimp who lets his wife decide for him what he wants to eat. I am an independent, strong-willed, free and unfettered individual who lets his wife decide for him what he wants to eat.

My mother isn't in the equation because she would never order a steak; she doesn't even like steak. She orders the trout. She always orders the trout. You could take her to Burger King and she'd order the trout. "I don't know what I want," she murmurs as she reads the menu. Everyone else knows, so we wait for her to decide. "Maybe . . . maybe the trout."

"The suspense was killing me," my dad says. We probably have this same conversation every time we go out.

"I also want a wedge of lettuce salad with blue cheese dressing, blue cheese crumbles, and a hypodermic injection of blue cheese," my dad says.

Okay, he doesn't say that last part, but I'm having such order envy, I'm hallucinating whole conversations.

My point in recounting this event is that we stood up at the end of the meal, we were all still alive—well, all of us except the trout, I mean. So if my dad can eat like that every night and he's still going strong, why can't I? Isn't it time I spoke up for myself and declared that I'm going to order a huge steak?

Would someone tell my wife?

Your Dog Is Calling

Last month a South Korean company began offering a service that will enable dog owners to communicate with their pets via cell phone.

Feel free to read the above sentence as many times as you need to.

Using a cell-phone-to-Internet connection, dogs will send their owners text messages like "I am sad" and "I'm borrowing the Cadillac." The owners can then respond with their own messages, which, according to the story I read, will be translated into "dog sounds."

Your reaction to this story is probably the same as mine: Oh, come on, this is unbelievable—I thought America was first in text-to-bark software! Here we've been pouring our money into technology to enable our refrigerators to contact us via e-mail—*Hello, you're low on milk, plus the lettuce is making faces at me again*—when other nations have wisely understood that if your dog can call you, *he* can check the milk!

As soon as this application is available in our country, I am going to sign up, in order to continue what my children have started, which is the transfer of every dollar I own to the cell phone companies. I look forward to having conversations like this:

Dog: Dad?

Bruce: Why are you calling? I was in the middle of an important meeting.

Dog: There's a squirrel in the yard!

Bruce: So?

Dog: There's a squirrel in the yard!

Bruce: Okay, I get it; what do you want me to do about it?

Dog: I tried barking and smashing my face against the window and slobbering all over everything and tipping over a lamp and smearing my paws on the glass, but it's still there! There's a squirrel in the yard!

Bruce: You knocked over a lamp?

Dog: Plus somebody's been eating garbage again. The trash can is tipped over and there are pieces of chewed-up paper all over the place. I'm just warning you now so that you have time to calm down and not be angry when you get home.

Bruce: What do you mean, "*Somebody's* been eating garbage again"? Who do you think might have done that?

Dog: Uh, the cat?

Bruce: The cat won't even eat *cat food*. I have to buy her salmon and tuna. The last thing she's going to do is root around in the garbage, eating some stale donuts.

Dog: That's not true, there weren't any donuts! The only things worth eating were half a ham sandwich and some pizza crust.

Bruce: Then why did you chew the paper?

Dog: To see if there was anything edible on them.

Bruce: So you admit eating the garbage!

Dog: I meant, to see if there was anything edible on them as part of my investigation into the cat.

Bruce: That makes no sense. You're going to be in big trouble when I get home.

Dog: How about if I eat everything I spilled?

Bruce: No! Then you'll just get sick all over the carpet.

Dog: Which should be all the proof you need that this cat is a big mistake!

Bruce: What's a big mistake is this technology that enables me to run up my cell phone bill talking to a dog.

Dog: Can you hold? I have another call coming in.

Bruce: What?

Dog: It's probably that malamute from next door. He's been calling all morning.

Bruce: What? Why?

Dog: Because there's a squirrel in our yard!

Bruce: You are not to use the phone to talk to other dogs. You are not to call me at work just because there is a squirrel in the yard. Your job is to guard the house while I'm away.

Dog: I'm bored. I barked at the mailman, but he left mail anyway. I took a nap, chewed a shoe, watched the fish, ate some snacks from the cat box, and now . . .

Bruce: Hold it! You chewed a shoe?

Dog: Uh . . . Want to go for a walk?

Bruce: Don't change the subject! What did I tell you about chewing my shoes?

Dog: Uh, Dad? I'd like to talk about this, but I can't.

Bruce: Why not?

Dog: Because . . . because there's a squirrel in the yard!

Voiceover Hiking

One of my daughters, I forget which, told me recently that she's worried about my short-term memory. To aid me in remembering things, she gave me a small digital voice recorder so that I can leave myself small verbal reminders, like "You parked in slot 73" and "Don't forget, if you go to the store, wear pants." The reminder that would have been most helpful is "You put the voice recorder in the silverware drawer," because that's where I found it when I was looking for my sunglasses.

I decided to take my recorder along on a guided hike that one of my daughters, I forget which, gave me as a present. Now, I don't normally need a guide: I'm an experienced woodsman and explorer who can go into extreme wilderness conditions and drive around as well as anybody. But I decided to go ahead and take this hike because the accompanying brochure contained photographs of the wonderful things I might see on my journey, like the guide, who resembles Jessica Alba in shorts.

11:16 a.m.: Packing to go on the hike. Can't find my backpack, so I'm taking a briefcase. Got pretty much everything I need in there, except that the donuts I bought specifically for the event won't all fit unless I take out the pie.

12:04 p.m.: Met the tour guide. Her name is Mandy, and she looks less like Jessica Alba and more like a girl I used to call Big Bad Brenda Bell, who beat me up when I was in the fifth grade. (She was the meanest third grader I ever met.) Mandy had a backpack for me, but it wouldn't hold everything from my briefcase, and she made me leave behind some pretty critical equipment, like the candy bars. Mandy said we might see a bear today; if we do, I'm putting my money on Mandy because she's stronger than most bears plus has thicker fur. Other people in the group seem mostly to be novices, who came in weird oversized boots and thick socks instead of the sandals I cleverly donned to keep my feet from sweating.

12:11 p.m.: Hike so far has been challenging but enjoyable. I am growing concerned, however, because we're leaving the parking lot.

12:32 p.m.: Is this a hike or a sprint? My legs are trembling and the sweat is pouring down my face. We just now pulled over so another group of hikers could pass us—I've never been so glad to see a Brownie troop in my life.

12:44 p.m.: We've paused again, this time to debate whether we should turn back because I heard a tiger. Mandy keeps saying, "There are no tigers in this park," which is, I've pointed out, the same thing they said on the *Titanic*. No one can think of an argument against this.

12:58 p.m.: Despite the blisters caused by her poor selection of a trail, Mandy refuses to carry me.

1:07 p.m.: When the search party finds this tape, they will file criminal complaints against Mandy for: speaking disparagingly of expensive sandals, making a certain person go hours and hours without candy, murder by thigh cramp.

1:31 p.m.: Mandy has halted the group to calm our widespread panic over seeing some kind of animal stalking us. I'm the only one who actually saw the predator, and dispute the idea that Mandy could tell from my description that it was "only a rabbit." Besides, a lot of rabbits carry fatal diseases. (The word "rabies" is, I believe, derived from a ferocious species of rabbits that would pounce on children in Europe. Mandy dismisses this even though she admits she's never been to the part of Europe where this happens.)

1:40 p.m.: We've stopped again. Hikers are complaining about "one person ruining the day for all of us" (without actually naming Mandy) and are giving me significant looks because I'm the only one with the courage to express to her the exhaustion and fear we are all feeling.

1:50 p.m.: I've been sent back down the hill because the pace I was setting was too tough for everyone else.

2:15 p.m.: Eating candy bars!

Woman Marries Dolphin

According to a January 3 AP news report, a woman from England named Sharon Tendler recently married a bottlenose dolphin named Cindy. No, you are reading it correctly: As ridiculous as it sounds, she married a human. In deference to Cindy, the wedding was held in the ocean off the coast of Israel, and by the end of the ceremony, there wasn't a dry eye in the place.

Guests described the whole thing as "not exactly your typical Jewish wedding."

Naturally, this event has caused a considerable furor among socially conservative dolphins. "I'm not Homo-sapiens-phobic, but marriage is supposed to be between a man porpoise and a woman porpoise. This human babe can't even breathe through the top of her head," snorted a spokesmammal for the aquatic species. More-liberal dolphins claim that what a husband and wife do underwater is their own business.

Humans like Sharon are thought to be nearly as intelligent as dolphins, with advanced language skills, except for American high school students. Training humans is pretty easy as long as the tricks are relatively simple, such as hand-feeding dolphins fish, or hand-feeding sharks hands. More complex tasks—such as eating a picnic at sea without tossing a bunch of plastic in the water—are generally considered beyond them.

This seems to be the first documented marriage between a human and a bottlenose, though in the movie *King Kong*, Naomi Watts winds up with Adrien Brody. In the movie *The Incredible Mr. Limpet*, Don Knotts becomes a cartoon dolphin-like fish, which is less plausible than a giant ape named King Kong but probably more plausible than Naomi Watts falling for Adrien Brody.

Why would Cindy agree to marry such a poor swimmer? "She gives me herring," explains Cindy. Humans from England are unable to cook pleasant-tasting food, so to them, herring is a real treat. Dolphins generally don't like herring, claiming it tastes "too fishy." Cindy, though, is a very unusual bottlenose dolphin, because she is actually a male.

Perhaps the gender confusion resulting from being a male named "Cindy" lies behind the dolphin's decision to wed someone not of his species. But if that's the case, how do you explain "Sharon?" (Though to be fair, I've been to England, and the place is rampant with gender confusion.)

Sharon originally spotted her future husband while snorkeling in the ocean. She swam over to him, and the longer she stayed with the bottlenose, the more her heart pounded. Love at first sight, or merely hypoxia? Apparently it was the former, though the two of them courted for nearly fifteen years, taking their time so they wouldn't do anything foolish, like marry a fish.

When Sharon finally decided to propose to the porpoise, she did it the old-fashioned way—by talking to Cindy's trainer. (Many dolphins have human trainers as personal assistants.) The trainer agreed that it was time for Cindy to settle down, get married, and raise a family, though Sharon wasn't exactly what he had in mind as the ideal wife. He finally consented when Sharon threatened to feed him herring.

Sharon wore a white-veiled gown, and all the women cried and said she looked beautiful, which only serves to demonstrate that when it comes to weddings, women have brain damage. It's worth noting, though, that when Sharon threw the bouquet, none of the single women tried to catch it. In fact, the guests responded by throwing Sharon, tossing her in the ocean so that she would quit blasting them with herring breath.

According to the report, Sharon, a wealthy music promoter and clothing importer, executed a prenuptial agreement with her groom, though experts doubt the validity of the document because (a) Cindy didn't have an attorney representing him, and (b) Cindy is a sea mammal.

A spokesperson for the Knesset, the Israeli parliament, when asked to comment about the marriage between Sharon and Cindy, said "Right, we *so* have time to worry about stuff like this."

(In the above story, I may have fabricated a few quotes, but I promise you the part about the woman marrying Cindy the male dolphin is true.)

Performance Review of Dad

The following is a verbatim transcript of my annual performance review as a father, relayed to me by my three children.

Older Daughter: Welcome to your annual performance review. We, your children, have prepared this review in order to help you become a better dad. It's not too late.

Younger Daughter: When we're done, you can make your lame excuses.

Father: Thank you for the opportunity to learn and improve. You are all grounded.

Son: Okay, that kind of joke isn't appreciated, Dad. First subject is "Paying Allowance." I need you to pay allowance because I am trying to learn how to be financially independent. Often when you pay allowance you want to talk about chores, which is a totally separate topic. This causes bad morale for me, and for the purpose of this review represents poor performance.

Older Daughter: I no longer get allowance, but I want to tell you it makes me feel bad when you want to talk about all the money you have loaned me, and making me feel bad is bad performance.

Younger Daughter: I don't see why I shouldn't get allowance. It's a lot more expensive to live in an apartment than you realize.

Older Daughter: She makes a good point. May still paid me allowance, I could pay you money I owe you.

Father: Or, here's an idea, you could just stop spending more than you make.

Older Daughter: So with that attitude, it is no surprise that when it comes to paying allowance, your performance is "needs improvement."

Son: The next element in your performance review is "Telling Stories." Like, about how hard it is in the "real world," which is unacceptable to us. Or how your parents would never have let you sleep in until noon on the weekends.

Younger Daughter: We have heard all of your stories about when you were growing up and they are not relevant because when you were a kid, *The Flintstones* was a reality show.

Father: So laughing and high-fiving each other is part of my performance review?

Older Daughter: We just wish you would stop trying to be instructive. You have no idea what it is like to be a young person.

Father: That's right, because the way we did it when we were kids was to skip youth altogether and go straight to middle age.

Younger Daughter: Wait, that's like, sarcastic, right?

Son: Your performance when it comes to telling stories is "please stop." The next one is "Talking to our Friends."

Younger Daughter: It takes a lot of work to make friends, and we don't want you ruining it by trying to be cool.

Older Daughter: When you say "wassup," it makes me want to scream. Or "dude." You should never try to use words you don't understand.

Son: One time he said, "Yo dog."

Younger Daughter: You have got to be kidding me!

Son: My friend was like, "Dude, did your dad call me a dog?"

Father: What's wrong with using your lingo?

Younger Daughter: "Lingo"! Oh my God!

Older Daughter: Dad, people your age use lingo. We do not use lingo.

Son: You always want to ask them about world events and politics and things that are irrelevant to our generation. Your performance on talking to our friends is "there's no reason to do this."

Younger Daughter: I still can't believe you say "lingo."

Older Daughter: So your overall rating is the same as last year, meaning, bad.

Father: Well, after trying so hard and failing for another year, I think we can all reach the conclusion that I am just not cut out for this job. Rather than be fired, I think I should just avoid the humiliation and quit. Of course, that means I stop paying allowance.

Son: What?

Father: Or making loans.

Older Daughter: Wait, I think I speak for everyone when I say we do not want you to quit.

Younger Daughter: Yeah, Dad, aren't you always telling instructive stories about how you should never give up?

Son: I'm changing my vote.

Older Daughter: Me too.

Father: Well, I thought you might feel that way. Once I used the right lingo.

Dinner at the Expensive Restaurant

I'm not the sort of person to avoid a five-star restaurant if someone else is paying for it. Otherwise, I would argue that happiness doesn't come from buying a meal that costs a day's wage—happiness comes from buying a meal that comes in a paper bag (why else would they call it a Happy Meal?)

From time to time, though, I can think of a good reason why I should eat someplace where the main attraction is not that you can order without leaving your car. My wife—my wife is the good reason. She says she wants to go someplace where she can wear her new shoes, and the way she says it suggests to me that I won't gain any points by arguing that if we hit the drive-thru, she can wear whatever she wants.

This is how I find myself sitting in a restaurant called "La Cena Meravigliosa Deliziosa" (literally, "The Really Expensive Restaurant"). I have been handed a menu that, in the dim light, looks imprinted with ant tracks.

"Any questions?" the waiter asks in high smug.

I nod. "Yes, are we planning to have a séance later?"

"Sir?"

"You could develop film in here."

"Bruce," my wife says. I hear a whole sentence in that single word and decide I need some points, fast.

"Your shoes look great," I say, peering down into the gloom at what are either her shoes or a couple of pointy kittens in leather.

"Perhaps you would like some piccoli morsi for the table?" The waiter suggests. I decide that "piccoli" means "piccolo" and "morsi" is from the latin "mort," which means "dead." The guy is asking me if we want dead piccolos on our table. I sadly shake my head, thinking how much happier I would be if I could just order a bag of tacos and some plastic forks.

"It means 'tiny bites,'" the waiter explains implausibly. He points to a section of the menu where every entry is \$22, which means as far as my wallet is concerned, these are *not* tiny bites.

The first item is a scallop served "lo spruzzo di limone," which the waiter explains means that as we cut into a delicate outer pastry, an "atmosphere of lemon" is released into the air.

"So as we eat the scallop, we get lemon juice in our eyes," I translate.

"Bruce," my wife warns.

"I suppose if I order the lasagna, some guy comes out and shocks me with a taser."

"We don't have lasagna," the waiter responds.

"An Italian restaurant without lasagna?" I shout, outraged.

"We're not actually an Italian restaurant," the waiter responds patronizingly.

"Oh, sorry, I guess I thought that because the menu is in Italian and the name of this place is the 'Deliziosa Dim Lit' that you're an Italian restaurant, but clearly I'm an idiot who doesn't understand how lucky I am that you're willing to serve me 'scallops di pepper spray.'"

It is, I'm informed, a "ristorante sperimentale," which means "experimental restaurant," though obviously one of the things they're experimenting with is the Italian language.

I try to order a "hamburger with di cheese di American," which isn't how you say "cheeseburger" in Italian, but hey, it's not an Italian ristorante, is it? I'm being sperimentale! They don't have cheeseburgers, though—too much like food, I suppose.

What I eventually order is a stew that is simmered near a photo of a rainbow and served with a "rumor of wine" and a "gasp of cherry." It is contained in a bowl so small (piccoli) it looks like the sort of thing you'd put your paperclips in if you only had like five paperclips. I stir the piccoli morsi of stew, seeing oak leaves and burnt toast, coffee grounds and pencil points, but no meat of any kind. I feel insert-Italian-word-for-sad, as if my stomach will soon be as mort as a piccolo.

My wife, however, seems to be happy with her broiled pears raised by singing children and nursed by organic angora bunnies and then served with a "vision of truth" and "chimes of swan feelings."

"How's your dinner?" she asks me.

"Nice shoes," I finally say. "Really nice shoes."

Old Age Is Inherited—
We Get It from Our Parents

According to pollsters, I am part of an "aging demographic." But who isn't?

I'm not worried about getting older; I'm worried that as I age, I will become more and more like my parents. I am, after all, the result of a scientific experiment in which their DNA was commingled by a process too hideous for any child to contemplate. In my youth, I overrode any inherited traits by applying judicious quantities of obnoxiousness, but lately I've noticed I'm spending a lot of time trying to find the car keys, a search to which my mother has dedicated most of her life.

A few years ago, my father mistook his hearing aids for peanuts and fed them to the dog. Does that mean I am automatically condemned to do the same thing? I was already condemned to hunt for the things a few days later out in the yard—a highly unpleasant task. Isn't that enough? (My father, by the way, was unenthusiastic about using them even after a cleaning, but the dogs were more than willing to eat them again.)

I don't have hearing aids, of course, but as part of my highly successful obnoxiousness program, I listened to loud rock music with headphones throughout my teenage years, ignoring my parents' advice that I was ruining my hearing.

"You were right. I never should have cranked up the volume through my headphones," I tell my father.

"What?" he asks.

"I said, you were right, I should have listened to my parents!" I shout.

He shakes his head. "Peanuts? I fed them to the dog."

On my mother's side, she often asks me questions like this: "Who was that actor, you know, he was in that movie about the dog?" (It turns out that the movie is *The Day of the Dolphin*, and the actor she's thinking of is Eddie Albert—who wasn't actually in that movie, which wasn't about a dog. The person who *was* in that movie, George C. Scott, looks a little like Eddie Albert, the way Spain looks a little like Canada.)

"Why did you want to know about Eddie Albert?" I ask my mom.

"I don't know," she replies. "Who?"

"He was in that movie about the dog," I tell her.

"The dog? Fed him my peanuts," my dad says. "You seen my hearing aids?"

Lately I, too, am finding names and faces to be slippery. I was at a shopping mall when a man tapped me on the shoulder. He looked familiar, so when I turned around, I put a pleased-to-see-you expression on my face, hoping he was someone I liked and not, say, the ayatollah. We exchanged pleasantries, remarking on how remarkably remarkable it was that there was weather outside, while I searched desperately for some sense of who he was. There was an air of authority about him, so I speculated to myself that he might be the mayor of San Diego.

"You don't recognize me, do you?" he finally said.

"Of course I do, . . . Senator, uh . . ." I said weakly.

"I'm your doctor."

"Right! Sorry, it's just that usually when I see you, I'm not wearing pants."

"I was calling to you; didn't you hear me?"

"No, where were you?"

"Standing right here behind you. I think I'd like you to come in for some hearing tests."

"Sorry?"

"Hearing tests!"

I agreed that this was a fine idea, shaking his hand as we said goodbye. "See you soon, Doctor . . . Doctor," I told him. I'm pretty sure he has a last name and that "Doctor" isn't it, but it was the best I could do at the time. He's a handsome man with white hair, sort of what you'd expect if Eddie Albert and George C. Scott had a baby.

So: I'm having trouble recognizing the people I'm having trouble hearing. I am, as it turns out, exactly what you'd expect if my mother and father had a baby.

There's no cure that I'm aware of for my increasing inability to recall faces and names, but luckily there's a technology for addressing my hearing issues. And I know right where to find it.

Out in the yard.

My Retrospective on 2011

It's a good time to look back on 2011—much better than it would have been last January, anyway.

The year 2011 was remarkable because it was the first year in the last decade where Britney Spears was not one of the top ten searches on Yahoo. She fell to thirteenth, which probably is why California radio preacher Harold Camping predicted the world would end on May 21. If people have so much ennui they can't be bothered to check in to see who Britney is marrying, surely it is a sign of the end of times.

Actually, the world almost *did* end on May 21, but at the last moment the legislature was unable to reconcile the two bills that were passed—the House of Representatives approved a measure called "The World Is Ending because of Barak Obama" and the Senate passed a competing bill called "The World Is Ending because of the Republicans." Both bills failed, leading the American public to conclude that the country would be better off if Congress were run by dead goldfish.

Desperate to improve the situation, Congressman Anthony Weiner flooded social media with pictures of himself in his underpants.

It didn't work.

In 2011, Kim Kardashian married the love of her life and spent seventy-two blissful days with him before filing for divorce, beating expectations. ("Kim Kardashian" was the number one "personality" search term in 2011, according to Google. Weiner should have sent pictures of *her* in his underpants; at least people would have appreciated those.)

Just because Kim Kardashian is listed in the "personality" category doesn't mean she has a good one.

In Los Angeles, residents experienced "Carmageddon," when construction on a single bridge shut down a single highway on the west side of town. Concerts were held to raise funds for the victims, food was donated by local farmers, and Anthony Weiner sent pictures of his underpants. People actually stayed home to view the "event" on television—for several hours, they sat and watched a live feed of an interstate with no traffic on it. (These are the same people who come up with ideas for reality TV shows.)

In September, scientists working out of the European Organization for Nuclear Research announced that they've observed neutrinos, which are particles that move faster than the speed of light. (Except in Los Angeles, where they would be held up in traffic.) This means that when a neutrino takes a trip, it arrives at its destination before it starts, which doesn't impress Kim Kardashian, whose marriage was over before it began.

Neutrinos may not have any real practical use of any kind, which is why several of them have announced they are running for Congress. (Neutrinos are so fast that they'll be able to send pictures of their underpants before they're even elected.) What does have practical use, though, is the Kepler telescope, which has begun identifying Earth-like planets in other solar systems. Harold Camping hasn't yet announced when *those* worlds will end, but careful scrutiny of the other planets reveals that we can't see anything happening. (Just like Carmegeddon.)

In 2011, millions of Americans purchased or were given e-readers, which are devices that enable you to read a book that your neighbor wrote about her cats. More people are e-publishing their e-books than ever before, absolutely flooding the market, so how you would find, say, *A Dog's Purpose* (my personal recommendation, though the cat book sounds good too) is anybody's guess. Probably the thing to do would be to go to a bookstore, find the book you want to read, and then download it, depriving the bookstore of any revenue. Next time you want a new book, you can do the same thing. The bookstores will be happy to stay open to accommodate you.

And 2011 will see the last full year of something that started in 1995: this column. After 668 straight weeks of using my internal Kepler telescope to try to spot something Earth-like to write about, it's going the way of Kim Kardashian's marriage. Next week will be my last column, just as Harold Camping predicted. I hope you'll do me the honor of checking in with me that one final time.

The Last Cameron Column

Ages and ages ago—like, 1993—people would purchase a PC, plug it in, and then stare in wonder at all the error messages. There wasn't much else to do with the things if you weren't part of the "information economy," though people gave it their best shot.

"Look!" Mom would cry, "I'm typing my recipe cards into the computer!"

"Wow," the children would say. "Mom is so smart." (Unless they were teenagers, in which case they would say, "Mom is such a dork.")

"From now on," Mom promised, "these recipes will be permanently stored in the computer until there's a hard disk crash and we lose everything. It's far superior to the old, unreliable system of index cards, some of which were handed down from your great-grandmother!"

The family would be eating dinner when suddenly the computer would announce, "You've got mail!" Everyone would bolt, racing to the monitor.

"Some generous person in China wants to sell us Viagra!" Mom would shriek excitedly.

Actually, no, that's not what the e-mail said. Back then, most e-mail said, *Tell me if you got this e-mail!* The unfortunately named "spam" hadn't yet become a feature in life, so e-mail was something of a joy. When your Uncle Fred passed along a joke someone had passed to him, you didn't write back *TAKE ME OFF YOUR LIST, UNCLE FRED.*

One of the things that Fred was kind enough to pass along was this oddity called "The Cameron Column." Written by some guy named W. Bruce Cameron, it was an e-mailed, opt-in newsletter that was random both in subject and publication schedule.

I was writing the thing and sending it out over the Internet because I wanted to write humor and hadn't been successful in getting my work published any other way. At its peak, "The Cameron Column" had 50,000 readers in fifty-two countries, if you count Texas as a country.

And then people's e-mail boxes started filling up, computers became more reliable, and Uncle Fred got indicted. The column fell from favor. Around that time, though, I wrote a column called "The Eight Simple Rules for Dating My Teenage Daughter." It was extraordinarily popular, to the point that thousands of people took my name off it and sent it around as if they themselves wrote it. It even showed up on Oliver North's website as something like "Colonel North's Rules for Dating His Daughter," which led me to conclude either that he had stolen my column or that I was Oliver North.

When I wrote to the colonel, he was immediately apologetic, explaining that he had a staff who edited the website and that he would make sure they were pushed out of an airplane. No, actually he made sure I got my byline on his site and promised me he would help me get syndicated, and that's exactly what he did.

Some things happened along the way to syndication: I wrote exclusively for the (now sadly departed) *Rocky Mountain News* for a few years, and, most significant for me, I was able to turn my *8 Simple Rules* into a successful book and TV show on ABC starring John Ritter. But since Creators began carrying my column, I've been appearing in somewhere around fifty newspapers in the US and Canada—probably, if you are reading this, I've been in your paper.

I've had several books published subsequent to *8 Simple Rules*, including my *New York Times* best seller *A Dog's Purpose*. Which leads me to where I am today: fortunate enough to have a couple more books in the pipeline, but so overwhelmed with all the work those commitments entail that changing gears every week for my column has become increasingly difficult.

This is my 689th weekly column, and I'm taking a break. Some newspapers have chosen to continue to run my column as a "best of" collection, and others are taking the position that none of my columns are "the best." After a rest, I may be back, but in case I'm not: Thank you for doing me the honor of reading my work all these years. Without you I'd still be sending e-mails, wondering if anyone was reading them. I am eternally grateful for your support.

Yours,

W. Bruce Cameron

A Final Word

There are a lot of habits that are fairly easy to give up—regular exercise, dieting, putting my dirty clothes in the hamper, etc. I certainly thought, when I bid farewell to my readers at the end of 2011, that the weekly habit of chronicling the events of my life would be one of those things I could walk away from pretty easily.

And yet it didn't turn out that way. Despite my effort to be the sort of person who just sits around being amazingly wealthy and who wins free vacations and is often called by the president for advice or just to crack jokes, my life continued in my post-column age with a lot of experiences that looked suspiciously as if I was trying to come up with more things to write about. These things leak out, in Facebook and other places, as writings that are basically new columns. I just don't call them that.

What follows below, a little column-like piece I posted to the "A Dog's Purpose" page on Facebook, is an example—it seems that once a columnist, always a columnist. Especially when the president forgets to call.

A True Crime Story

We shop at two grocery stores: Ralph's, and Whole Foods. The first one is for when we're feeling broke and the second is to make us actually broke.

A few days ago I was in Ralph's (true fact: No one named "Ralph" works there) and decided that I had done such a good job sticking to my diet at lunch that I deserved another lunch. I went to the deli section and speculated that I was hungry enough to eat two fried chicken thighs, so I ordered three of them.

The flirty woman behind the counter then said something very sexy and provocative to me, which was, "Did you know that for an extra dollar you could have *six* chicken thighs?"

Well, I didn't really want that many, so I said yes.

So then I'm sitting outside eating these chicken thighs, which I am actually very talented at doing, and I see a guy sort of watching me. He was a little unwashed looking, with a scraggly beard, so I figured him for either a homeless person or a studio executive. And then suddenly he bolted straight at me, snatched up a chicken thigh, and ran off with it!

I have very quick reflexes, so within seconds I spilled my iced tea. Then I stood, and it was on my lips to cry, "Stop, thief!" Except I don't know if anyone in the world has ever actually shouted that, and I didn't want to sound like an idiot. Besides, I would feel pretty bad if someone ran after the chicken snatcher and wrestled him to the ground and my food got all dirty.

Without a backward glance, the man vanished around the corner. I sat back down, feeling numb except for where my pants were soaked in tea. That part felt cold.

The guy, I mused, must have been pretty hungry to have pulled off such a daring kidnap in broad daylight from someone with such quick reflexes as myself. And truthfully I didn't really miss the thigh, being a little full from the other five and also from the first lunch I'd eaten, the "prelunch," as they call it in medicine, which consisted of me sticking strictly to my diet except for dessert.

But shouldn't I report this to the police? What if the thief was part of a vicious crime ring that had descended on the city, stealing chicken parts from all sorts of defenseless people? This possibility was, well, really stupid. More likely it was just what it appeared to be: high thighs and misdemeanors.

In the end, I decided to rewrite the exchange in my mind. It hadn't been a crime: I had given the thigh to the man, albeit at high speed, and because of my generosity, I now had room for dessert. I found myself hoping that whoever he was, he found a way back on his feet, or had better luck with his next movie, whichever it was.

About the Author

Author's Note: it is traditional for an "About the Author" to be a brief summation of facts, all of them written in the third person. Like, "*Author McAuthorson is a member of the Automobile Club of America. He has been to Wisconsin. This is the first novel he has written that is not about a long running argument with his mother. He lives down the street from a gas station in Texas with his wife of three years, the lovely former Miss Duluth.*" I'm going to keep the third person convention because I was asked to find someone else to write about me, and the only person I could think to ask was my wife, who edited this book and has already done enough work. I suppose I could have asked my kids, but then you'd get this: "*W. Bruce Cameron snores during football games. He traumatized us our whole life with chores which were not fair and rules which were not fair. His idea of what is dinner is deplorable. When he dances at weddings it makes us want to cry and then throw up.*" So read this and pretend it is someone else writing it, like, the Nobel Prize Committee, who I keep expecting is going to call me any day now.

About the Author

New note: I know I already said About the Author once already, but it seemed like the author's note should come before About the Author.

About the Author, written in the third person by the Nobel Prize Committee

W. Bruce Cameron should win the Nobel Prize because it's worth about a million bucks and, let's face it, he could use the money. But only to do good things with it! He would benefit all of humanity, pay off his credit cards, probably get in some skiing, stuff like that.

He has won prizes before, so the Nobel thing wouldn't be that unusual. He won the Robert Benchley award for humor and was the National Society of Newspaper Columnist 2011 Columnist of the Year. His Uber rating is 4.8 stars.

He does not snore during football games.

His book, *8 Simple Rules for Dating my Teenage Daughter*, went on to become a TV series of the same name starring John Ritter on ABC. Cameron wrote for the show in its final season and consulted on the pilot episode. His novel *A Dog's Purpose* was developed for the big screen, with a release date of January 27th, 2017. Cameron and his wife of less than a year, writer/director Cathryn Michon, were the first screenwriters on the project.

Cameron's novel *The Dog Master* is set in Europe at the beginning of the last ice age and is based on Cameron's experiences as a cave man. So, if the Nobel thing falls through the Pulitzer looks like a sure bet, plus there is a petition to get him on Dancing with the Stars.

Pretty much every important person in America wants Cameron to come over for lunch.

When he is not writing, Cameron likes to relax by climbing mountains, fording every stream, following every rainbow, until he finds his dream. Or maybe just taking a nap, whichever is easier. The point is, there's a lot of dreaming involved.

Cameron lives in California, Colorado, and Michigan, which makes it really hard for him to remember where he put his glasses. He likes to visit his fans when they fly him to Hawaii. First class, if you're thinking of doing this, because in his defense it is a long flight. Also Cathryn needs to go with him and what about his dog, you need to figure this stuff out. If this strikes you as pretty complicated, just remember that the Nobel Committee has it a lot worse and you don't hear us complaining.

You can find Cameron's books in the bookstore in the "good" section. Visit Cameron at www.adogspurpose.com or his author site, www.wbrucecameron.com. Or follow him on Facebook. Or follow him on foot, it's not hard, his dog makes him stop every fifteen feet to mark territory. The dog does the actual marking.

--November, 2016

About the Editor

Cathryn Michon is an award-winning comic, actress, improviser, film director, screenwriter and book author. Along with the author of this book, she is a screenwriter of the DreamWorks film *A Dog's Purpose* starring Josh Gad and Dennis Quaid. She has written and produced Emmy-nominated episodes of television for a wide variety of hit series. She is the author of the bestselling chick lit series of **Grrl Genius Guides** and for two years was the writer and star of the cult hit AMC series *Grrl Genius at the Movies*. Along with Mr. Cameron she co-wrote and produced the feature film comedy *Cook Off!* which has an all star cast including Melissa McCarthy and Ben Falcone. She also co-directed, and is one of the stars of the film. Cathryn wrote, directed and starred in award-winning feature film *Muffin Top: A Love Story,* which was released in the fall of 2015. She is the proud, if somewhat delusional, dog mom of Tucker, 24 lbs of suspect DNA and the actual boss of the Cameron household.

Okay, all of the above is true and this was written by a very professional publicist, but I think it's pretty boring and doesn't give you really important information. Here's my (Bruce's) "about the editor." (I wrote it in third person to make me sound important. At the end of it, if you're thinking, "this Bruce person sounds really important to me" then you read it correctly.)

Cathryn Michon consistently wins the Most Important Woman in Bruce's Life award (people biologically related are not allowed to enter the contest). Though prone to lapses in judgement (she married Bruce Cameron, for example) she has contributed to his body of work by reading and giving notes, and edits everything he has written since the moment they met. She's just kidding about not liking any of her husband's sweatshirts—they're *classics*, some of them, and if you don't like the Broncos one it's like saying you're not a Bronco fan, which everyone knows you really are even when you pretend to not like football. She should listen more patiently to his political lecture series on How Much Better The World Would Run If Everyone Voted Like I Do. She should stop interrupting when he is making a point that she says he has made before— obviously, it must be a *very good point*. She's got to be pretending to enjoy romantic comedies more than movies where people shoot at helicopters. What do you mean it is the same as in some other movie? In that movie, the helicopter was a completely different color! Anyway, Cathryn Michon is W. Bruce Cameron's writing partner, his business partner, his life partner, and very possibly the reason he switched from writing humor books to novels like *Repo Madness* and the *A Dog's Purpose* series. His life is better because of his (award winning!) wife.

CPSIA information can be obtained
at www.ICGtesting.com
Printed in the USA
LVOW07s1729051217
558726LV00005B/1124/P